SYRACUSE UNIVERSITY
The Shaw Years

Select titles about Syracuse University . . .

Syracuse University,

    Vol. 1, *The Pioneer Days* (1952)
      W. Freeman Galpin

    Vol. 2, *The Growing Years* (1960)
      W. Freeman Galpin

    Vol. 3, *The Critical Years* (1984)
      W. Freeman Galpin and Oscar T. Barck Jr.; ed. Richard Wilson

    Vol. 4, *The Tolley Years* (1996)
      John Robert Greene, with Karrie A. Baron

    Vol. 5, *The Eggers Years* (1998)
      John Robert Greene, with Karrie A. Baron, Debora D. Hall,
      and Matthew Sharp

SYRACUSE UNIVERSITY

Volume Six · The Shaw Years

DAVID T. TOBIN

With a Foreword by Chancellor Kent Syverud

Syracuse University Press

This book is published with the assistance of a grant from Syracuse University.

∞ The paper used in this publication meets the minimum requirements
of the American National Standard for Information Sciences—Permanence
of Paper for Printed Library Materials, ANSI Z39.48—1992.

For a listing of books published and distributed by Syracuse University Press,
visit www.SyracuseUniversityPress.syr.edu.

V. 6. ISBN: 978-0-8156-1104-2 (hardcover)

Library of Congress Cataloging-in-Publication Data
Galpin, William Freeman, 1890–1963
Syracuse University.
Vol. 3 rev. and edited by Richard Wilson, from a text prepared by
W. Freeman Galpin and Oscar T. Barck, Jr.
Includes index.
Contents: v. I. The pioneer days.—v. 2. The growing years.—
v. 3. The critical years.
I. Syracuse University—History. I. Wilson, Richard, 1920–
II. Barck, Oscar Theodore, 1902. III. Title
LD5233.G3   378.747   52-2118
ISBN 0-8156-8108-9 (v. 3)

V. 4. The Tolley years
ISBN 0-8156-2701-7 (cl.)
V. 5. The Eggers years
ISBN 0-8156-0549-8 (cl.)

Manufactured in the United States of America

For Maria. You inspire me again and again.

Contents

Illustrations

Foreword

M ORE THAN SIXTY-FIVE YEARS AGO, Syracuse history
professor W. Freeman Galpin and Syracuse University Press
published the first volume of a history of the university, titled *The
Pioneer Days*, covering the years from the founding of the university
through 1894. Four more volumes followed, with various authors,
carrying the history up through the 1991 conclusion of Chancellor Melvin Eggers's leadership. The last volume published exactly
twenty years back.

A lot has changed in the world and at Syracuse since 1991. I am
grateful that this sixth volume of Syracuse University history, *The
Shaw Years*, recalls the great reinvigoration of the university under
the leadership of Chancellor Kenneth Shaw during the years 1991–
2004. This volume captures the tone of those times at the university
and the leadership culture that Chancellor Shaw and his wife Mary
Ann sought to build here. It is a chronicle of many successes, often
in the face of adversity, and always accompanied by a deep commitment to our school as a student-centered research university.

By the end of his service as chancellor, this volume reports, "the
budget was in the black, new creative programs were being launched,
major construction was underway, and a healthy culture of frankness and caring was in place" (p. 245). Of course, so much more
is documented in this volume about the events and challenges and
accomplishments of this era, but I particularly admire that healthy
culture of frankness and caring fostered by Buzz Shaw. It was hard
to achieve and was of enormous value to the university. It was a
product of effort and sacrifice from people across the university,

including trustees, alumni, faculty, students, staff, and members of the wider community.

It was a similar team effort that produced this volume. In 2014, then-chair of the Board of Trustees Richard Thompson encouraged and supported the commissioning of this history, and engendered support from fellow trustees and from his successor as chair, Steven Barnes. Overall support and direction for the work was provided by David Seaman, dean of libraries and university librarian, and by Alice Randel Pfeiffer, director of Syracuse University Press. Thanks are also due to Kevin Quinn, senior advisor to the chancellor for executive communications and public affairs, who served as a liaison between the author, Syracuse University Press, and the chancellor's office.

Most important, the university is fortunate to have Dave Tobin as the author of *The Shaw Years*. Dave experienced Chancellor Shaw and the university firsthand through his two decades as a reporter for the *Syracuse Post-Standard*. His work here captures an era vividly and accurately and is based on so much time spent listening carefully to those who participated in it. The result is history worth reading, and a book that is itself a fine contribution to Syracuse University and all who care about it.

—*Chancellor Kent Syverud*

Acknowledgments

A S A CENTRAL NEW YORK JOURNALIST who covered Syracuse University for several years and had read SU historian Bob Greene's enlightening volumes on the Tolley, Corbally, and Eggers years, I began this exploration thinking my familiarity with SU would give me a leg up. Then SU Archives were opened to me, and the university sprawled like an uncharted mountain range. Skilled guides would be needed to assist my understanding of the years between 1991 and 2004, and there were many, in large part because this book would be about an era that numerous people remembered fondly, and they were eager to talk.

I extend my deepest thanks to the more than one hundred people who generously gave their time to be interviewed and respond to email queries, sometimes repeatedly. Caring was an SU value that Buzz Shaw often talked about, and I saw its vibrant existence in nearly everyone I encountered.

It was an honor and delight to work with Buzz and Mary Ann Shaw, who were every bit as warm, gracious, kind, funny, and thoughtful as people had reflected. I thank them for their generous cooperation and patience.

This book would not have been possible without Chancellor Kent Syverud and former chair of the Board of Trustees Dick Thompson, and I am grateful for their support and confidence. Kevin Quinn, senior advisor to the chancellor for executive communications and public affairs, and his assistant Patricia Pitzeruse were consistently helpful navigating the labyrinth of details and approvals necessary to get this project off the ground and to sustain it.

SU Archives holds the voluminous raw material of the university's history, and I grew to appreciate fondly the dedicated people who keep it in order and make it accessible: Lucy Mulroney, Nicole Westerdahl, Margaret Mason, and especially Mary O'Brien, a living repository of SU history.

I am especially grateful to Donald Haviland, SU alumnus, who generously consented to let me draw from the research and observations of his doctoral thesis. His work provided a degree of analysis of Shaw's restructuring that would not have existed otherwise.

One of the great privileges of researching and writing this book was getting to know and rely on some brilliant scholars and administrators, without whose help this book would be far thinner; among them: Tom Walsh, John Palmer, Eleanor and Ben Ware, David Smith, Gershon Vincow, Deborah Freund, Shiu-Kai Chin, Cathryn Newton, Sam Gorovitz, and Barry Wells. Linda Pitonzo, Gretchen Goldstein, and Bob Heaphy also generously lent their understanding about this era to the project.

I owe a debt of gratitude to Sheila Pitt, my assistant since July 2016, whose initiative and encouragement helped sustain me through long days and whose familiarity with SU yielded surprising insights. Professor William Coplin graciously referred to me some of his top student teaching assistants when I needed help. Chief among those was Hannah Danielle Johnson, who transcribed hundreds of hours of interviews while working toward her 2017 degree in policy studies.

When the time came for their input, Suzanne Guiod, my editor, and Kay Steinmetz, my copy editor, both with Syracuse University Press, offered wise suggestions in a gentle, kindly manner, and this book is much stronger for their keen ears and sharp eyes.

From first research through to final editing, I was struck by the generosity, the care, and the commitment of Syracuse University people to see this book through. Efforts to bring this book to fruition proceeded quietly for years as a true, university-wide project, and I am grateful for the privilege of having been in the midst of them.

Maria DeMitchell, my life partner, brought her unfathomably joyful spirit to my days with unwavering support and encouragement and provided wise comments on early drafts. This would have been a far more arduous project without her.

We are the sum of so many influences, the people who inspire, lead, shape, suggest, and encourage us to start and finish a project such as this, whose support is profound yet indirect. In that regard, I am beholden to Sean Kirst, Michael Connor, Mark Fohs, Paul Elice, and my personal distractor, J. P. Crangle. In these days when so many rely on a personal trainer or guide, J. P.'s services were particularly grounding.

Lastly, I want to acknowledge my two children, Celia and Will, who venture forth boldly in their creative adult lives, modeling equanimity in calculated risk-taking. They continue to teach their parents well. Thank you.

I N 1991, facing a $38 million deficit that was projected to worsen, Syracuse University hired an unusually seasoned administrator to extract it from its predicament. At fifty-two, Kenneth "Buzz" Shaw had spent fourteen years running campuses or university systems, including five at one of the largest public university systems in the country, the twenty-six-campus, 165,000-student University of Wisconsin system. Nine chancellors had led SU before Shaw but never one with as much administrative experience.

The uncertainty faced by the nation was echoed by circumstances facing colleges and universities. The US military had driven Iraq's army out of Kuwait, and many of the 500,000 troops deployed there were returning home. In the 1980s, we saw double-digit interest rates and the collapse of the savings and loan system, prompting students and parents to think long and hard about a private college degree when state university systems offered degrees for a fraction of the cost. Disillusionment with the quality of higher education was being stoked by books like *Profscam*, which criticized university professors for being more interested in their own research and careers than in their undergraduate students.

Furthermore, a significant demographic decline among college-age men and women was forcing many colleges and universities, especially those in the Northeast, to cut spending. Even Yale University was cutting its academic and administrative departments between 5 and 10 percent.

When Shaw arrived, all of this and more was coming to bear on Syracuse University, whose economic difficulties were more serious than those of many peer institutions: it faced a bloated enrollment, anemic academic quality, a bland reputation, sinking faculty morale, and a weak endowment.[1] In short order, Shaw identified core issues that were dragging Syracuse down, and without assigning blame or purging top administrators, he drew the best out of the people he had, setting the institution's course in a promising direction. In a matter of years, the university would log an impressive list of corrective measures that put its finances on a positive track and raised SU into the upper rankings of the best colleges in the nation.

Shaw, the sandy-haired, blue-eyed, genial Midwesterner who was more manager than academic, oversaw improvements in academic quality and the university's reputation, deliberately reduced enrollment, and corralled sacred cows in athletics. The university community's mood lifted in an atmosphere that was cooperative and collegial.

As Shaw orchestrated the most comprehensive financial and academic restructuring since the university's founding, he brought to the process a refreshing candor. He was forthright about finances, budget trade-offs, and policy decisions, and resisted the impulse to increase enrollment to increase revenue—a strategy his predecessors engaged whenever budget difficulties arose. Highlights of Shaw's restructuring process are explored in chapter 2, and further restructuring details can be found in appendixes A–D.

He identified a market niche for SU that was unique, and that resonated with what families of college-bound students were clamoring for after the inflationary 1980s: a solid education at good value. Syracuse University achieved national recognition for its focus on student achievement. It led the way, regionally and nationally, with initiatives to support diversity, and it became an institution acutely aware of its place in the community, with a reputation for kindness, fairness, and respectfulness.

Shaw was a man who spoke his mind, who, in one memorably blunt remark, told SU football fans to "get a life." Years later, he would reflect that his choice of those three words was a stratagem to divert attention away from a coach beleaguered by the insults and barbs of disappointed fans, and to draw that anger toward himself.

Conflict did not fluster Shaw, and pressure did not inhibit or intimidate him. He was the former college athlete who knew how to rally himself and others, who had learned how to get large, diverse groups of people working like a team and moving in the same direction. Behind Shaw's "get a life" statement was a deep and sincere message, one he delivered in various ways over and over throughout his SU chancellorship: get past your resentments, your rancor, your turf battles, and petty preoccupations. Focus on the big picture, on making the world you are a part of a better place.

SU's restructuring changes did not come without pain. Some colleges spent years recovering from deep financial hits, hundreds of staff were let go, and hundreds of faculty accepted generous severance packages. Through it all with great equanimity, Shaw conveyed confidence that the process of working with a clear mission toward a clear vision would lead to success. "What you saw with Buzz was what you got," said John Palmer, Maxwell School dean during Shaw's tenure. "He was straightforward. He was focused. He knew what to do."[2]

"Buzz" Shaw became a familiar and welcome presence on campus, his name a household word throughout greater Syracuse. His time at Syracuse cannot be considered apart from his wife Mary Ann, the first chancellor's wife ever paid at SU. She was an understated, determined force in her own right—far more than a spousal confidant—who forged a broad-based community service initiative at the university, engaged alumnae in unprecedented ways, and played a powerful role in fund-raising. She built relationships among and between students, faculty, administrators, staff, trustees, and community leaders that few others could.

By the end of the Shaws' thirteen years at Syracuse, the university would have more than a decade of financial stability, its administration and fund-raising would become more professionalized, and its Board of Trustees would be more diverse and national. Major and much-needed building projects would be underway or planned, as would groundwork for the next major fund-raising campaign.

At the start of the twenty-first century, Syracuse University would be stronger in traditions that had guided it for more than 125 years. After a decade of steady gains in academic quality, it was poised to accomplish the goal set by Shaw's predecessor, Melvin Eggers: "to reach the next level of academic and research excellence."

SYRACUSE UNIVERSITY

The Shaw Years

O N T H E C L O U D Y S A T U R D A Y M O R N I N G of May 4, 1991, Chris Witting, SU's chairman of the Board of Trustees, introduced Kenneth Alan Shaw to the full board as the university's tenth chancellor. Witting was a dynamic leader in his own right, a former chairman and CEO of Crouse-Hinds Company, a Syracuse-based electrical and lighting equipment manufacturer that he had built into a Fortune 500 company.[1]

Before Shaw had entered the room at the Sheraton Hotel Inn and Conference Center, all forty-four board members had confirmed his appointment. Outgoing chancellor Melvin Eggers was at the meeting and gave his final address to trustees and the several members of his cabinet who were there, including three who had applied for Shaw's job: Gershon Vincow, vice chancellor for academic affairs, Louis Marcoccia, senior vice president for business and finance, and Lance Baker, senior vice president for university relations, were among the 190 names the search committee had reviewed. Shaw, who welcomed dissenting opinions and was not threatened by challengers, would keep all three in his cabinet.

The candidate pool had been more diverse than ever, with thirty-six females and nineteen minority candidates, a trend that would continue, search committee staffers predicted. "Future search committees will have access to increasing numbers of qualified women and minority candidates," wrote Michael Sawyer and Bruce Hamm in a debriefing report about the search process.[2]

H. Douglas Barclay, a Syracuse University College of Law graduate and a former ten-term Republican New York state senator, had led the nineteen-member search committee. Shaw had been nominated by a woman he had hired at the University of Wisconsin, Donna Shalala, another SU graduate. Shalala had earned her PhD from the Maxwell School of Citizenship and Public Affairs in 1970, and she was a valued and devoted alumna. During Shaw's tenure at Syracuse, President Bill Clinton would appoint Shalala US secretary of health and human services.

Before Shalala nominated Shaw, she had been identified as a potential candidate and was contacted by the search firm Russell Reynolds Associates, Inc. of New York.[3] "Every time there was an opening at Syracuse they approached me," she said.[4] She was not interested, but she thought her boss might welcome the opportunity to work at a private university and be a good fit. She wrote Shaw a glowing recommendation, and when he made it to the committee's short list, she reiterated her praise.

"Buzz was a very gifted manager and knew how to delegate," she recalled saying. "He knew how to hire very good people. He didn't pretend he was the intellectual leader of the institution. He made sure that he had the right people in place."

Barclay had to woo Shaw, who had spent his entire career working for public institutions and was not looking for a new job. "I was exploring, and we'll see what happens," Shaw said. The University of Wisconsin president made his first trip to Syracuse in mid-March, while Syracuse University was hosting the first two rounds of the regional National Collegiate Athletic Association (NCAA) men's basketball tournament. He came under the guise of being a consultant to guard against any appearance of seeking to leave Wisconsin. He stayed and met with search committee members at a Carrier Circle hotel, was given a quick drive around campus in the dark, and headed back to Madison.

He had been impressed by Barclay and other search committee members. They seemed deeply committed to the university and had "at least a general understanding of where it needed to head," Shaw said. Barclay, a straight talker who had a knack for breaking down complex issues and strategizing solutions, hit it off with Shaw. They would forge a working relationship that would be key for the university's progress moving forward.

Barclay brought Shaw back a few weeks later, this time with Mary Ann. They had dinner at Pascale's, on Hawley Avenue, along with Douglas Biklen, professor of education, and trustee Renée Schine Crown. Shaw "was very quick, had a great sense of humor and a breadth of experience," said Biklen. Search committee members were struck that Shaw had succeeded so well at the prestigious University of Wisconsin system, negotiating a difficult state political system led by Republican governor Tommy Thompson.

Back in Wisconsin, the more Shaw read about Syracuse, the more the job intrigued him. "Their challenges, as they understood them, were ones that fit my skill set," he said. "And if you follow my career you'll see that I was pretty much invited places where they had some serious challenges. But challenges that could be dealt with."

So on that mild, May morning, as soldiers were returning to Fort Drum from Desert Storm and newscasters were priming people for the day's Kentucky Derby, the newly appointed chancellor assured trustees that he accepted "the challenge of downsizing faculty and staff." Shaw gave no indication how he would undertake the downsizing or how quickly and decisively he would act. With a candor that would define his chancellorship, however, he described his administrative style: He would bring an openness to the job, a willingness to listen to different viewpoints and to express his. He did not mind being disagreed with and believed ideas come from all directions. Decisions should be made as far down (the seniority chain) as possible, and he knew "where the buck stops." He would begin August 20, 1991.

In a first for Syracuse, Shaw's wife, Mary Ann, was hired as the chancellor's associate and would receive a salary, a deal Shaw had negotiated with Witting. It was a bargain considering the skill set Mary Ann Shaw brought and the role she would play in the life and community of Syracuse University. Shaw brought no one else with him.

Mary Ann was not present at the meeting, missing the modest pledge her husband offered trustees: "If you [trustees] do your part and pull together through some difficult times in the first part of the decade, Syracuse University will come out stronger than when it went in." A host of obstacles had to be overcome. An entire university had to be restructured.

*   *   *

Kenneth Alan "Buzz" Shaw was born January 31, 1939, in Granite City, Illinois, across the Mississippi River from St. Louis. His father, Kenneth W. Shaw, an "inveterate" reader and a dreamer, applied his high school education to jobs as a bank teller and sheriff's dispatcher and worked for an electrical parts manufacturer. Shaw's mother, Clara Helen Lange Shaw, went as far as the eighth grade, clerked at a Ben Franklin variety store, and advanced to become its bookkeeper, with responsibilities for several stores in the chain.

Shaw is seven years younger than his sister and only sibling, Elizabeth, which ensured him his parents' undivided attention. When young Kenneth was learning to speak and understand himself as a "brother," his pronunciation of the word sounded to his father like "buzzer." So the elder Shaw took to calling his only son "Buzz."[5]

Edwardsville, Illinois, next door to Granite City, was where Shaw grew up, and in 1950 its population was 8,700, half the size of Syracuse University's enrollment at that time. Close relationships in the small, working-class city shaped Shaw's character and values. He was well behaved and preternaturally responsible—an "old soul" at six years old, running errands for neighbors or taking a neighbor's baby for walks in a stroller. "I never got into any trouble. [Never] got caught, anyway," he said.

His grandfather, William Shaw, worked as a superintendent at the brass works of N. O. Nelson Manufacturing Company, which had been founded by the son of Norwegian immigrants and became a progressive social experiment. The company established its own village of LeClaire, offering its workers affordable homes, free education, health services, and bowling alleys. By the time Shaw was born, LeClaire had been annexed by Edwardsville, and its progressive values had seeped into Edwardsville life.

Although racism and discrimination of blacks were entrenched in southern Illinois in the 1950s, Edwardsville was actively reformist.

Shaw's playground mates were black and white, and racially segregated elementary schools merged when Shaw was in sixth grade. On the newly integrated Edwardsville High School basketball team, Shaw played starting guard with two black students, Mannie Jackson and Govoner Vaughn, both of whom went on to play for the Harlem Globetrotters, with Jackson eventually becoming the Globetrotters' owner.

The first in his family to attend college, Shaw enrolled at the state's oldest teaching college, Illinois State University at Normal, on a basketball scholarship. He played point guard and set freshman and sophomore records for foul shooting—83 percent his best year. He credits his high school coach, Joe Lucco, with teaching him the benefits of discipline and hard work. "I was a gym rat," Shaw said. "I would have slept in the gym if they had let me."[6]

One "old soul" trait of young Shaw was self-awareness—his ability to learn from and carry forward early life lessons. After receiving a bachelor's degree in history from Illinois State University, he taught history and physical education at the newly formed Rich Township High School in Park Forest, Illinois. Students so exploited his need for approval that it kept him awake at night, and he learned that being liked "is something you can't have if you're going to be a leader. By the time I got to Syracuse, I had no need to be liked."

Through stints as dean of academic affairs, college president, and chancellor, he learned leadership fundamentals and life skills, including how to use his time and the importance of scheduling unstructured time. "I wouldn't have survived otherwise," he said. "And I learned very early on how to work in groups, to work with groups. It was intensified at Syracuse because I played a much more direct role in a lot of things. By the time I got there, I'd learned I didn't want a chief of staff. I didn't want to have the dean of students reporting to the provost."

James Fisher, a college administrator who gave Shaw his first big break, was an important mentor. Fisher met Shaw when he was a basketball player at Illinois State University. Fisher was vice president and executive assistant to the president and would go into the locker room to congratulate players when they won. It was one of several Fisher practices that Shaw would emulate at Syracuse. Years

*As a basketball player at Illinois State University, Shaw
met James Fisher, a college administrator there who
would become a lifelong mentor to him. Courtesy of
University Archives, Syracuse University Libraries.*

later Fisher would influence one of Shaw's critical hiring decisions
(explored in chapter 11).

Shaw wanted to be a counselor and earned a master's degree in
education at the University of Illinois and a doctorate in the School
of Humanities, Social Sciences, and Education from Purdue University, where he took a special interest in the psychology of change.
At twenty-six, Shaw was hired at Illinois State as assistant to the

president, where he worked close by Fisher for three years. Fisher had recommended Shaw to the president, Robert G. Bone, to whom both Fisher and Shaw reported.

When Fisher was hired as president of Towson State University in Baltimore, he asked Shaw to join him as interim vice president for academic affairs. Fisher was not sure Shaw could keep the position permanently, but he told him he would find something else if it did not work out. "He took a chance on me," Shaw said. "He probably saw things that I didn't see in myself." Mary Ann, who had just given birth to their third child, also saw her husband's potential. Shaw was uneasy about taking the new job, and yet, with a newborn, Mary Ann encouraged him to go for it and to move some eight hundred miles away from their families.

Towson was another public university that had begun as a teachers', or normal, school. No academic powerhouse, its emphasis on training teachers had evolved toward broader liberal arts offerings.

Fisher, eight years older than Shaw, had a Kennedyesque charm and good looks. He was a skilled administrator who made working with him fun. He taught Shaw the importance of vision, of having good people working for you, and of the need to "hold their feet to the fire" while giving them flexibility. The Shaw/Fisher friendship grew closer when the Shaws bought a house down the block from the Towson president and Shaw coached Fisher's sons in basketball and baseball. With Fisher, he played tennis and poker—never bringing much money, losing quickly, and eating lots of food, Fisher said. An apocryphal anecdote, perhaps, meant to illustrate Shaw's frugality.

Eight years into his job at Towson, Shaw received a call from Southern Illinois University at Edwardsville, his hometown, asking him to interview for the presidency. The offer surprised him; college president was not a position to which he had aspired. Fisher encouraged Shaw to apply and offered some frank, much-needed advice: shed the Midwestern vacuum salesman look, shave the mustache, buy a blue suit, white shirt, and red tie for his interview, and work on table manners—wait until the hostess begins to eat before taking a bite. "I learned there are things you can't change about yourself," Shaw said, "but there are those things [you can change], and

I learned that they are important. You might think they are superficial. But for a lot of people, they are very important."

Shaw spent three years as president of Southern Illinois University Edwardsville and seven years as its first chancellor. The university had two main campuses that included medical, dental, and nursing schools.

In 1986, he became president of the University of Wisconsin system, one of the largest public university systems in the country, with twenty-six campuses and 165,000 students. In Wisconsin, Shaw further developed a skill that Fisher helped tutor him in: working state legislators and the governor. In his first year, he initiated one hundred policy changes. He championed free tuition for minority students and expulsion of students found guilty of racial harassment.

By the time Shaw reached Syracuse, the first and only private institution he would work at, the university was ready for change. Shaw was an anomaly at SU, whose previous nine chancellors had been ministers and scholars, products of an elite, buttoned-down academia. Shaw possessed an executive outlook shaped by twenty-two years of administrative work that emphasized good management and process.

Following Eggers, who was seventy-five and had been chancellor for twenty years, Shaw brought vital energy and confidence to the job. A lifelong athlete, he expected people to work as a team. He was diligent about getting daily time on the treadmill or tennis court and had a competitive streak that made it hard for him to turn down a challenge. Plainspoken, easily approachable, and without pretentions or airs, Shaw established open office hours Friday afternoons, when anyone could, and did, make an appointment to see him. He was as down-to-earth as the farmers who sat on the board of directors of Agway, a farming cooperative, said Eric Mower, a trustee and advertising executive who had Agway as a client. "You didn't need a contract with these guys; their handshake was their bond, and Buzz could be on the board of Agway."[7]

In May 1991, not long after the trustees appointed him, Shaw directed Eleanor Gallagher, who had been designated his on-campus liaison, to poll administrators for their views on a chancellor installation. Should it be modest or grand? November or April? SU had not had a formal installation since John Corbally's in April 1970, which was an elaborate event at the War Memorial for 2,000 people, with representatives from over one hundred universities and colleges. Eggers did not have an installation, deeming a celebration inappropriate during a time of turmoil.

Given the financial austerity SU was under, most deans and administrators recommended a modest "in-house" ceremony in November. And so it was, on November 8 at Manley Field House, Shaw was installed as SU's tenth chancellor, with both Melvin Eggers and William Tolley present. Invitations for 4,300 had gone out to all SU employees, several hundred student leaders, and city and county officials.

Mary Ann

One of Shaw's conditions for taking the job was that the university hire his wife, Mary Ann, then fifty. It would be a first for SU, a chancellor's wife being paid, but Shaw well knew the expectations put upon chancellors' spouses and the unacknowledged work they did. At Wisconsin, a public university where thirteen chancellors reported to him, state law did not allow chancellors' spouses to be paid, but Shaw made sure that they received library and parking passes, trip mileage reimbursement, and honorific titles.

The couple had a rich and balanced life in Madison. Mary Ann was a director on the board of the First Wisconsin National Bank of Madison, and vice president of development for the United Way, which she successfully led through a $6 million campaign. The University of Wisconsin provided the Shaws with a car and a house—the mansion of a former lumber baron. The Shaws' son, Kenneth William, lived above the carriage house/garage with his new wife and young daughter; their daughters, Susan Lynn and Sara Ann, had their own rooms when they came home to visit. It was a lot to give up, so Shaw made Mary Ann's salary a deal breaker. "I wasn't going to go if she [Mary Ann] didn't have a staff position," Shaw said. "First of all, she had a very responsible job. Secondly, it wasn't fair. And if she wasn't going to have a position, we might as well stay in Wisconsin. I wanted her to be happy."

Hired as associate of the chancellor, Mary Ann Shaw was the first wife of an SU chancellor to be paid a salary. Courtesy of University Archives, Syracuse University Libraries.

As associate of the chancellor, Mary Ann's responsibilities on paper were fund-raising and event planning, but she stepped in where she saw a need, confident she could make a positive difference. Nine years after her hiring, her salary was $65,000, the *Chronicle of Education* reported. That Mary Ann was receiving a salary was not broadcast but was generally known on campus. Although some resented her being paid for presumably doing what chancellors' wives always had—holding teas and greeting guests at events—others applauded her compensation. "It's about time," said a Women's Studies professor at a University Senate meeting during Shaw's first year. Equal pay and treatment of women in the workplace still had a long way to go. In 1998, only 4 percent of 894 colleges and universities paid spouses of presidents and chancellors, according to the College and University Personnel Association.

Mary Ann's partnership with Shaw made him a more engaged chancellor. Better than he was at remembering names and details, she was more gregarious and sophisticated, and could smile graciously through social activities longer and more easily than her husband ever could. Her pleasant manner, lively curiosity, and formal title gave her easy access to anyone at the university, as well as in the broader Syracuse community, and enabled her to forge relationships and learn about both on her own terms. She was driven to help her husband improve the university and saw herself as a matchmaker, connecting people with similar interests who might never otherwise come in contact: alumni and faculty, community leaders and deans. "My goal always has been to help people do what they want to do, and become the people they want to become," she said.[8] Beholden to no school, department, or office, she could enlist people from anywhere on campus and seized opportunities to strengthen and initiate student-centered programming.

She had an office with staff in the chancellor's residence and an assistant who had an office in the Tolley Administration Building. Her staff organized trustee events and alumni and special guest visits to every home football and basketball game, researching and tracking all special attendees.

In her first months on campus, Mary Ann asked to ride along with Thomas Cummings, vice president for enrollment, to a high school reception in Rochester for prospective students. As Cummings spoke to parents and students, Mary Ann sat quietly, not wanting to be introduced, but during the drive back, she asked "thousands" of questions, Cummings said. She was determined to learn firsthand and to draw her own conclusions about SU's student recruitment process.

A Chicago native and the second of four children, Mary Ann Byrne had wanted to be a teacher. Her mother, Rita Patterson Byrne, had graduated first in her class from Mundelein College, a private Roman Catholic women's college in north Chicago. After graduating high school, Mary Ann's father attended night school while selling stocks and bonds during the day, but when World War II intervened, he was called to work as a machinist in a factory. After the war, he went on to make his career in the textile business as a manufacturer's representative and salesman.

Mary Ann attended the University of Illinois at Urbana–Champaign for two years, leaving school to work, and it was then that she was introduced to Shaw on a blind date. Eight months later, they married; he was twenty-two, she was twenty-one, and over the next eight years, they had three children.

At Towson University, Mary Ann returned to college, earning a bachelor's degree in sociology and elementary education, and a master's degree in reading education. While there, she put her education into action and problem-solved childcare for their youngest, Sara Ann, by helping organize Maryland's first state-licensed nursery school for two-year-olds.

When the Shaws moved to Edwardsville, Mary Ann developed and ran her own business, the Reading Center, which provided reading, writing, and math tutoring for three-year-old to college-age students, with special focus on students with learning disabilities. She served on the board of the Oliver Anderson Hospital, outside of Edwardsville; was an elder and Sunday school teacher in the Presbyterian Church, a member of the League of Women Voters, and president of the Edwardsville YMCA; and served on the advisory board of the Friends of the Southern Illinois University Library. All of her engagement provided a foundation for the fund-raising and public service work Mary Ann would do in Syracuse.

Two years after the Shaws arrived at SU, they purchased a house in Skaneateles, half an hour's drive from the university. The mid-century modern house at 12 Gayle Road, with its quiet, wooded backyard and access to the lake, would become an important refuge for the couple, who would drive there Saturday afternoons after football or basketball games. "We'd be, like, on vacation for a full day and then come home [to the university]," said Shaw. "It was wonderful. I tried very hard, and I always advise CEOs, presidents of campuses, and chancellors to set aside a day when nobody can get to them, except for emergencies. That was Skaneateles."

*   *   *

The day after Shaw was appointed chancellor, he asked the university's vice presidents to submit to him a SWOT report, a self-analysis of their divisions' strengths, weaknesses, opportunities, and threats. Additionally, he asked for each vice president to request SWOT reports from every manager who reported to them. As the reports came, Shaw read them all, highlighting points and scribbling comments. "Reads like it was copied from a manual," he wrote across the report from the Office of Facilities Management, which was run by Harvey Kaiser, senior vice president. A report on the Dome, written by Athletic Director John J. "Jake" Crouthamel, listed among the Dome's weaknesses its air-supported roof and the kinds of events that could not be held there. No professional wrestling. No Grateful Dead concerts.[9]

Some of the reports went on for dozens of pages and revealed more about the writer than about the division. Typically, the strengths of each division included the wonderful people on its staff, and weaknesses stemmed from inadequate funding. Some writers were critical of specific people in their divisions. To their chagrin, Shaw passed the reports around, sharing them with the other chief authors. "I was used to being in a public setting where just about anything sent is a matter of public record," Shaw said. "It didn't dawn on me that people would not want anything they said revealed to other people. Had I thought about it, I might have said, 'Please know that I might share these with other colleagues.' They had some justification for being concerned."

The most insightful SWOT report came from John Hogan, the university's director of budget and planning. A graduate of Adirondack Community College and Bryant University, a small private school in Smithfield, Rhode Island, Hogan came to SU in 1974, starting as a budget analyst and then becoming budget director, and in 1985, he was named director of budget and planning. Before coming to Syracuse, he had been a supervisor of budgets and records at Brown University and worked as a quality control auditor at General Electric Co.

In five succinct pages, Hogan defined the major issues that Shaw would grapple with over the next five years and proposed the strategies Shaw would use to deal with them. He questioned why certain things were not being considered for budget cuts—like audits, legal work, subsidies for Syracuse University Press, and the yearly transfer of money to a reserve for "bad debt." He cautioned against cutting the budgets of the Development and Admissions offices and physical plant maintenance, noting that those offices critically protected the university's revenue. The timing was opportune for major changes, he said, because everyone—students, faculty, and staff—was facing financial hardship, either through enormous tuition hikes or wage freezes, and they would be amenable to changes. Eggers's 1990–91 wage freeze had jolted faculty and staff, whose salaries had been increasing an average of 6 percent annually, with 8 percent increases in 1988–89 and 1989–90.[10] Academically, the university was trying to be too many things to too many audiences, Hogan wrote. "Program quality suffers because of it." He continued, "Highly marketable programs should be added or expanded if they fit with the university's overall areas of strength." Also, to lessen the pain of staff reductions, Hogan recommended tapping a financial reserve known as the "Plant Fund."

Hogan had been closely monitoring SU's operation in all of its budgeting details for the better part of two decades, and he was now offering Shaw a game plan that he summarized in his conclusion: "to define what Syracuse University is going to be, what segment of the student market it will attempt to attract and what societal needs it will attempt to fulfill . . . to articulate the mission of SU and to sketch out the strategic plan that will get us there." Hogan's ideas were still being debated by a committee that had been appointed to recommend financial changes to the university, changes that would soon be revealed to the entire university.

Cabinet

A month before taking office, Shaw had identified SU's major problems along with a strategy and a timetable to address them, and shared his ideas with the cabinet members he had inherited from Eggers: Joan Carpenter, vice president for human resources; Lou Marcoccia, senior vice president for business and finance; Edward Golden, vice president for student affairs; Lance Baker, senior vice president for university relations; Eleanor Gallagher, executive assistant to the chancellor, executive director of government relations, and secretary to the Board of Trustees; John Hogan, director of budget and planning; Harvey Kaiser, senior vice president for facilities administration; and Gershon Vincow, vice chancellor for academic affairs.[11]

Shaw's plan and timetable were remarkable for their specificity at such an early stage and for how closely they would be followed in the months ahead. Decisions in one area would affect others, Shaw told cabinet members, and they had to work as a team. They would be kept informed of everything, and Shaw directed Marcoccia to simplify and fully disclose the budget so that everyone on campus could understand it and no one would think some fiscal remedy lay hidden in budget details.

A month later (August 26, 1991), at his first official cabinet meeting as chancellor, Shaw exuded confidence in the restructuring process. It would proceed briskly and on a firm schedule, pay raises would be restored, and tuition increases would be brought down to 6 percent, which would be the target going forward.

He also introduced a timely management principle: "Making Conflict Work for You," which was the title of an article he had written at the University of Wisconsin, and he distributed copies to cabinet members. Like most of Shaw's writing, it was simple and direct. "Conflict is inevitable and should be viewed as constructive."[12] Conflict could be resolved by listening carefully, observing body language, and repeating what you heard. He explained: If employees begin complaining about each other, stop them before they finish and ask them to speak to the person they are complaining about. If that does not resolve the issue, both parties could bring the issue back to him. "The last thing the contending parties want is a decision on a matter of such personal importance to be made by a busy president who is uninterested in hearing the details," he wrote.

Practicing the transparency and candor Shaw championed could be awkward. When cabinet members' divisions received cuts, he told them they could appeal to him for special treatment, and their appeals would be discussed by the entire cabinet.

*   *   *

Few understood the depth and scope of the university's problems when Shaw was introduced. SU's prevailing narrative about itself had been conveyed in a blithely upbeat prospectus for chancellor candidates written a year and a half earlier. Referred to as "The Book," the sixty-page document described Syracuse University as a "major research university" with 16,000 students, a $417 million budget, and 4,600 faculty and staff. Its finances were "stabilized," with balanced budgets the previous eighteen years.

Computer science and engineering were SU's flagship programs. Incoming student quality was "steadily improving," with average SAT scores in the university's fourteen colleges ranging from 1,183 in public communications to 954 in nursing.[13] Successful men's athletics programs in football, basketball, and lacrosse served as "unpaid advertising" for student recruitment. Undergraduate enrollment was expected to remain at current levels for the foreseeable future. Graduate student enrollment was expected to expand modestly. "There is no compelling reason to believe that the current undergraduate recruitment strategy should be discarded nor radically changed in the near future," The Book said. A new leader at the helm would merely have to hold the university on course, the document augured.

One weakness persisted, The Book acknowledged: fund-raising. Syracuse ranked 120th in endowment per full-time student among private universities. Fund-raising was improving, though, and the Division of University Relations, which oversaw fund-raising, had "capable and stable leadership" and an expanded budget and staff. It was in the midst of a five-year, $100 million campaign.

The Book was anything but a hard self-assessment and reflected aspirations that had guided the university through the 1970s and 1980s. In the year between its early 1990 publication and the winnowing of chancellor candidates in early 1991, the university's shaky financial circumstances had become undeniable and were partly self-made. By loosening admission standards through the late 1980s, SU had shielded itself from the enrollment losses that other universities were experiencing. The number of college-age men and women, which had been dropping since 1980, would continue to decline until 1995 or 1996, census data indicated.[14]

The Book did not anticipate 1990–91's grim outlook: a projected 20 percent decline in undergraduate enrollment and estimated budget shortfalls totaling $38 million by 1996. It carried no hint that Syracuse University would need to undertake the most substantive across-the-board changes in its history. Overall enrollment had declined 2.7 percent in 1990–91, with the number of new freshmen declining by 330 from the previous year to 2,770. A decline of 300 students carried through four years would mean a $15 million revenue loss over that period, and 73 percent of the university's revenues came from tuition.[15]

For the moment though, the university was in the black, having just completed its nineteenth year (1990–91) with a balanced budget and a $133,000 surplus.[16] A whopping 9.94 percent tuition hike had made that possible, which had followed a 12.4 percent hike in 1989–90 and a 9.6 percent hike in 1988–89. Tuition increases that were two to three times the rate of inflation could not continue without driving students away. In fact, after four years of exorbitant increases, they *were* driving students away, forcing Eggers to freeze salary and operating budgets for the 1991–92 year and to cut parts of the budget by 4.5 percent. Months later when it was clear that big cuts were coming, Tom Cummings, vice president for enrollment management and continuing education, told the *New York Times*, "We did not see any pattern suggesting an enrollment downturn."[17]

Enrollment declines were not the only troubles. New York State governor Mario Cuomo was proposing cuts in Bundy Aid, a state funding stream to private institutions that had been in place since 1969. The university estimated it would lose $30 million from state cuts by 1994.

At the May trustee meeting where Shaw was introduced, outgoing chancellor Melvin Eggers said the university's top priority was to "restructure" its academic programs. That meant cutting programs, cutting jobs. Without strategic restructuring, across-the-board cuts would have to be made for years, as the number of college-age students in the Northeast, and SU's enrollment, continued to decline. The Northeast was still the university's principal source of students. Maintaining current job levels while steadily losing revenue was a formula for collapse.

With job cuts, it would be important to minimize sinking employee morale, Eggers noted. He suggested rewarding and recognizing those leaving, as well as those remaining, because their workloads were going to increase. Supervisors would have to be trained to deal with the trauma of staff reductions. Faculty, staff, and graduate assistants were already protesting the salary freeze. Dozens from the School of Education and the College of Arts and Sciences signed a petition protesting the wage freeze and other budget cuts while campus construction projects continued.

"We can look out our windows and easily see that this hardship does not extend to the massive building construction campaign that has been underway," they wrote, noting plans for and construction of a $25 million addition to Maxwell Hall, a $5 million parking garage on Irving Avenue with a pedestrian bridge to campus, and a $3 million deal with the city of Syracuse to lease and reconfigure College Place and University Place, two streets running through campus.

Implementing this restructuring would be a job for Eggers's successor, but Eggers had laid the groundwork. After twenty years as chancellor, he was troubled by the university's predicament and searched for reasons behind it. "Almost every unit says it does not have enough resources. University lacks a clear statement of its goals/mission," he wrote in a 1991 note."[18]

At the page's bottom: "Next steps for the Ad Hoc Advisory Group." Eggers had just appointed the Ad Hoc Advisory Committee, or group, and entrusted its members to identify problems and suggest changes that would "preserve the most central and highest quality elements of the University." Robert Allen, the trustees' Budget Committee chairman, was named the Ad Hoc Advisory Committee chairman.

Some of the university's best and brightest deans and professors served on the committee: Susan Crockett, dean of the College for Human Development; Cynthia Hirtzel, department chair of chemical engineering (in the College of Arts and Sciences); Howard Johnson, professor of mathematics and associate vice chancellor for academic affairs; John Palmer, dean of the Maxwell School; Gary Radke, director of the Honors Program and associate professor of fine arts; David Rubin, dean of the Newhouse School; Ben Ware, vice president for research; and Michael Wasylenko, professor of economics and chair of the University Senate Budget Committee.[19]

Staff members were budget director Hogan and Eleanor Gallagher, executive assistant to the chancellor. Palmer and Ware were co-chairs and drove the analysis. The committee would have unprecedented access to information about budgets, staffing,

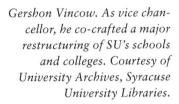

*Gershon Vincow. As vice chan-
cellor, he co-crafted a major
restructuring of SU's schools
and colleges. Courtesy of
University Archives, Syracuse
University Libraries.*

student demand, and various measures of quality and performance. Conspicuously missing from the committee was someone who knew more about each college's academic strengths and weaknesses than anyone at the university—Gershon Vincow, the soft-spoken vice chancellor for academic affairs.

A slight, elfin man who was detail oriented and analytical, Vincow approached issues with the measured deliberation of Talmudic inquiry. Programs and initiatives were often better for having endured his scrutiny. "You better not put numbers in front of him that didn't add up," said David Smith, dean of admissions and financial aid, "or ideas that didn't make sense. He would, in a very civilized way, cut you to ribbons." But Vincow had a hard time saying "no," a quality that would lead to difficulties through the restructuring process and beyond.

Vincow grew up in the Bronx and Brooklyn. At Columbia University, he graduated first in his class, majoring in chemistry. He earned his master's and doctoral degrees at Columbia, specializing in electron spin resonance spectroscopy. He was offered a research job at Bell Labs, in New Jersey, but passed it up to take a teaching position at the University of Washington, in Seattle. SU hired him in 1971 to chair the Department of Chemistry, a job he held until 1977. He was subsequently named vice president for research and graduate affairs, dean of the College of Arts and Sciences in 1978, and vice chancellor for academic affairs in 1985.

Why was Vincow not part of the Ad Hoc Advisory Committee? Eggers wanted the analysis to be ruthlessly rigorous and suspected Vincow might be defensive about programs and policies, said several committee members. Furthermore, Eggers knew that Vincow was applying for chancellor jobs and might leave. Vincow had applied at the University of Pittsburgh, Iowa State University, Georgia Institute of Technology, Brandeis University, and Syracuse University. He had interviews at several, but not Syracuse. Eggers insisted, however, that Vincow be given weekly updates about the committee's work. Whatever the committee recommended, Vincow would consider and have a hand implementing, or not.

On September 11, 1991, the much-anticipated report of Eggers's Ad Hoc Advisory Committee was released and printed in the *Syracuse Record*, the university's official newspaper. That same day, Shaw gave his first address to the University Senate, the academic governing body of faculty, students, staff, and administration members. Shaw told the senate that in addition to the $21 million already cut by Eggers (which included the wage freeze underway), $28 million more would be cut over three years. Citing the advisory committee's priorities, Shaw described how cuts would be decided and the timeline, with the final plan announced in early 1992.

*   *   *

The Ad Hoc Advisory Committee's report was a remarkably rigorous self-analysis, and although its premises would be debated for years—things such as whether research grants should be included in a school's income—its conclusions were the foundation for the strategic decisions credited to Shaw. During five months of work, the committee received some hundred letters from faculty, who overwhelmingly requested strategic cuts instead of "across-the-board cuts."[20] The $28 million question was, what to cut? The advisory committee's report, which laid bare schools' relative performance, set the stage for those decisions: the merger of two colleges, budget cuts totaling $8.1 million for ten colleges, increased budgets totaling $1.7 million for four colleges, and job cuts for faculty and staff.[21]

The committee reached its recommendations by assessing each college using three criteria—*demand, centrality,* and *quality* (see appendix A)—the university's strongest schools would have high degrees of all three. The criteria were the same that Eggers had used for at least a decade to determine how much to invest in academic programs. The difference now was that Eggers's ambition to improve SU's research stature was not driving recommendations; the looming fiscal crisis demanded a hard, objective analysis, school by school.

Most important, the committee assigned to each college an analytical metric that indicated its fiscal health. The number, which was called Implicit Fringe Benefit/Overhead (FB/OH), became as crucial a measure of colleges' health as blood pressure readings for patients and was used throughout the Shaw era to evaluate their performance. Each college's FB/OH was monitored, and each college had its own FB/OH target. The number was also confoundingly impenetrable and became "one of the dirty words of the era," said Ben Ware.

Its originator at SU was John Palmer, who had been hired as dean of the Maxwell School in 1988. A skilled analyst and administrator, he was uniquely equipped to assess institutional performance. He had earned his bachelor's degree in mathematics from Williams College and his PhD in economics from Stanford University. At twenty-eight, he was a senior economist and director at the US Department of Health, Education, and Welfare (HEW), and worked there during the administrations of presidents Richard Nixon and Gerald Ford. He did a stint at the Brookings Institute and later was named assistant secretary for planning and evaluation at HEW under President Jimmy Carter, where he oversaw 300 employees and a $100 million budget.

When he came to SU, Palmer observed that Maxwell professors seemed to be teaching a disproportionately high number of students compared to other schools, yet the university was only modestly increasing Maxwell's budget, and he concluded the school was

*John Palmer, dean of the
Maxwell School. Palmer
applied administrative
experience he gained in the
US Department of Health,
Education, and Welfare to
a fiscal and performance
analysis of SU's schools
and colleges. Courtesy of
University Archives, Syracuse
University Libraries.*

getting shortchanged. To support his request for more money, he
used a version of the FB/OH index, and when he joined the Ad Hoc
Advisory Committee, he brought the index with him.

The committee did not explicitly call for closure of programs or
schools, but it supported the idea. "The elimination of a program
that is below average in quality raises the average quality of the
institution." Money should be allocated to schools using a *student-
centered* criteria that would provide "the best experience to the
greatest number of our students," the committee's report said. The
university should not abandon its unique blend of professional education with traditional liberal arts education and should not let faculty scholarship and doctoral programs decline, even though both
needed substantial subsidies.

The committee ranked schools into three categories according
to their fiscal strength or weakness, recommending more money
for strong schools, cuts and other strategies for weaker schools.
(For a list of each school's category, budget cuts, and add-ons, see
appendix B.) Several consolidations were recommended: education,
human development, nursing, and social work schools could be

combined into one college, and the School of Information Studies
and the School of Management could be merged.

The committee's disclosures and recommendations prompted
anger, anxiety, and disbelief for some faculty and deans. "You could
have knocked me down with a feather," one dean said. "My only
reaction was: it has to be wrong."[22]

Shaw and Vincow spent the next several months meeting with
deans, faculty, and University Senate committees to discuss the
report and the trade-offs of various cuts and to ask for input, but for
the most part, decisions had already been made. "He [Shaw] really
never left it to them [faculty and deans]," said Vincow. "But he provided opportunities for input for every one of the colleges. And they
appreciated it. Because at the end, they had been consulted about the
financial problems of the university."

Faculty and deans asked why they were being singled out for
major cuts and not the administration or academic auxiliary offices,
like University College and the Division of International Programs
Abroad (DIPA). They had a point, Shaw conceded, and he directed
Gallagher and Ware to arrange for consultants to examine the rest
of the university's operation. Ware, a quick study with a broad intellectual range, was tapped whenever the university found itself facing
the unfamiliar. He had been a co-chair under Eggers on the advisory committee and would, under Shaw, lead the university into the
computer age.

Ware grew up in Ponca City, a small city in northern Oklahoma.
He graduated first in his class from Oklahoma State University,
majoring in chemistry, and earned his PhD in biophysical chemistry
from the University of Illinois, in Urbana. He taught chemistry at
Harvard University before being hired as professor and chair of the
Department of Chemistry at Syracuse in 1979. He was named vice
president for research in 1989 and, additionally, vice president for
computing in 1992.

Ware hired seven outside consultants to analyze the administrative units' efficiencies (see appendix C). The consultants compared SU's administrative and auxiliary operations with those at
forty-nine other private universities that had enrollments of 5,000
or more, including Yale, Cornell, Princeton, and Brown. Allen, the

Ben Ware, vice president for research and computing, was called upon whenever the university found itself facing the unfamiliar. Courtesy of University Archives, Syracuse University Libraries.

trustee Budget Committee chair, who oversaw the Ad Hoc Advisory Committee, oversaw this committee as well, and his understanding of the process would be essential for getting full Board of Trustee support for the restructuring plan.

The consultants' findings were released September 30, and they recommended an average 16 percent cut for administrative and auxiliary divisions with two exceptions: admissions and enrollment management. They found that SU had relatively little long-term debt compared to other private universities, where average debt was five times higher than SU's, a testament to Eggers's conservative fiscal management and careful campus stewardship.

The report confirmed yet again SU's poor endowment and its need for a consistent, steady enrollment. SU's $144 million endowment compared to an average of $417 million at other private universities. Endowment income provided Syracuse with just 2 percent of its budget, compared to an average of 7 percent.

At SU, 16 percent of all financial aid was going to scholarship athletes. The consultants recommended that athletic scholarships be funded not out of the financial aid budget but out of the athletic budget and that the university increase financial aid "to attract and retain undergraduates."

Stabilizing enrollment with better-quality students who stayed through to graduation was becoming a priority. Cummings suggested to Shaw in the early fall of 1991 that SU bring in an enrollment consultant who worked at Northwestern University and had written a book on the topic, William Ihlanfeldt.[23] Coincidently, Shaw had worked with Ihlanfeldt at one of his first jobs after college, when they both taught at Rich Township High School, an hour south of Chicago. Ihlanfeldt coached football there, and Shaw worked as his assistant for one year. At Northwestern, Ihlanfeldt was vice president for institutional relations in the admissions office. Shaw invited him to Syracuse, and he stayed two nights at the chancellor's house and talked to some fifty people on campus.[24]

Ihlanfeldt's report substantiated much of what administrators already knew: that SU was high priced and of only middle-market quality, and was graduating a lackluster 65 percent of new freshmen in five years and only 40 percent of minority students (blacks and Hispanics). Both figures were unacceptable, Ihlanfeldt said, and programs to retain students should be put in place.

He also discovered some other areas of need: the bursar's and registrar's offices were unresponsive to students and tended to give them the runaround. "The people are rude and obnoxious," one student told him. SU's approach toward minority students was clumsily homogenous. A spring weekend program for minorities had grouped together Asians, blacks, and Hispanics, provoking resentment from Asians who did "not view themselves as disadvantaged" and were offended by being included in a special minority program. Also, the admissions office staff had a high turnover, lacked enthusiasm, and had few SU graduates. The alumni coordinator of the admissions office was a longtime employee who did not have a degree.

Two of Ihlanfeldt's recommendations would become mainstays in the effort to improve student quality: provide a limited number of $5,000 merit scholarships to exceptional students and make the undergraduate experience, particularly the freshmen year, more gratifying and rewarding. "This will attract better students," Ihlan-feldt wrote.

In just a few months on the job, Shaw had gathered critical as-sessments about nearly every aspect of the university. Selecting the most cogent and penetrating of those, he would act on them just as quickly, and, in some cases, he had already begun.

CHAPTER 2

Restructuring

Building on Strengths

Core Values

Among Shaw's first requests after he was appointed chancellor was to receive a copy of SU's core values. Eleanor Gallagher, who served as Eggers's executive assistant and was the university's liaison to Shaw, told him she did not know if core values had ever been identified. "Well, we better get some," she recalled Shaw telling her. Having clear values was a stock management strategy for Shaw. As chancellor at Southern Illinois University, he had identified five institutional values that became pillars of his leadership approach there.

From Wisconsin, Shaw sent Gallagher an article he had written about values and how once identified, they should be reinforced through speeches and award ceremonies. Southern Illinois's values were caring, quality, service, opportunity, and comprehensiveness.

Gallagher shared Shaw's value-quest with Palmer, who as cochair of Eggers's Ad Hoc Advisory Committee, had been thinking a great deal about the essence of Syracuse University. Over a weekend, Palmer came up with five: quality, caring, service, diversity, and innovation.[1] His first three overlapped with three at Southern Illinois, and Shaw liked them all. They became his moral compass as he set a direction for the university—when issues arose, he would turn to SU's core values for guidance.

Another Shaw request was for "zingers"—positive and concrete things about the university, as well as things that needed to change—ideas around which to shape action plans and goals. He asked cabinet members and department heads to submit five of each.

"I want to make sure people understand that everything else doesn't stand still while we deal with restructuring," Shaw wrote in a September 1991 memo to cabinet members.

Shaw rolled out SU's newly minted values in his November 8 convocation speech at Manley Field House. "We are different because we are an institution committed to values—values that drive everything we do," Shaw said. For each value, Shaw recited a litany of positive examples, as well as things that needed improvement, all drawn from the zingers he had received. In the same speech in which Shaw laid out his aspirations for the university, he identified the value dearest to him.

"The one that needs the most attention, in my opinion, is caring," Shaw said. "The caring value is diminished when we become indifferent to the problems of others. Indifference, not hate, is the opposite of love." Shaw addressed recent examples of caring's diminishment: thirty false alarms to campus security over one weekend; rowdy house parties in the neighborhood around the university; racist, hateful, and homophobic slogans on T-shirts. Incidents of this sort had plagued SU for decades and were symptomatic of the indifference and hostilities that afflicted nearly every higher education institution in America. Never had they been characterized as sins against one of Syracuse University's core values.

By October, layoff and faculty severance plans had been drawn up. The process would be painful, and many were dreading it. Morale was sinking, staff felt underappreciated, and attendance was slim at University Senate forums about the restructuring. Yet Shaw brought an equanimity to the process, attempting to lighten the atmosphere with droll, Will Rogers–like quips. Restructuring was like sausage making, he said. "Even with the most carefully chosen and healthy ingredients . . . sausage making is an ugly process to witness. But after all the slicing, chopping, blood, and gore, the end process can be delicious, nutritious, and of remarkable quality."[2]

Shaw used the sausage-making metaphor in speeches and introduced it as an agenda category in weekly meetings with his cabinet. "The sausage-making process has begun," Shaw declared at the September 11 cabinet meeting.[3] While Shaw's use of "sausage making" referenced restructuring's messiness, another sausage-making attribute made his use of the term particularly relevant: little is wasted when sausage is made. Leading up to restructuring, Shaw used most of the ideas that came to him. Core values and zingers evolved into his "33 Initiatives," which he laid out in his Chancellor's Report of February 17, 1992. Each initiative had a timeline, and completing initiatives would involve more sausage making.

To some, it seemed as if Shaw was pulling recipes from a university administrator's cookbook, and they doubted whether his methodical, formulaic approach would work. "I recall being a little concerned that some of this was a little too simplistic," said Palmer. "But I came to see the value of it. Because if you're going to take an amorphous institution of this size and diversity and get everybody on the same page, you have to have some simplicity of goals, characterizations, language."[4]

Creating What?

On December 16, 1991, Vice Chancellor Vincow presented a proposal for budget cuts and increases. Ten schools' budgets would be cut, some by up to 40 percent—millions of dollars over three years. Two, engineering and computer and information science, would merge; four schools' budgets would increase. The College of Law's budget would remain the same.

Additionally, eight schools (including the College of Law) were charged with increasing enrollment at a time when the university's overall enrollment would be deliberately lowered and when their own college budgets were being cut. It was a bitter pill to swallow and, in some particulars, seemed nearly impossible.

Knowing the sausage making would generate resistance and criticisms, Shaw stayed in the background, letting Vincow serve as the stalking horse. Vincow's proposal was part of Shaw's measured rollout for cuts, reallocations, and mergers. Assessing reactions to it would help Shaw adjust the final plan and craft his message.

Vincow's proposal was more than a budget-cutting plan. Entitled "Restructuring Plan for Academic Affairs," it took up twenty-one broadsheet pages in the *Syracuse Record* and presented a new vision for Syracuse where students' learning needs would take precedence over everything else and even affect how research was conducted. It appeared to be a profound shift for Vincow, a research chemist who as vice chancellor for academic affairs had played a major role strengthening the research university that Syracuse had become, especially through the hiring of deans and professors.

Syracuse had spent considerable money over the previous decade hiring star professors to enhance its research reputation. Among them were Roger Penrose, an English mathematical physicist, mathematician, and philosopher of science, who shared his time between Oxford University and Syracuse and in 1988 was awarded the Wolf Prize in Physics, which he shared with Stephen Hawking, the English theoretical physicist and cosmologist; Nicholas Cabibbo, president of the National Institute of Nuclear Physics in Italy, hired as Distinguished Visiting Professor in Physics; Per Brinch Hansen, SU's Distinguished Professor of Computer and Information Science, who previously had been chair of the Computer Science Department at USC; Charles Long, a professor of religion, formerly at the University of North Carolina at Chapel Hill; Melvin DeFleur, a leading scholar in the field of media research and sociology at the Newhouse School; Janos Fendler, Distinguished Professor of Chemistry, who was helping SU develop its Center for Membrane Engineering and Science; and Robert Birge was hired away from Carnegie Mellon University to establish SU's Center for Molecular Electronics.

Becoming a top-tier research university was the golden ring beyond Syracuse's reach. The university was too dependent on tuition. Syracuse had financed the hiring of faculty stars and the expansion of select research programs by increasing undergraduate enrollment and raising undergraduate tuition. The year Shaw was hired at a salary of $209,628, one professor, John Alan Robinson, who taught logic and computer science, was earning $228,000, the equivalent of $409,773 in 2017. Fendler's salary that year was $157,411, or $282,907 in 2017 dollars.[5]

In the five years before Shaw arrived, tuition had increased an average of 9.2 percent a year. Increases topped out at 12.4 percent in 1989–90, far outpacing inflation and median family income growth.[6] Undergraduate academic quality had slid, and Vincow had been in charge of academic affairs for six years.

Did Vincow believe what he was saying? Could he effectively lead deans and faculty in a direction that seemed contrary to everything he represented? Would Shaw keep him? After all, Vincow had applied for Shaw's job. Shaw and Vincow confronted the questions during the summer, when Shaw came to Vincow's modest office in the Tolley Administration Building, down the hall from Shaw's new office suite. "There may have been some people who expressed doubts about me," Vincow recalled. "I assured him that, yes, I was able to deal with this."

Shaw saw in Vincow someone who knew the institution well. "I've always felt that I was the outside change agent," Shaw said. "I needed somebody on the inside who understood the place and understood how to get things moving from here to there. That was Gershon. Early on I could see that Gershon could do this. Early on I could see that Gershon *wanted* to do this. He was going to be my person."

Vincow's proposal had Shaw's fingerprints all over it. He and Shaw were creating a new vision together. "Things that were in my report, well, they were created in collusion [with Shaw]. That's the beautiful part," Vincow said.

Vincow referred to the core values Shaw had introduced in November. He stressed the need to improve graduation rates and student retention through closer monitoring of student success and better advising. He previewed Shaw's ideas for a fund to improve undergraduate teaching and for bringing a corporate-style quality improvement program to campus.

Criticisms of all sorts followed Vincow's proposals from faculty and deans in more than 300 letters to Shaw's office: There was nothing new, and Vincow's rhetoric—balancing teaching and research—was the same lip service to teaching that administrators had been spouting for years. Engineering's financial standing was misrepresented because sponsored research money was not considered, and engineering had brought in millions of dollars in prior years. The Maxwell School received favored treatment to the detriment of the College of Arts and Sciences, while categorizing schools created winners and losers. Enrollment projections were too high, and Vincow offered no backup plan. People who had served on Eggers's advisory committee wrote that more schools should be closed or merged.

Just two months remained, Christmas break included, before Shaw would announce his final plan. In the home stretch, Shaw turned to the four people he had come to trust most during his first eight months: Gallagher, Hogan, Vincow, and Ware. Shaw sent a university-wide order for feedback on Vincow's proposal: deans and supervisors would send feedback to vice presidents, and vice presidents would send summaries to Shaw's office. His four cabinet members would read and summarize reports from their divisions and read *each other's* reports and give him feedback on those. Meanwhile Shaw had a university to run, an NCAA investigation to see through, and alumni and trustees to meet and get to know.

In December, Shaw traveled to California for four days. After Christmas, there was a six-day trip to Florida for the Hall of Fame Bowl in Tampa. In January, Shaw took a five-day trip to visit alumni in Cleveland, Chicago, and Pittsburgh. Staggered deadlines for reports ensured he would have new ones in hand when he flew off on each trip.

The sausage making was getting ugly. With the proposed selective cuts and increases, long-standing institutional resentments that had been building for years were on full display. "Syracuse University faculty morale sags," concluded a *Syracuse Herald American* Sunday story after a faculty survey.[7]

His closest advisors were more pointed, telling him that serious troubles lay ahead unless he vigorously and confidently introduced specific action plans to create a student-centered culture. Hogan specifically identified several areas of concern, including a schism between liberal arts and professional school educators. "This does not bode well for the goal of blending," Hogan said. Furthermore, "teaching" faculty resented "research" faculty, feeling that they were paid less and had inferior facilities. For all the money that had gone toward research, the university had few areas of national research prominence, teaching faculty held. And, academic affairs people lacked respect for student affairs people.

Hogan warned of a morale crisis: "There's a lot of hostility on the part of the deans toward the vice chancellor and in some cases

toward one another. The level of hostility of some deans is so great
that it must be percolating through the colleges. If these negative
attitudes haven't reached our students by now, I would be surprised.
This is a bad situation. We all have to start pulling in the same direction or we will pull ourselves apart."[8]

Shaw Report

Shaw began his restructuring announcement with grimmer news
than expected. SU's projected deficit had grown by one-third since
August, from $28 million to $38 million. Student application
demand was softening. The university was lowering its enrollment
target and, therefore, its projected revenue. Where would money
come from? Athletics, for starters, the one area where Syracuse's
national reputation was riding high. Shaw cut $2.1 million from the
Department of Athletics budget. For the first time in the university's
history, Shaw demanded that athletics begin covering some portion
of scholarships for their revenue sports—football and men's basketball. He also took $5 million from the department's reserve fund to
cover general university scholarships.

Money would also come from SU's $108 million reserve, or Plant
Fund. Eggers had built it up with yearly transfers of $15 million. Its
existence had been rumored as a deferred maintenance fund, but
its true worth was known only by those in Eggers's inner circle. By
revealing the Plant Fund's value, Shaw had established a new trust
between the chancellor's office and the rest of the university, which
facilitated candor in discussions about budgets and programs. Portions of the Plant Fund would pay for increased financial aid, capital improvements, severance packages for laid-off employees, and
retirement incentives for faculty. Yearly $15 million transfers to the
Plant Fund would end.

The bulk of the deficit would be made up through cuts to personnel and programs, projected over five years—fiscal year 1993
through fiscal year 1997. The academic side, which included faculty
and staff in the schools and colleges and had a reducible base of
$112 million, would be cut $12.7 million, roughly 11 percent. The
administrative side, which included everything that did not directly

support teaching, had a reducible base of $49.3 million and would be cut $9.4 million, roughly 19 percent.[9]

Just as Vincow's plan had described two months earlier, colleges and schools would *not* be treated the same: some saw their budgets increased, most saw their budgets cut. The amounts were nearly identical to those in Vincow's proposal, with slightly less cut from social work, nursing, music, information studies, and computer and information science.

Only engineering and computer and information science were merged, as per Vincow's plan. No colleges were closed. Vincow had argued against any closure: "Once you close colleges at a restructuring, it has a kind of an effect on your reputation," said Vincow. "And it has an effect on the faculty. 'Oh, close the nursing school . . . who's going to be next?'"

Overall, the cuts and increases shifted money from weak schools and colleges to stronger ones. The plan demanded that the weak ones get stronger, increase their enrollments, and become more profitable. Corporate-style accountability had come to SU's academics.

With morale low, Shaw's speech needed to bring faculty and deans on board. He addressed that by restoring wage increases—4 percent on salaries and 1 percent for fringe benefits for the first year—and saying that the university would strategically increase salaries to bring them more in line with those at similar universities. He allotted $340,000 for a faculty diversity initiative and to hire faculty in the African American Studies department. He committed more money for scholarships, especially merit scholarships for talented but not necessarily needy students. He also announced the creation of a $2 million Chancellor's Innovation Fund that would provide grants to faculty to support their ideas to improve undergraduate instruction and advising over the next two years.

Shaw offered few details about how research and graduate education would be strengthened.

The campus culture had to change, he said. Students had to embrace learning and move away from partying. Faculty had to shift from emphasizing scholarship and research to focusing on undergraduate teaching. "Our commitment to becoming a learning and student-centered culture within a research institution is the answer to the challenges we face. . . . We will . . . become a national model," Shaw said.[10]

The criticisms and suggestions that followed Vincow's December proposal became to-do items in Shaw's February proposal. "I knew exactly where the touch points were," Shaw said. He wanted Syracuse University to look differently when new students arrived for the fall 1992 term. Besides identifying cuts, he presented 33 Initiatives (appendix D) that were already underway or about to begin. The initiatives turned criticisms into proactive goals. Each would have a task force with deadlines, and most were designed to support the "student-centered research university," a brand that Syracuse would own.

The 33 Initiatives would serve as a kind of scorecard for Shaw's student-centered mission.[11] It fell to Vincow to identify and categorize the initiatives under the five core values and to begin pursuit of them right away. "Buzz told me 'I want things that can be done and I will insist that they be done with first reports within six months. Let's move it, so there's no possibility of falling back.'"

Shaw's restructuring plan could proceed, it seemed. One obstacle remained, however. University Senate leaders wanted to vote whether to endorse Shaw's plan, which concerned him. He chaired the senate and knew how angry some faculty were about the cuts. Although the senate's vote could not block restructurings, a negative vote could hinder implementation.

Shaw told James Wiggins, co-chair of the Senate Committee on Academic Freedom, Tenure, and Professional Ethics, that as senate chair he (Shaw) would not bring up the resolution.[12] "The people who are going to be hurt by this—almost everybody with the exception of Maxwell and Newhouse—are going to be opposed to it. It creates all kinds of 'us and them' with schools and colleges." And yet, Shaw knew he had to demonstrate trust in the process. "Nothing can keep *you* from doing it," Shaw told Wiggins.

The afternoon of February 19 (two days after Shaw presented the restructuring plan), eighty-four members of the University Senate met in room 101 of the Physics Building. Shaw was not there, and Vincow presided. Wiggins presented a resolution offering the senate an opportunity to declare its support for Shaw's plan.

"The Syracuse University Senate declares its support for chart-
ing a new course designed to change the culture of Syracuse University and commits itself to continue to cooperate and participate
in considering and in initiating proposals aimed at accomplishing
those culture changes. Further, the senate commends Chancellor
Shaw for his leadership in the restructuring process." The resolution
passed. The exact vote count was not recorded.

*   *   *

What were students' responsibilities in a student-centered research
university? Shaw wanted students to agree to a statement of responsibility. Crafting that statement was a task delegated to Ronald
Cavanagh, vice president for undergraduate studies. From the out-
set, Shaw and Cavanagh disagreed over what the statement should
be called. Shaw wanted a "student contract." "I didn't like that language at all. I *did not* like the language," said Cavanagh, a former
dean of the Department of Religion. "I wanted 'covenant.'"

In Shaw's office, the two debated, their voices getting louder and
louder. Shaw's secretary, Marlene Carlson, walked by and said, "I
suggest you try 'compact.'"

Cavanagh looked at her and asked, "Like the Mayflower?"

"Yes," she said. "That will do."

By summer 1992, after more than one hundred drafts, Shaw
accepted this version of the Syracuse University Compact:

> We the students, faculty, staff, and administrators of Syracuse
> University will:
> - support scholarly learning as the central mission of the
>   University.
> - promote a culturally and socially diverse climate that sup-
>   ports the development of each member of our community.
> - uphold the highest ideals of personal and academic hon-
>   esty, and
> - maintain a safe and healthy environment for each member
>   of our community.
>
> In all aspects of university life, we will work together to reach
> these goals.

At campus meetings about the compact, students, faculty, and staff were encouraged to personalize those goals and share them. It began to change the way people saw each other. "Listening to [students] talk about things, listening to other groups, I got to know the campus in an altogether different way than ever before," Cavanagh said.[13]

*   *   *

A number of introductory, fall orientation programs for freshmen were introduced in Shaw's first year that linked small groups of students with faculty to build student–faculty relationships and to strengthen the student-centered emphasis. Since students in different colleges had different academic profiles, the programs differed slightly.

The College of Arts and Sciences called its program a Freshman Forum. A small-scale, experimental version had begun in Eggers's last year (fall 1990), and the program was expanded to all 390 incoming first-year students at the college in 1991. Each forum section had a maximum of fifteen students and was taught by a full faculty member; even deans and vice presidents led it. Each section met once a week for eight weeks in the fall. Meetings were informal and interactive, with a focus on student concerns, rather than on academic matters. Students were encouraged to journal. Forum sections might have dinner at a faculty member's house or a restaurant, attend a Syracuse Stage production, tour the Dome, or visit the Everson Museum. One vice president took a group camping on the Lake Ontario shore for a weekend. "The point is that students need some warm, guiding experience that can be helpful to them in an institution," said Vincow, who led a Freshman Forum section. Faculty learned things about students they would not have otherwise—those on Ritalin, their homophobia, their homesickness.

The School of Management and Newhouse called their programs the Freshmen Advocacy Network (FAN), with groups of five students each. The College for Human Development offered a gateway course for freshmen that not only worked to develop faculty–student relationships but addressed study skills and the ability of students to work together as a team.

Disney Deaccession

Like a laid-off worker looking for ways to pay the bills, the university looked everywhere for onetime income. On March 2, 1994, the university sold for $1 million its collection of Disney animation cells and drawings.[14] Donald W. Wheaton, a 1955 graduate of the School of Management, had donated the collection in 1968, when it was appraised for $21,800. The collection contained 556 items, including original animation cells, preparatory drawings for the cells, storyboards, pastels, and watercolors from *Snow White*, *Pinocchio*, *Fantasia*, *Dumbo*, and *Bambi*.

The buyer was Jeffrey Lotman of Philadelphia, the son of Herb Lotman, a food industry magnate who built his family's wholesale beef business into Keystone Foods Corporation of Bala Cynwyd, Pennsylvania. Among Keystone's food industry breakthroughs was to use cryogenics to distribute McDonald's food products in the late 1960s. Keystone also helped conceive the Chicken McNugget in the 1980s.

SU's proceeds were used to create a quasi-endowment to support the university's permanent art collection. The sale was a significant revenue bump at a time of major budget cuts.

Faculty Awards

The institution-wide shift to a student-centered focus prompted the introduction of faculty awards for teaching. The Laura J. and L. Douglas Meredith Professorships of Teaching Excellence were the largest and most impactful teaching award. It gave two tenured professors in any field a bonus of $25,000 annually for three years— $20,000 as salary and $5,000 for professional development. Two new recipients are named each year, and there could be six Meredith Professors at any one time. Three were named the first year, in 1995: Linda Alcoff, professor of philosophy, William Coplin, professor of public affairs, and William Glavin, professor of magazine journalism.

The Meredith Professorship was one of the first endowed professorships at SU not awarded for research, and it bolstered faculty morale by recognizing teaching in a way that had not been done

The first Meredith Professors. Standing: Linda Alcoff, philosophy; William Coplin, public affairs; William Glavin, magazine. Sitting: Jerry Evensky, economics; Samuel Clemence, civil engineering. Courtesy of University Archives, Syracuse University Libraries.

before. Supporting it was an unearmarked $2.6 million bequest from the estate of Dr. L. Douglas Meredith, a gift that came at just the right time, enabling Shaw to put money behind his talk about emphasizing teaching. Meredith was a 1926 graduate of the College of Arts and Sciences who later became an SU trustee, and the professorship was named for him and his wife, Laura J. Meredith.

Endowed professorships can help attract outstanding professors to come to a university or, in the case of those already there, keep them. Since outstanding researchers are nationally recognized and generally have higher market value than outstanding teachers, most endowed professorships are for research.[15] So the Meredith Professorship was a distinct departure from the accepted economic rationale of paying more to outstanding researchers than to teachers.

Another new faculty award to recognize teaching was the William P. Tolley Distinguished Teaching Professorship in the Humanities, named for SU's chancellor from 1942 to 1969. It provided an annual salary supplement of $12,000, plus a $12,000 summer stipend to develop innovative curriculum and new instructional techniques.

In addition to these sizable grants, a number of smaller programs with financial incentives to improve instruction were launched or expanded through the Center for the Support of Learning, which came under Cavanagh's oversight. Among them were the Faculty-to-Faculty Teaching Consultancy, which matched seasoned teachers with new faculty members, and an expanded version of the Gateway Fellowships, a program that had started in 1989 to improve the quality of large-class, introductory undergraduate courses. Under Shaw, Gateway expanded and faculty competed for awards of $3,000–$5,000. The Gateway program expanded again in 1994, offering luncheons three times a semester, at which Gateway Fellows would share their teaching innovations with other faculty. Topics included such things as using the internet, interacting with students, active learning strategies, and grading philosophy.

Outside speakers like Ernest Boyer, an educator, author, and former commissioner of the US Department of Education, were invited to speak. Such programs encouraged and incentivized professors and even staff to initiate ways to improve teaching and fostered conversations about teaching across departments and schools.[16] A similar but much more structured quality program for staff and administrators, called SUIQ (Syracuse University Improving Quality), will be explored in chapter 9.

Supported Resignations

The day following Shaw's restructuring speech, the *Post-Standard*'s front-page headline focused on the speech's immediate, hard news: "SU's Vision Focuses on Lay-Offs."

SU's layoffs were all anyone was talking about. Allen, chairman of the trustees' Budget Committee, sent Shaw a note, newspaper headline included, saying that the high aspirations of Shaw's speech, so critical for SU's long-term success, were being lost in public discourse. Shaw's vision needed to be "carefully prepared, aggressively pursued, and successfully promulgated," wrote Allen, the former chairman and CEO of Carrier Corporation. He understood marketing and encouraged Shaw to seek "the very best outside [public relations] help we can get" to promote SU's new vision.

The vision, however, could not be executed without the layoffs. At a cabinet meeting weeks later, on March 16, the tenured faculty reduction program, referred to as "supported resignation," was the focus of attention. They were meant to be layoffs without the sting.

One hundred and twenty-two tenured faculty with at least ten years of service signed up. Their ages ranged from forty-two to seventy-two; one hundred seven were men, fifteen were women. These volunteers accepted a generous program designed to persuade them to give up their tenured positions. Two years of salary and three years of health insurance were the enticements. Professors who took the offer could still receive emeritus status upon recommendation of their school or college. One faculty member, John Alan Robinson, a British-born philosopher, mathematician, and computer scientist, received a $300,000 payout.[17]

Vincow had directed Michael Flusche, associate vice chancellor for academic affairs, to design the severance program to reduce the number of faculty in a collegial and community-supported way. Flusche consulted counterparts at other universities and decided on a priority system for ranking faculty according to quality that identified who the university was willing to see leave and who to discourage from leaving.[18] "We discovered . . . who was above-average and therefore someone we wanted to keep," said Vincow. "We didn't want to give them two years and let them run away to Harvard."

Shaw set no dollar target for how much should be saved; he wanted to see what the result would be, Flusche said. The university spent $30 million from its Plant Fund to pay for the supported resignation and severance programs, an amount recovered in one year with fewer faculty and staff on the payroll.

In the end, the program prompted the self-selection the university was after. No one who applied for the program was denied, Flusche said. Whether or how many valuable faculty were lost is debatable and depends on who one asks. Vincow remembers three top faculty members leaving. Flusche said no top faculty departed: "When people say we lost some of our best, it's simply not true."

For staff departures, two different programs were put in place. A target of 474 people would be laid off, with a projected one-year savings of $12 million. Some layoffs would be involuntary, others would be voluntary departures with a severance payment based on length of service. Some long-term employees would receive as much as two years' pay. The total cost of staff severance payments was estimated at $12.3 million.

Making layoffs as "painless" as possible and demonstrating to staff that Syracuse University was a caring institution were the university's goals, according to an Office of Human Resources document, and the generous terms helped do that.[19] Laid-off employees who did not find other work would receive up to a year's health care, life insurance, and disability coverage if they paid their share; tuition benefits for dependents already attending SU would continue; and remitted tuition for employees and their spouses would continue for a year after the layoff date. Involuntarily laid-off employees could be rehired, so it was possible for an employee to receive a severance payment and then be rehired. Most layoffs occurred in the first year.[20]

Salary Adjustments

For the university to improve after restructuring, faculty salaries needed to increase. The salary freeze (1990–91) had ended, but it was understood that faculty in some schools earned considerably less than their counterparts elsewhere. Shaw had addressed the importance of competitive salaries and benefits in his February 1992 restructuring speech. He also had a history of advocating for faculty. At the University of Wisconsin, Shaw had, with some success, persuaded the governor and state legislature to increase faculty salaries to make them more competitive—no small achievement.[21]

At SU, Shaw created a task force, chaired by Martin L. Fried, a professor at the College of Law, to study salary inequities. SU's faculty salaries were roughly 4.5 percent below its competitors, Fried's task force found. However, SU spent roughly 2 percent more of its payroll on pension contributions. Faculty salaries in architecture, human development, nursing, and visual and performing arts were significantly lower than their competitors. Within those schools and colleges, faculty faced even greater disparities.

Shaw agreed to increase salaries strategically in those four schools. Totaling approximately $513,000 in 1993–94 dollars, the increases would be phased in over three years. The money was given to the respective deans and distributed on a merit basis. The source of money for the first-year installment (1994–95) was the Plant Fund. Money for second- and third-year increases would come from incremental reductions (one-third of 1 percent) in overall faculty salary budgets. "I recognize that this will involve sacrifice," Shaw said, "but I hope you will agree that it is necessary for the well-being of our entire community."

Staff salaries, which also had disparities and were generally viewed as being less than competitors' salaries, would be examined the following year with an eye to making them fair and competitive, Shaw pledged.

Eggers Hall

The one school that came out of restructuring the strongest was the Maxwell School, which received an extra $1.08 million a year *and* was getting a new six-story building, Eggers Hall. The new building would be attached to the renovated Maxwell Hall by a glass-enclosed, three-tiered atrium. Total cost for construction and renovation would be $25 million. The building commitment was made by Eggers, who pledged the $1 million naming gift.

Site preparation involved the dramatic relocation of Holden Observatory, built in 1887 and one of the oldest buildings on campus. In June 1991, the firm L. D. Dexheimer and Son moved the 320-ton limestone observatory 190 feet, at a rate of four inches an hour, a move that took three days. Groundbreaking for Eggers Hall took place on May 9, 1992.

For all the anticipation that generally accompanies a new building's construction, the Eggers Hall work was played down. Shaw's construction progress report to trustees in May 1994 came with a caveat: "In the near future, though, we will see very little, if any, new construction." Once it was finished, celebrations were held, starting with an official opening January 7, 1994, at which Chancellor Emeritus Eggers was honored. The entire Maxwell School complex was dedicated October 6–7, 1994, as part of a year-long celebration of SU's 125th anniversary.

The enlarged Maxwell School complex (Eggers Hall was 84,000 square feet) brought together departments and programs that had been scattered among ten buildings and increased the school's space by roughly 45 percent. Eggers Hall was the first academic building on campus with a cafeteria, an amenity that became standard in academic buildings that followed. The $25 million to be raised for the building was to be matched by another $25 million to fund new programs.

Leading up to the restructuring process the Maxwell School had been deemed one of SU's strongest schools, and it became even stronger. In 1995, Maxwell was rated first in the United States for public administration schools by *U.S. News & World Report.*

Facilitated Communication

Amid restructuring anxieties in the fall of 1991, a new program in the School of Education, led by Professor Douglas Biklen, was getting national attention. Biklen was director of the Division of Special Education and Rehabilitation, and was promoting a technique said to enable people with autism and limited communication skills a means to express themselves articulately. It was called facilitated communication (FC), and its results seemed miraculous.

FC had the potential to change the theory and definition of autism. People with severe disabilities who some thought might not have feelings or an ability to empathize suddenly had means to express intelligence and emotion. Using the technique, nonverbal people with autism were solving math problems and writing poetry.

FC required a teacher or speech therapist to support the hand or arm of an individual with autism as he or she pointed to a letter on a keyboard or alphabet display. By pointing to letters, the person was able to spell out responses to questions and converse with others. Biklen had been introduced to FC by Rosemary Crossley, its original developer, on a trip to Melbourne, Australia in 1988. He brought it to Syracuse, taught the technique to parents, teachers, and teacher aides, published an article in the *Harvard Educational Review*, and began to draw attention from the national press, most notably an enthusiastic feature on the ABC news program *Prime Time Live*, with Diane Sawyer. That summer, Biklen formed the Facilitated Communication Institute at SU.

With SU's budget woes generating plenty of dire news, the positive publicity about FC seemed a public relations gift. Riding the wave of good news, Lance Baker, senior vice president for university relations, secured from Shaw's office a $248,240 loan to pay for the editing and production of five, twenty-minute training videos for Biklen's Facilitated Communication Institute and said that his office would make "its top fundraising priority the generation of funds necessary to repay this loan."[22]

However, SU colleagues questioned Biklen's techniques, which they said were not being rigorously tested. A small group of faculty had met with Shaw during his first semester on campus and encouraged him to prohibit the practice of FC at the university, according to Bruce Carter, an associate professor of psychology at SU who specialized in child development.[23] Shaw stressed that the tradition of academic freedom allowed faculty to pursue what they desired and did not intervene.

In the fall of 1993, a PBS *Frontline* episode called into question Biklen's claims of a breakthrough. Parents, siblings, grandparents, and teachers were being accused of sexual abuse by children using FC techniques "being promoted at Syracuse University," the episode said.[24] Accusers were being pulled from their families and put into foster homes. Courts had to decide whether to admit testimony created through FC, and most decided against it.

"Syracuse University is now in the position of having an institute dedicated to researching, teaching, and promoting a technique that all the scientific evidence says is not real," the program's narrator stated. *60 Minutes* followed with its own report questioning the technique's validity.

Biklen defended FC, saying that anxiety-producing experimental conditions likely led to its failure. Shaw assured trustees that the university's position was to encourage research and investigation and to allow the marketplace of ideas to determine the efficacy of FC. In May 1994, Syracuse hosted a national conference on FC attended by some 900 parents and providers.

The broadcasts set off a firestorm of criticism, with letters to the university accusing it of supporting pseudoscience. Faculty pressed Vincow to have the university at least take a more neutral stance toward FC. Robert Hill, vice president of public relations, reached out to Diane Sawyer, encouraging her to do another positive story on the technique, and contacted television critics and public television stations in San Francisco and New York telling them *Frontline* reporting had been unbalanced.

At a cabinet meeting, Vincow expressed concern that, by helping promote FC, the university was opening itself to being sued, and in 1994 it was. Mark Storch of Red Hook, New York, accused the university and Biklen of fraud after Storch was falsely accused through FC of sexually abusing his daughter. The lawsuit was dismissed in 1995. "There is simply no basis for placing responsibility for these events on the shoulders of the man who brought the theory to this country and touched off the debate surrounding its efficacy," wrote the judge.[25]

Although FC was widely and repeatedly discredited, Biklen and his institute stood by it as a learning technique that helped people with autism communicate and integrate into mainstream life, and the institute continued to explore validation tests and to strengthen training techniques for facilitators. After Shaw left as chancellor, Biklen was named dean of the School of Education, an announcement met with "disappointment and dismay" by the Commission for Scientific Medicine and Mental Health.[26]

Engineering

No school or college had a more profound takedown under restructuring than engineering. For decades after World War II, when the university's mission had been to advance to the next tier of research universities, the College of Engineering had been SU's entrepreneurial flagship. In 1971, SU became the second university in the United States to offer an accredited computer engineering program.

The college expanded as the electrical and computer engineering industry grew in upstate New York. It offered master's degree programs at IBM's and GE's corporate offices and in Rome at Rome Air Development. The corporate–college partnership was enhanced with the opening of the CASE Center (Center for Advanced Technology in Computer Applications and Software Engineering) in 1984, run by Bradley Strait, who had been dean since 1981.[27]

Off-campus programs were big revenue generators for the college. Corporations paid the full cost of master's degrees for their employees. Tenured engineering faculty, who originally received bonuses for teaching at the off-campus sites, were picked up by limousine (sent by IBM from Endicott and Owego), took a train, or flew in a chartered plane to classes in Poughkeepsie.[28]

Demand for the off-campus engineering programs waned during the 1980s, after SUNY Binghamton's Watson School of Engineering (named for IBM Corporation founder Thomas J. Watson) opened in 1983 and as both IBM and GE began downsizing operations in New York.[29] Spending continued, though, within the College of Engineering. In the six years before Shaw became chancellor, engineering's budget grew 21 percent (to $6.3 million), and its faculty increased by 9 percent (to 99), while the number of undergraduate credit hours taught (14,936) declined 40 percent.[30] According to the FB/OH assessment tool, engineering had a low score (-36 percent), which meant the rest of the university was heavily subsidizing it.

Shaw's restructuring slashed engineering's budget, cutting $2.8 million over five years, while demanding that engineering generate an additional $550,000 through increased graduate enrollment. Increasing graduate enrollment seemed a pipe dream; off-campus demand had virtually disappeared, and competition from other engineering schools across New York State had changed the landscape.

Shaw merged the College of Engineering with the School of Computer Science—the only SU school with a worse financial profile than engineering. Computer science's FB/OH was -48 percent. Together, engineering's and computer science's budgets were cut 41.3 percent, more than $3.8 million. Faculty numbers (instructors and professors) went from 108 in both in 1991–92 to sixty-one in 1996–97 in the merged program.[31]

The merger had been suggested by Eggers's advisory committee. "One of the things that we discovered in Engineering, if you looked at the number of students and number of faculty, it looked reasonable," said Ben Ware, a chemist, vice president of research, and a leader of that committee. "But they had a huge number of paid staff—technicians—on salary, not on grants. So their overall costs were really high. And they'd gotten used to living like that. It's a nice way to live, if you have somebody to do a lot of the technical work; then the students and the faculty don't have to do it. But it was an overbearing expense that had to be cut drastically."[32]

The cuts reverberated beyond the university and took an emotional toll on faculty and deans, a toll that persisted all through Shaw's tenure. For people inside the College of Engineering, their distinguishing feature—their research infrastructure of people with time to stay on research tasks—was being gutted. "We would go out to conferences and colleagues would say, 'We hear you're shutting down,'" said Shiu-Kai Chin, then a newly tenured professor of electrical engineering and computer science. "It was very clear, to the outside world, this wasn't the place to be."[33]

Strait, the college's dean, was one of the first to accept the supported resignation program offer. He was only 60, and SU was in his blood—his grandfather, father, mother, and brother had all graduated from SU. A Navy veteran who served during the Korean War, Strait knew that engineering faced big cuts and felt he could lead the way by accepting the resignation offer. "I'm thinking if I take this, everybody will think it's OK, it will be easier to sell," he said.[34]

For some in engineering and computer information science, the cuts and merger were part of a narrative that began before Shaw and would continue after him—the waning of research at SU. Engineering's part of the story began in the 1970s, when student war protests prompted the university to disaffiliate itself from the Syracuse University Research Corporation (SURC), an arm of SU that conducted research for the US Department of Defense. That decision began a slow decline of research opportunities from which SU never fully recovered, say professors and deans in the combined school.

Eggers's ambition to raise SU to "the next tier of research excellence" led to the creation of the Northeast Parallel Architecture Center in 1987—with the help of a federal grant—and to the hiring of star faculty. But SU did not have the endowment muscle to sustain research faculty at the levels to which it aspired. Supporting research with more and more undergraduate tuition revenue weakened the university's core. Shaw's cuts in research-heavy schools, undertaken to direct more resources toward the education of undergraduates, amounted to a tacit abandonment of the institution's research ambition, the narrative goes.

When Strait resigned, the national searches for new deans, which had been a core initiative of Vincow under Eggers, were suspended. It would be hard to recruit an outsider to take over two schools whose combined budgets had been cut by almost half.

To replace Strait, Vincow submitted a list of internal candidates. At the top was Steven V. Chamberlain, a professor of neuroscience, who was named dean of the newly merged College of Engineering and Computer Science. Chamberlain served as dean until 1996, when he resigned.[35] He was replaced by Edward Bogucz, a mechanical and aerospace engineer who had been at the university since 1985 and who had some heavy lifting to do to bring the struggling school forward.

School of Information Studies/iSchool

Shaw's restructuring decisions about which school budgets to cut and which to invest in were more conservative than visionary. He largely implemented the plan that was given to him, in which schools that were making money with high demand and high quality received more money, and those that were being subsidized had their budgets cut and were expected to improve their bottom line. That strategy missed an opportunity.

The School of Information Studies, which was later rebranded the iSchool, was a small, reinvented upstart when Shaw arrived, poised to capitalize on the explosive growth of electronic data that would soon dominate our lives. Its trend lines were positive. By the chief determinant of restructuring, FB/OH, however, it was deemed a poor performer and placed in the lowest tier of Category 3 schools (appendix B).

The dean, Donald Marchand, had been hired in 1987 to launch the school's undergraduate program and to strengthen its master's program. He had come from the University of South Carolina's

College of Business Administration, where he founded the Institute for Information Management, Technology, and Policy. In 1986, he had coauthored a book, *Infotrends: Profiting from Your Information Resource*, and was seen as future-thinking and progressive.

The school had begun as the School of Library Science in 1914. Nearly eight decades later, it still offered a master's degree in library science, but its focus was becoming more entrepreneurial, with an emphasis on grooming graduate students for private sector information management work. The year Marchand began, the iSchool welcomed its first freshman class with twenty-three students who would work toward a bachelor's of science in information management and technology. Nearly all of those first students had been "steered" to the iSchool by the university's alternate admissions offer.

SU's alternate admissions policy was an enrollment strategy to capture applicants who were not accepted at their first choice of SU colleges, usually Newhouse. After freshman year, if their grade point average was in the high 3s, they could apply to transfer to their first-choice school. Since the iSchool had just begun its undergraduate program, student demand from direct, or primary, applicants was almost nonexistent, a strike against it in the restructuring process.

The ad hoc report suggested the iSchool merge with the School of Management or Newhouse or Maxwell, where its computer and information management work would complement those schools' curriculum.

In Vincow's proposed restructuring cuts, the iSchool was slated for a budget decrease of $150,000 over three years. Marchand fought the cuts and merger ideas and unsuccessfully argued for a budget increase like Maxwell, Newhouse, the School of Architecture, and the College of Visual and Performing Arts were getting. "Growth doesn't come free," he told Vincow.

Within the iSchool, Marchand was espousing the same qualities that Shaw was promoting for the whole university: quality in teaching, research, and service. The iSchool was at the cutting edge of data analysis and could be one of SU's flagship schools, Marchand maintained. Its graduates were getting high-paying jobs at firms like Morgan Stanley and Goldman Sachs. He pushed iSchool faculty to work cooperatively with other programs and offices, and as one example, the iSchool developed a joint program with Maxwell for executive training in Washington, DC, for information resource management.

In 1991, a young assistant professor, Liz Liddy, who had earned her doctorate from the iSchool when Marchand was dean, was awarded her first big ($680,000) research contract from DARPA (the US Department of Defense's Defense Advanced Research Projects Agency). By 2004, she had brought to the iSchool more than $13 million in research money from Department of Defense agencies and had started her own company, TextWise, LLC, which at its peak employed fifty.

Marchand left SU in 1994 for a faculty position at IMD International, one of Europe's leading business schools, in Lausanne, Switzerland. Two years later, under Dean Raymond von Dran, the iSchool was rated fourth in the nation for its master's of library science program. In 1999, the iSchool's FB/OH was 168, far exceeding the balanced expense income factor of 100.

Marchand was pleased with the iSchool's considerable progress during his time as dean. His frustration that the university would not put more resources into the school, however, contributed to his decision to leave. Would more investment in the school have yielded even bigger results? "They didn't have a vision of the impact of technology and IT on the world in terms of government, commerce, society," he said.

Scholarships

Enrollment was the fuel that powered Syracuse University, and in 1992, the university was facing an enrollment challenge unlike any in recent memory. In Shaw's first year, applications for the freshman class of 1992–93 were 20 percent fewer than the previous year, when SU had admitted 89.1 percent of applicants. Among those it admitted, only 24.6 percent committed to Syracuse, the second-lowest rate of commitment in a decade.

Shaw determined that SU would not lower admission standards further to maintain a freshmen enrollment near 3,000. On the other hand, if SU admitted the same percentage of applicants as it had been—roughly 85 percent—its fall 1992 entering class would be 2,400, an unsustainable number.

Pressure to maintain enrollment was nothing new at Syracuse. During World War II, when SU's enrollment declined, Chancellor Tolley found nontraditional students to offset it—servicemen and men and women headed into the military. SU developed special classes in subjects like Russian and Slavic languages, meteorology, and map reading to appeal to this group.[36] After the war, SU accepted veterans by the thousands.

Now, SU faced the challenge of maintaining enrollment while also attracting more high-achieving students. The university had developed a reputation as a "safe school" to which nearly anyone could gain admission. "Good students didn't apply, because anybody could get in," said Vincow. "If anybody could get in, you didn't want to be there."

Poor student academic achievement weighed on faculty. Cathryn Newton, who started at Syracuse in 1983 as an assistant professor of geology in the College of Arts and Sciences, recalled that roughly one-third of her student advisees through the 1980s had GPAs below 2.0 and were on academic probation. Initiatives to improve SU's quality and reputation would take years to yield results. To woo quality students immediately, SU offered strategic financial aid.

The university had been stingy with its financial aid. In 1989–90, among comparable institutions, Syracuse's discount rate (the aggregate of financial aid) was among the lowest: 17.5 percent versus an average 26.3 percent. SU's competitors had been increasing financial aid both to needy students and to talented, financially well-off students. SU would do the same, offering merit scholarships of $5,000 for students who ranked in the top 20 percent of their high school classes, had SAT scores of 1200 or higher, and did not qualify for need-based financial aid.

Over five years, Shaw directed $37.2 million from the Plant Fund to be spent on financial aid, raising SU's discount rate to "a competitive 28.5 percent." Shaw also took money for academic scholarships from the Department of Athletics, which had its own plant fund of $10.7 million.[37] When SU received a Fiesta Bowl windfall of $1.5 million in January 1993, Shaw directed most of the money to undergraduate scholarships.

David Smith, dean of admissions and financial aid. Courtesy of University Archives, Syracuse University Libraries.

*   *   *

Opinion research studies of accepted students revealed another image problem: SU was perceived as having a culturally and geographically homogenous student body that came mostly from Long Island. That was not true—the largest majority of students came from Onondaga County—yet the perception was deterring some admitted students who were seeking more diversity from enrolling. "It told us we had to change our messaging," said David Smith, dean of admissions and financial aid.

Investigating further, admissions staff found that high schools in the greater New York City area were flooding SU with applications and that accepted students usually did not enroll. "There was this phenomenon of Syracuse being a doormat," said Smith, who spent the first few months of 1992–93 traveling to schools in the greater New York area, telling high school principals that Syracuse was playing a new game. His message: "We are not going to admit forty-seven people in order to get three people. Don't send us

Thomas Cummings, vice president of enrollment management and continuing education. Cummings and Smith tailored SU's admissions program to increase the academic quality of incoming students. Courtesy of University Archives, Syracuse University Libraries.

fifty-five applications to make yourself feel good. Because none of them are going to get in if that happens."[38]

The messaging and increased merit scholarships yielded results—SU began admitting more high-academically achieving students, applications increased, and the admit rate declined. Contrary to what merit scholarship critics had predicted, offering financial aid regardless of financial need did not result in a surge of smart, wealthy students. "What you're really doing is giving a whole bunch of money to smart people," said Smith. "Some of them are rich, some are poor. What you're doing with the poor people who happen to be smart is sweetening the deal. We discovered that it was the smart people who were poor who were far more responsive and price sensitive than it was the rich people who were smart."

CHAPTER 3
Image Making
Shaping and Promoting the New SU

To SELL SU'S NEW EMPHASIS on educating, Shaw branded SU as the leading "student-centered research university." But years before he arrived, many at the university were concerned, or at least aware, that SU's research emphasis was hurting undergraduate instruction and could threaten enrollment. SU was competing for students with state universities, especially the State University of New York, which were offering college degrees for half the cost of an SU degree.

Soon after Vincow was appointed vice chancellor by Eggers in 1986, he created a new position to strengthen teaching: vice president for undergraduate studies. Into that position he put Ronald Cavanagh, former professor of religion and chair of that department, who had worked as assistant dean for arts and sciences when Vincow was its dean. Vincow gave Cavanagh a diverse portfolio of responsibilities: ROTC, the Division of International Programs Abroad, the Office of the Registrar, and, to address teaching, the Center for Instructional Development.

The Center for Instructional Development assisted faculty in developing curriculum and improving teaching methods. The center's founder and director was Robert Diamond, associate vice chancellor. Diamond had come to the university in 1978 and had a reputation for being difficult to work with. Cavanagh, his new boss, joked that it often seemed that *he* was working for Diamond. "He was a pain in the ass, but very good. And he attracted a bright, innovative staff."[1]

In March 1989, Diamond asked faculty in a survey how they perceived the balance of research and teaching, which direction SU was headed regarding this balance, and which direction it should go. The survey results were not a surprise—research was perceived to be overemphasized at the expense of teaching, and most faculty wanted to strengthen teaching. Over the next several years, Diamond worked to achieve that, organizing discussions among deans that sought better ways to evaluate and improve teaching. Tenure and promotion guidelines were modified to help incentivize teaching and advising.

Shortly after Shaw began, Diamond learned about a new, national competition for colleges and universities that recognized those programs that most improved teaching. The competition was sponsored by TIAA-CREF, the nation's leading retirement provider for teachers and professors. SU had to win it, Diamond determined, so he and Cavanagh pitched the idea to Shaw.

"This is a reach," Shaw told them.

"You're never going to grab it if you don't reach," Diamond said.

Shaw was already asking faculty and staff for a lot of extra work, he told Diamond. If Diamond wanted to apply, he would have to do it on his own, which Diamond did, repeatedly. In 1993, SU was named a runner-up and awarded a certificate of excellence for TIAA-CREF's Hesburgh Award, named for Syracuse native Rev. Theodore M. Hesburgh, CSC, president emeritus of the University of Notre Dame.

Diamond needed stronger proof that the university was significantly increasing its emphasis on teaching, so in 1995, he conducted the same survey he had conducted in 1989, asking the same questions about the balance of research and teaching. This time, teaching was clearly identified as the main focus by faculty and deans.[2] With that and other documentation, SU won the top Hesburgh Award in 1996, which recognized "faculty development to enhance undergraduate teaching."

Diamond's successful application told the story of SU's steady and continued progress to improve teaching, starting in Eggers's last years and continuing through Shaw's first years. He cited a slew of concrete initiatives to improve the undergraduate experience, which included the $2 million Chancellor's Fund for Innovation, the Meredith Professors program, the Gateway Fellowship,

Robert Diamond, director of the Center for Instructional Development, helped bring national recognition to SU's mission to be a leading student-centered research university. Courtesy of University Archives, Syracuse University Libraries.

and a university policy requiring courses with more than fifty students to have corresponding sections with no more than twenty-five students. He mentioned the Freshman Forums, the fund to support the development of interdisciplinary courses and programs, new courses and programs for academically at-risk students, and a midsemester "early warning" system to identify and support students in academic difficulty. Diamond also made the case that SU's campaign to become a student-centered research university had made "a significant contribution to the national change agenda in higher education."[3]

The Hesburgh Award was national validation of Shaw's drive to make SU a leader among student-centered research universities. Further good news came from *U.S. News & World Report*'s rankings, in which SU's stature markedly improved.

In September 1992, *U.S. News & World Report* had grouped SU with "best of the rest" with 179 other universities and 115 liberal arts colleges. SU's average SAT score at the time was 1095, with an acceptance rate of 72 percent and a graduation rate (within five years) of 74 percent.

Three years later, Shaw proudly announced that SU had broken into the *U.S. News*'s top fifty, ranking forty-ninth in America's
Best Colleges category and thirty-fifth in Best College Values. The
merit scholarships that had been introduced were improving student
quality and making SU more affordable than its peers. Even better, among specialty schools, Maxwell was rated first in the United
States for public administration schools, the School of Architecture
seventeenth (schools of architecture), the College of Visual and
Performing Arts (fine arts) was rated twentieth, and the School of
Education was rated twenty-eighth (education). The first three had
received budget increases under restructuring.

SU's rankings continued to improve for several years: in 1996,
it was rated forty-fourth among the top fifty universities; in 1997,
it was rated fortieth overall and twenty-seventh for best value, the
highest ranking ever for Syracuse.

Even as SU celebrated its higher rankings, Shaw cautioned trustees that college rankings were like the report cards their children
brought home.[4] "If the grades were As and Bs, I'll bet you thought
the teacher's assessment was right on target," Shaw said. "If there
were Cs and Ds, you might have said that grades can never really
measure your child's true potential." Nevertheless, the *U.S. News
& World Report* system was the most accurate, the most widely
quoted, and most widely read, Shaw said. Stronger students and
their parents paid attention to rankings, he told trustees, and "being
among the top fifty national universities is a real advantage." Shaw
concluded his ranking commentary with a remark that would prove
prescient for SU. "It's always better to have a high ranking—no matter how disputed the rankings are—than to have a low one (unless
it's party school ranking)."

In 1998, SU's rankings began to decline, and in 2000, SU
dropped out of the top fifty. The *U.S. News* rankings were important enough to Shaw that, in 2002, he and Sandra Mulconry, associate vice president for university communications, met with a *U.S.
News & World Report* editor to discuss the magazine's criteria for
ranking schools and why its criteria were unfair to SU.

They argued, for example, that average faculty compensation
was low because the cost of living in central New York was low and

because SU did not have a medical school; SU had a lower percentage of faculty with doctorates because of its professional schools like Maxwell and Newhouse, where top faculty had experience but not always doctorates. Shaw and Mulconry suggested that *U.S. News* give more weight to factors such as small class sizes and low faculty/student ratios. It is not clear if the meeting changed anything about the way *U.S. News & World Report* rated universities.

Seal and Logo

If SU was to be the nation's leading student-centered research university, all aspects of its branding had to reflect that. One that concerned Shaw was SU's letterhead and business logo, which had been redesigned in 1989 to make it more contemporary and edgy. Yet, the new, white-on-orange logo had become an object of derision on campus; its swooping white *S* with an orange *U* shape inside it was abstract enough that some saw in it two ducks in courtship.

Shaw, who had noticed the logo on correspondence before he was hired, thought that it looked like a logo of a community college or shopping center and that it did not help a creeping perception that SU was a state school welcoming anyone who applied. Soon after arriving, he asked about the logo. "They gave me this explanation that took like five minutes. 'That line means progress. And that line going up there means something else.'"

Shaw directed that the university would again use SU's historic seal, which is classic and distinctive: a laurel wreath, symbol of victory; inside is the university's motto: *Suos Cultores Scientia Coronat* (Knowledge Crowns Those Who Seek Her). Encircling the wreath is *Syracuse University: Founded A.D. 1870*. Under the 1989 reimaging program, the official seal had been preserved exclusively for diplomas.

By December 1992, Shaw had "released" the seal for use on stationary, business cards, and publications, but did not mandate that people had to use it. The swooping SU logo continued to be used in commercial and athletic imaging.

As the university seal became more widely adopted, it came under criticism from Donna E. Arzt, a College of Law professor, who wrote Shaw in early 1998 objecting to the seal's incorporation of the abbreviation A.D., which stands for the Latin *anno Domini*

The Syracuse University logo created in the late 1980s, which Shaw said looked like a shopping center logo. Courtesy of University Archives, Syracuse University Libraries.

(in the year of our Lord) "and could offend people of cultures and religions who do not see Jesus as 'Lord.'" Arzt included with her letter a 1997 *New York Times* column by William Safire, an SU trustee, which she said supported her view of the seal's inappropriateness. Safire had reflected that in his earlier career as a White House speechwriter, he had a hand in writing the text on the plaque marking the spot where Apollo 11 astronauts first set foot on the moon. The plaque's inscription includes "July 1969 A.D." Safire said he inserted A.D. as an "unobtrusive reference to God." Decades later, though, Safire was reconsidering its appropriateness.

"A.D. is another story," he wrote.[5] "Dominus means 'lord,' and when the lord referred to is Jesus, not God, a religious statement is made. Thus, 'the year of our Lord' invites the query 'Whose lord?' and we're in an argument we don't need."

Facing an argument *he* did not need, Shaw delegated three faculty members, one each from the Departments of History, Philosophy, and Religion, to investigate the A.D. conundrum. They surveyed official seals of fifty other colleges and universities, including several that were religiously affiliated and found that none used A.D.

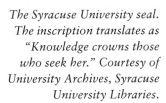

The Syracuse University seal. The inscription translates as "Knowledge crowns those who seek her." Courtesy of University Archives, Syracuse University Libraries.

They also identified the cost of changing SU's seal—creating new dies and printing new stationery—would be about $80,000.

Shaw began his response letter to Arzt with characteristic wryness. "If the University were starting over with a new seal or logo, this issue would be a simple matter. We could eliminate the A.D. on the seal, confident in the assumption that no one would become confused and believe that SU was founded in 1870 BCE and was now a ripe old 3,740 years old."[6]

The faculty researchers had also determined that A.D. had taken on a "purely conventional significance," and its original religious meaning had all but evaporated; that A.D. had historical significance for Syracuse, as it was first used when the university was founded as a Methodist institution; and that changing the seal so soon after changing from the swooping logo would "give the impression that we cannot settle on an identity and stick with it."

Shaw's decision, firm yet considerate, was that SU would not remove A.D. from its seal. "In spite of some ambivalence on the matter, I am most attracted to the *Chicago Manual of Style* position that A.D. has reached a conventional rather than religious status."[7]

Utica College

Utica College was a holdover from SU's postwar expansion. Chancellor William Tolley had founded the school in large part to serve

returning veterans, and Utica College continued to operate with
SU's support. When Shaw arrived in 1991, nearly every aspect of
running Utica College was dependent upon Syracuse University.

SU's trustees were Utica College's trustees, and Utica College
was part of SU's charter and bylaws. Their identities were intermin-
gled with insurance policies, union contracts, state and federal reg-
ulation compliance requirements, tax obligations, bank accounts,
motor vehicles, and even bookstore fixtures. New degrees at Utica
were approved through SU's University Senate, and SU chancellors
attended Utica commencements. Utica College employees could get
remitted tuition for SU classes and SU scholarships for their children. Utica College did operate its own budget and paid its own
way, but its president was on SU's payroll.

In his November 5, 1991, convocation speech, Shaw mentioned
Utica College once—in a reference to a US Department of Education grant that would provide four years of co-op funding (student
employment money) to programs on the SU campus and at Utica
College. Tolley was at the speech, as was Eggers, who had maintained SU's close relationship with Utica, handpicking Lance Baker,
the superintendent of Jamesville–Dewitt School District, to serve
as Utica College's fifth president in 1982. Eggers would later select
Baker as SU's senior vice president for university relations.

Given the need to strengthen SU's core programs, separating
from the much-smaller Utica College made sense.[8] The relationship
that had once served both institutions so well had become complicated and less useful; untangling it would take time, and Shaw
moved the process along as he did so many other changes, with slow
deliberation. Days after his speech, he told trustees that the supported resignation program for professors would not apply to those
in Utica.

In June 1992, a *Syracuse Post-Standard* headline highlighted
the risk of the two institutions' continued entanglement: "Assistant
Professor of SU's Utica College Charged with Rape." The assistant
professor was indicted by a grand jury in Montgomery County.
While the incident did not involve a student, the potential existed
that in a similar instance a court of law could clarify the ambiguity
of the relationship to SU's detriment. "The ambiguity could lead, if

they had serious financial problems, to us accepting responsibility for them," Shaw said in an interview.[9] One risk was that SU guaranteed Utica College bonds, although SU did not have access to Utica's assets in the way of property or building ownership.[10]

Over monthly meetings, Shaw persuaded Utica College's president, Michael K. Simpson, to work toward separating the two institutions. In essence, they were moving toward a divorce, but Simpson did not see it that way at first.

Simpson's own career reflected the conjoined institutional relationship. He had an MBA from SU and was resident director of SU's program in Strasbourg, France, when Eggers appointed him Utica College president in 1988, after pulling Baker into the SU university relations job.

Simpson formed a committee to explore the separation and its ramifications. Utica College, however, was not ready to make a clean break from SU. "Our intent is to remain a college of Syracuse University," Simpson wrote in a 1992 letter to community members.[11] A few months later, Simpson reiterated Utica's determination to "award the Syracuse University degree."[12]

By September 1994, SU's law firm, Bond, Schoeneck and King, had drawn up a detailed separation task list and timeline for Utica College to establish its own board of trustees and its own charter and insurance; to be responsible for its own workers' compensation claims; and to purchase its own diplomas.

On July 1, 1995, nearly half a century after its founding, Utica College stood on its own for the first time with its own board of trustees. It was still mentioned in SU's charter. Utica College students still received an SU degree (from Syracuse University at Utica College, and later, Utica College of Syracuse University) at a lower cost—in 1994–95, tuition at Utica was $12,680, compared with $15,150 at SU. Full separation would not be finalized until after Shaw left office, but the steps were laid out, and SU had one less concern to worry about.

Otto

In the fall of 1994, Lou Marcoccia, senior vice president for business and finance, had an idea for boosting SU's revenue—a new mascot.

Otto, originally created by SU cheerleaders, was preserved by Shaw as SU's official mascot, despite a study panel's recommendation to replace Otto with a wolf. Courtesy of University Archives, Syracuse University Libraries.

SU's existing mascot, Otto the Orange, had had a tentative beginning. The creation of SU cheerleader Eric Heath, "The Orange" (as it was first called) had stepped up to fill a vacancy and had never been officially approved.

The Saltine Warrior, which depicted a tomahawk-wielding Native American, had been retired in 1978 after nearly fifty years. The warrior was replaced by a Roman-style gladiator that was booed and laughed off the field.[13] Other characters had stepped up to rally fans: the Dome Ranger, wearing an orange cowboy outfit and blue mask; Dome Eddie, who flaunted orange sweats, oversize Elton John glasses, and an incandescent orange wig; and the Beast from the East, an electric-green monster. At some games, all four vied for attention.

The Orange, however, was the only mascot that was trade-marked by SU for use on licensed merchandise. Cheerleaders had dubbed it "Otto" after a brainstorming session at a Tennessee cheer-leading camp in 1990. In terms of revenue, however, Otto was not pulling his weight. Trademark revenues were declining, though poor performances by the football and basketball programs did not help, Marcoccia acknowledged. Vendors were saying that Otto was a kids' character, "restrictive, unattractive, and difficult to market on imprinted merchandise."

Marcoccia formed an eighteen-member committee, chaired by Athletic Director Jake Crouthamel and Peter Webber, director of auxiliary services, to come up with a new mascot. Alumni were clamoring for the return of the Saltine Warrior, SU's mascot for forty-seven years (1931–78), years that included SU's 1959 national football championship under Ben Schwartzwalder and the dazzling running of Jim Brown, Ernie Davis, Larry Csonka, and Floyd Little. However, focus groups in Syracuse and New York City led the committee to conclude that the logo should be gender- and ethnically neutral, and powerful, whether it be a character or an animal, and the warrior did not fit the committee's ethnically neutral criteria.[14] Wolf and lion rose to the top, but Orange had to stay a part of the name. To develop new prototype mascots, the committee paid roughly $50,000 to Sean Michael Edwards Design, Inc., of New York.

The committee issued its report in November 1995, and unanimously recommended the wolf—that way SU could keep the trademarked nickname "Orange Pack," which was also the name of SU's umbrella group for athletic fund-raising.[15] The Orange—the committee did not refer to it as Otto—could remain an unofficial mascot, like Dome Eddie or the Dome Ranger.

The committee's rationale began by pointing out that the 1994 football team had worn T-shirts with a wolf image under their jerseys, with the words, "For the strength of the pack is the wolf, and the strength of the wolf is the pack."[16] The following year, the team's football T-shirt bore a rendering of two wolves, scarred and supporting each other, with just one word: "Family."

There were innumerable reasons why the wolf should be the mascot, the committee said:

The wolf, used as an athletic mascot by only two other Division I institutions, was once indigenous to the lower 48 states. It is now an endangered species in all but one of those states. Victim of

A year-long study group recommended this new logo for SU, which Shaw rejected. Courtesy of University Archives, Syracuse University Libraries.

myth and merciless slaughter, recent studies reveal that the wolf is a complex social animal: highly intelligent, alert, energetic, and playful. The male and female are similar in appearance (although the female is smaller; the photo reference for the wolf illustration on this season's football poster was in fact female). Wolves usually mate for life, and all of the wolves in the pack, male and female, raise the young.

A pack comprises three to twenty wolves, and pack members show a great deal of affection and care for each other. Successful hunts depend on how well the wolves work together. Both males and females hunt. Wolves are good communicators and tireless runners. Pack survival rests upon cooperation and mutual respect. The interaction and interdependence of wolves in a pack are the essence of team philosophy. The social behavior of wolves and their pack/family structure mirror, in many ways, the best of qualities of a society.

As for the logo itself, the committee had multiple suggestions: a wolf in front of an orange sunset or a wolf depicted as "noble and mysterious, fierce and dynamic," or a child-friendly version of a wolf cub. And as for promotions, students in wolf costumes could form "the Pack" at athletic contests, a share of licensing revenue could go to wolf recovery efforts, and a cooperative education program between the university and Burnet Park Zoo (now Rosamond Gifford Zoo) could enlighten children about wolves. The zoo could even designate a live wolf family to represent the Orange Pack.

Months before the committee's announcement, word began circulating that Otto was out. Students rallied support for Otto with petitions and letters to the *Daily Orange*. On October 21, during a Carrier Dome football game against West Virginia, students staged a mock brawl between a wolf and Otto. The Orange won.

It would fall to Shaw to decide whether a growling wolf or a fuzzy orange would rally SU into the future. At the start of the process, Shaw had told Webber, his tennis partner and the committee's co-chair, that any proposed new mascot would have to "be a slam dunk" for him to abandon Otto.[17] After reading the mascot committee's report and gauging student sentiment, Shaw decided Otto the Orange would stay as SU's official mascot.

CHAPTER 4

Making Connections

Public Service and the Digital Age

THE INHERENT AND ANCIENT TENSIONS between universities and outside communities raise questions about their connections: How does a university best engage with the world? Where
are its points of contact and boundaries of engagement? When do
outside connections strengthen the university, and when does the
university extend itself so far—in financial resources, energy, commitment of personnel—that it begins to undermine its own identity
and mission?[1] In the broadest sense, this chapter touches on those
issues, exploring three very different kinds of expanded connections
that occurred during the Shaw era—public service, deepening connection with the Jewish community, and the wholesale computeriza-
tion of the campus, which expanded its connection with the world
through the internet.

Center for Public and Community Service

On one of Mary Ann Shaw's first days on campus, William Coplin
invited her to lunch. Coplin, professor of political science and public
affairs at the Maxwell School, had been at Syracuse since 1969. A
contrarian, outspoken and engaging, he taught classes that thrust
SU students into Syracuse's inner city to work with social service
agencies and local high school students. In his own classes, he men-
tored his top students to teach for him as he stood by. "Action is how
you learn," he would say.

Coplin had been challenging SU's emphasis on research to the
neglect of teaching undergraduates. He questioned the notion that
college was good for everyone. During Eggers's years, he advised a

student group, Undergraduates for a Better Education (UBE), that clamored for smaller classes taught by full professors, not just teaching assistants. One parents' weekend, UBE students awoke before dawn and posted signs around campus that read, "Are you getting what you're paying for?" Eggers had janitors tear the signs down.[2]

So the Shaws' arrival on campus, with their focus on strengthening undergraduates' learning experiences, and Mary Ann's experiences with literacy training and community outreach, fit right in with Coplin's agenda. In 1992, Coplin introduced Pamela Heintz, one of his students, to Mary Ann. The women were just four years apart and shared a deep interest in community service. Heintz had studied economics at Smith College before leaving to start a family. She had raised three children, sold real estate, and served on village boards in Skaneateles before enrolling at SU part-time to get her bachelor's degree in public policy, which she received in 1991. She had been active in community organizations, including the Junior League in Syracuse, an organization of women that promoted voluntarism.

"Service learning," the idea that community service work could help make classroom learning more relevant while providing assistance to community organizations, was taking root at universities nationwide. By 1994, President Bill Clinton's administration was requiring a share of federal work-study payments to colleges be applied to community service work, and his administration was rolling out AmeriCorps, which provided modest pay and student loan forgiveness to college-age volunteers.

Mary Ann Shaw was determined to strengthen SU's community service engagement, and she asked Heintz to help. Small planning meetings led to campus-wide meetings, which were well attended, in part because the chancellor's wife was hosting them. Mary Ann had a knack for drawing people out, negotiating competing interests, and mobilizing people. "She would plant a seed and do all the watering and the sculpting, and everybody else would just nurture it," said Heintz. "Before you knew it, it happened. And no one had any idea that she'd been managing the whole thing by supporting when support was needed."[3]

Syracuse University students were already doing community service work through programs at Hendricks Chapel, through internships in the College of Nursing and Schools of Education and Social Work, and through programs like Coplin's. The Volunteer Center, a community organization in downtown Syracuse, often assisted. On campus, though, there was no coordinating volunteer hub. That is what Mary Ann wanted—a place where faculty could find out about programs where they could place students, where students wanting to volunteer could learn about community initiatives that fit their interests, and where community agencies could find volunteers. It would be an office with no political or religious agenda. "There's a difference between just being charitable, which is fine and good, and having students learn things that will help them function well in the communities that they end up in," said Heintz. "We wanted them to have a broader understanding of complex social issues."

Meanwhile, Mary Ann was making connections with the greater Syracuse community. She had been appointed to the United Way of Central New York board as soon as she arrived in Syracuse and was pushing for Syracuse to adopt Success by Six, a new literacy and developmental initiative for preschoolers that she had worked with in Madison. She held luncheons that brought together top women business and civic leaders in Syracuse.

SU, of course, was strapped for money, undergoing buyouts and layoffs. Nevertheless, the chancellor quietly allocated money to hire Heintz for one year. She would establish a small office in the Schine Student Center. Shaw stipulated that she would have to pursue grants to fund continued work. A search committee would look for a permanent director, and Heintz could apply.

In early 1993, SU received a $1.5 million windfall—its take from winning the nationally televised Fiesta Bowl. On New Year's Day, SU's sixth-ranked football team beat the thirteenth-ranked University of Colorado. Shaw directed that the winning proceeds go not to athletics but to academic programs, to undergraduate scholarships, and to the new Center for Public and Community Service (CPCS) to buy a van that would transport student volunteers to work sites in the city. "With gratitude to the Fiesta Bowl," was painted on the van's panels.

Further funding came in 1994 from the Carrier Corporation, where trustee Robert Allen had been chairman and CEO. Shaw had called Allen to make the pitch, and Carrier donated $60,000 for three years to the CPCS. New York Telephone donated $50,000, which CPCS used to encourage faculty to incorporate community service into their courses. Faculty could use the money to help cover transportation costs or hire an undergraduate teaching assistant.

The center's programs grew to include student literacy tutors in the Syracuse City School District and SU's School of Management students advising not-for-profit organizations. It received a boost in 1996, when Clinton announced the federal government would pay 100 percent of wages for students who tutored preschool and elementary school children.

In 1999, Karen Binkoff Winnick, an author and illustrator of children's books and a 1968 graduate of the College of Visual and Performing Arts, along with her husband, Gary Winnick, committed to donating $100,000 per year to the CPCS to pay for permanent staff to administer SU Literacy Corps, which sent SU students into city schools to tutor.

Soon after Deborah Freund came on as vice chancellor for academic affairs in 1999, the CPCS linked itself with that office. The move more closely tied community service work to classroom teaching and learning. Just as important, it raised the center's institutional stature. "In a research institution, if you're not connected to the academics, you don't have the credibility or value," said Heintz. Students, paid through federally assisted work study, were scheduling volunteers and arranging transportation.

That same year, Shaw boasted to trustees that service learning at SU was "blending theory and practice." Some 5,000 students had provided more than 500,000 hours of community service the previous year. Another 3,400 students had completed community internships in their fields of study. As many as 125 courses included some community-based learning component.

For all the support Mary Ann and Buzz Shaw gave the Center for Public and Community Service, there was little funding that came directly from the university. When Heintz asked Shaw about expanding the program, he was encouraging. He did tell her he was not going to increase her budget, so what piece of her budget did she want to shrink to pay for the expansion? Heintz wanted nothing cut and searched for outside money. "[Mary Ann and Buzz] supported us in making appeals and providing the resources on campus to write grant applications or to promote the program. But you had to make your own way. We're not part of any college," said Heintz.

By the time the Shaws stepped down as chancellor and associate in 2004, service learning had been fully institutionalized at Syracuse University. Thousands of SU students were volunteering in the Syracuse community each year, learning about themselves, the city, and its challenges, as well as becoming comfortable off-campus—a trend welcomed by the city's apartment developers and restaurateurs. Classroom work became more relevant because students had grappled with social problems and tested solutions. Before Mary Ann Shaw left campus, the Board of Trustees officially put her name on the center she had created: the Mary Ann Shaw Center for Public and Community Service.

Hillel Center

Under the broad mission of creating a student-centered university, one opportunity came along that had not been on anyone's radar—a new center for Jewish students.

Behind it was Karen Winnick, who had been active with Mary Ann Shaw in funding SU's Literacy Corps and in creating the Winnick Family Endowed Scholarship Fund, which supports a freshman who comes from a public high school. Winnick and her husband Gary, a venture capitalist who chaired Global Crossing, were friends with Marty Granoff, a textile executive and a major donor to new Hillel Centers at Brown and Tufts Universities. SU's Hillel Center was an office in the basement of Hendricks Chapel.

Knowing about the centers at Brown and Tufts, the Winnicks offered to make a $2 million naming gift for a Hillel Center at Syracuse. It would be built on property at 102–104 Walnut Place, which SU sold to Hillel for $480,000. SU took the lead, raising $6 million for the Hillel Center, a campaign that lasted several years.

The Hillel endeavor drew in a number of new donors, among them Edgar Bronfman Sr., head of the Joseph E. Seagram & Sons Co. and president of the World Jewish Conference. Bronfman was a major supporter of Hillel around the world, and though he had no direct affiliation with SU, he visited campus on April 18, 2001, which that year was Holocaust Remembrance Day.

For Bronfman's visit, which included a dinner, the kitchen at the chancellor's house was made kosher for the first time. New cookware and eighty place settings were purchased, the kitchen counters were covered, the kitchen was blessed, and SU caterers prepared the meal. Afterward, the items were donated to Hillel. The building, which includes an auditorium/sanctuary, library, computer and study areas, meeting rooms, fitness center, student lounge, and kosher dining facility, was dedicated November 16, 2003.

Computing

Of all the changes that came during Shaw's time, the inexorable and most pervasive one was bringing the university's computer system into the twenty-first century. Faster communication, greater connectivity, and easy access to vast information resources were all coming; big investments in hardware, wiring, and software were needed; and everyone would be expected to become computer literate and would require substantial training. No one was sure about the details, how much it would cost, or what the end results would look like, but it was clear the changes would be big and disruptive.

In 1993, a personal computer costing $2,000 had the same processing power as a mainframe computer costing $2 million.[4] Computers had been at SU since 1957, when a first-generation IBM 650 was installed in Machinery Hall. Retrieving information or crunching numbers involved submitting a job to the mainframe computer staff for batch processing and waiting a day or two for results, or directly accessing the mainframe through SU's network.[5] SU had two separate computer divisions, one academic and one administrative, each with its own mainframe and networks.

SU had been one of the first universities in the nation to connect to the internet in 1985, and its mainframe capabilities were substantial—they provided the computer power for the Northeast Parallel Architectures Center (NPAC), which formed in 1987 to design, evaluate, and program parallel computer systems, and for the Center for Advanced Technology in Computer Applications and Software Engineering (CASE Center), which opened in 1984. Both centers continued bringing in millions of research dollars through the Shaw years.

By the early 1990s, central servers built with microprocessors were coming into wide use, doing the work of mainframes at a fraction of the cost. Instead of terminals connected to a mainframe computer, university-owned desktops connected to servers provided connections through what was called client-server computing, and it offered users more independence—they could seek and retrieve information on their own without the need for an intermediary at the mainframe.

SU shut down its room-sized, water-cooled, academic mainframe, an IBM 3090 known as SUVM, in June 1995 and shut down its administrative mainframe computer, an IBM ES9000, in 1998. Both were replaced with client-server systems. Information stored on the mainframes had to be "migrated" to the servers, a job that in some cases took years because programming languages on mainframes and desktops were different and because the new client-server software had to first be tested for security and integrity so data would not be lost.

SU needed a coordinated approach for the new era, and Shaw put Ben Ware in charge of it as vice president for research and computing, a new position. Ware was the first ever to take a university-wide look at SU's computing environment and its future needs, with responsibilities for both academic and administrative computing as well as telecommunications.

From an administrative standpoint, SU's computing had evolved piecemeal, school by school, department by department, though some barely had any computing at all. When Ware inventoried the systems and support teams in place, he was surprised to find "a bizarre labyrinth of organizational hierarchy." About 40 percent of the people in computer services were managers, with as many as six layers of management in some departments, he wrote Joan Carpenter. "We need to reduce management layers, put former managers to work, and empower workers."[6] Ware's consolidated computing services department (a few years later it would be called the Computer and Media Services Department) reduced the computing budget 18 percent and eliminated twenty-seven jobs, leaving a combined staff of 116.

In an overview of SU's computing status entitled "'93 Forward!,'" Ware described a future just five years off when most students would have their own computers and people could send messages across the world. Students would be able to access their grades and financial status and communicate with their professors via computers; some would take classes through their computer without even being in Syracuse. All of this would save time and stress, it was promised, though getting there, making the technology widely available, would create many new stresses. Some 400 computing stations existed around campus, gathered in fourteen clusters. Few classrooms had computing facilities and no dorms provided network access. Wiring dorms was estimated to cost $10 million.

Wiring classrooms began with proceeds from SU's Fiesta Bowl win. Residence halls would be wired in phases, starting with Kimmel and DellPlain. A monthly internet access charge would help pay for wiring costs. "The time has come when virtually all students should acquire a computer of their own," Ware wrote. Computer literacy was becoming essential for study in most disciplines, even for basic communication through email.

Not everyone embraced the changes. "I just didn't have the time for it," Shaw said. He recalled one cabinet meeting that ended with an agreement to share reports before the next meeting. Shaw told the group that his driver, Jack McNulty, could deliver copies to each person. Someone suggested using email and asked how many had it. Everyone but Shaw raised their hand. "The shock I had, sitting there, realizing, 'My God, everyone's got email.'"[7] Others were put off by the way the university's new "voice response technology," which worked off of personal computers, was being used. "What I am observing and experiencing is the substitution of voice mail for human contact," David Smith, then dean of admissions and financial aid, wrote Shaw.[8]

While university-wide upgrades were underway, the Computing Services staff was guiding faculty, parents, and students about which computer to buy. A 1994 mailing to parents recommended purchasing an IBM DX2 desktop, which had 8 MB of RAM, a 212 MB hard drive, and an internal 3.5" floppy drive. With keyboard and mouse, it went for $1,849 at the bookstore.

Upgrading the university's computer systems was not only a matter of acquiring better technology or needing to stay competitive. The impending century change posed an enormous challenge for computerized institutions like universities, banks, and schools whose mainframe data included calendar years expressed with two digits, as in MMDDYY.

The calendar issue, known as the Y2K bug, was real, as was the media-induced mania around it.[9] People feared bank computer systems would lock up, and the Federal Reserve distributed $80 billion in currency—four times its usual amount—to handle panic withdrawals from banks. SU's mainframe was not going to work on January 1, 2000, without major retooling, which was estimated to cost at least $1 million. The integrity of SU's records was at stake, especially student records. "[The student record system] is really more sensitive than our financial systems," said Ware. "We can recover from a financial disaster. But if the transcripts you see from Syracuse University are not reliable, we go out of business. Those systems were touching everybody."[10]

SU contracted with PeopleSoft, an up-and-coming software company that was designing client-server programs for colleges and universities to handle student records and payroll.[11] In 1996, SU paid $800,000 for PeopleSoft programming and became one of the company's "charter customers," receiving beta versions of software that enabled it to get a head start addressing year 2000 issues.[12] It also meant that SU would help instruct PeopleSoft about what a university needed in its software. When the conversion was complete, SU had spent some $23.2 million to move from mainframes to client-servers, most of it to pay outside consultants. Dozens of SU staff were taken off their jobs to help get the new programs running, and part-time people were hired to fill in for them.

Frustrations abounded. Adapting SU's systems to the software demands of PeopleSoft required that hundreds of the university's most fundamental processes had to be reassessed, usually by committees. In some instances, not all faculty had the appropriate computer hardware and network access to do what they needed. During the first online registration in the spring of 1999, some students were locked out of their accounts.

Students in the state-of-the-art College of Visual and Performing Arts computer lab in the Shaffer Art Building, October 2003. Courtesy of Steve Sartori.

As expensive as the conversion was, it began a new era of ongoing computer expenses for schools and departments. Every new computer product needed to be replaced every three to five years, and the university had to build a training infrastructure for students, faculty, and staff. By 1998, 75 percent of SU students brought their own computer to campus, and the university was spending $25 million a year on computer technology.[13]

In 2000, SU was not yet accepting admissions applications online, but students could register, drop and add classes, or check out library books. Getting online was getting faster: logging in took five minutes in 1999 and only one minute fifteen seconds in 2000.

Significantly, the university successfully avoided any Y2K meltdowns. That May, Shaw told trustees "It's been a long, hard slog to get to this point—Ben Ware promised us pain—and he delivered."

Computer information advances that now seem modest were initiated all through the 1990s. In 1994, a new campus-wide system named SyraCWIS was launched that provided an electronic academic calendar, Syracuse weather, SU job opportunities, and access to the newly opened internet. Its first administrator was Deirdre Stam, the wife of University Librarian David Stam. A few years later, the School of Management contracted with Caliber Learning Network Inc., an internet-based learning service provider, to develop online learning modules for its MBA Upgrade Program.[14]

The struggle to keep up with rapid advances in data transmission was constant. In August 2001, SU discontinued offering outside internet access through its dial-up lines because SU's dial-up capacity got bogged down by people using it to surf the internet.[15] With the elimination of internet access, the university's dial-up system provided access only to sites ending with syr.edu. The upside was that users no longer got kicked off an syr.edu site after an hour; they could stay for four.

CHAPTER 5
Campus Life
Managing the Village

In 1993, Vice Chancellor Vincow spoke to faculty and trustees about the different ways current students' experiences compared with their college experience, and among those he cited was the "near absence of in loco parentis guidance and restrictions by the institution."[1] The Latin phrase, meaning "in the place of a parent," referred to what had been a guiding principle for schools and colleges for centuries, allowing them to act, sometimes forcefully and unilaterally, in the best interests of students as they saw fit. Schools had rules for behavior and violators were summarily punished, often by expulsion.[2] The evolution of civil liberty protections had weakened the hand of institutions and complicated the ways schools managed their environments to ensure students' health and safety. Like all chancellors, Shaw faced the student concerns and circumstances of his particular time and place—student protests, public safety, fraternity hazing, excessive drinking—and sometimes it got messy.

Student Activism

Student protests had plagued Eggers's years. There were protests over divestiture from South African investments, over rapes on campus, over anti-Semitic graffiti, racism, and tuition costs. Student sit-ins at the Tolley Administration Building occurred several times, filling the lobby and the stairs up to Eggers's office.[3]

Student activism would continue to challenge his successor, Eggers predicted in his final report to the trustees' Executive Committee. His concern over student protests was not helped by his vice president for student affairs, Edward Golden, who expressed a sense of powerlessness in his June 1991 briefing to Shaw about student dissent. "Students see rallies, protests, and 'demands' as the only way to influence the agenda of the University," Golden wrote. "The cycle is entrenched, difficult to break, and adds enormous complexity to already challenging issues."

But Shaw encountered a fraction of the protests about which Eggers had warned. At campus forums each semester, Shaw couched a warning about the consequences of protests as a lesson in civil disobedience, reminding students that Martin Luther King wrote one of his most powerful tracts from the Birmingham Jail. "Yes, there are times that morally you have to violate rules," Shaw recalled saying. "But he [King] also wrote that you should expect that you will be punished for it. If you're not willing to do that, and you *will* be punished if you violate the rules, then you shouldn't be protesting."

Still, one of the first student actions was a sit-in protesting proposed cuts in the School of Music's budget. For two days, some forty students occupied the Office of the Dean of the College of Visual and Performing Arts, Donald Lantzy, in Crouse College.[4] No students were disciplined, and administrators afterward realized the university had no plan for responding to a student occupation of offices, not even a phone tree.[5]

Shaw's first direct student confrontation came in February 1993, when student demonstrators marched to his office angry about the 6.5 percent tuition increase. Shaw met with thirty-four students in the Tolley Building's admissions office conference room and listened to their grievances: They wanted no tuition increase and the library opened more hours. They complained about the cost of food at Kimmel and Schine food courts, the large number of athletic scholarships, and special treatment given basketball student-athletes. Shaw told protestors that most of the tuition increase was going toward increased financial aid and that if they could find $11 million in savings, he would eliminate the tuition increase.

That students had so quickly filled the stairwells of the Tolley Building concerned Shaw, and he directed staff to assemble a protocol to employ during sit-ins or demonstrations: Move personnel, shut down computers, secure records, and lock rooms. Protests continued, especially over the way the administration responded to concerns about rape and nonconsensual sex. At the center of it was Golden, whose response to such protests, as well as the language he used to talk about them, was defensive and reactive.

His SWOT report to Shaw about student affairs included passages that were so critical of his department it seemed as if he was not the one in charge. "Staff is singularly lacking in diversity and breadth of background . . . ," he wrote, "and are not prepared to respond to the uniqueness of the years ahead." He observed that student affairs had adopted a reactive rather than a proactive approach to issues and that "preventative outreach programs are lacking in the health areas particularly." That was not all: "Student organization advising is weak. The overall effectiveness of the office is diminished by a staff that is not cohesive and minimally able to form effective working relationships with students."

Golden was also dismissive of student movements demanding education about sexual safety and gender identity. Reporting on the Student Government Association (SGA) election results in 1992, he told cabinet members that the new president, Joseph Shields, and comptroller, Desmonique Bonet, were "part of a small clique of eight to ten students who have ties to S.C.A.R.ED (Students Concerned about Rape Education) and the GLBSA (Gay, Lesbian, Bisexual Student Association). They are not likely to get groundswell support, and the potential to self-destruct exists."[6]

In the fall of 1992, for the first time, SU published a campus crime report, fulfilling a requirement of the Clery Act. No rapes had occurred on campus the previous year, the report said. Meanwhile, the RAPE (Rape Advocacy Prevention and Education) Center reported six women had been raped, and eight others said they were sexually assaulted.[7] The RAPE Center reported attacks upon SU students on- and off-campus, which SU was not required to do.

A few months later, in December, one hundred students rallied to accuse the administration of underreporting sexual assaults on or near campus. They also complained that the university's judicial process, headed by Golden, allowed rape suspects to escape appropriate punishment.

Golden had been chairing a Task Force on Student Rights and Responsibilities that was reviewing the way the university's judicial

hearing board, which was composed of students and which he ultimately oversaw, responded to rapes and sexual assault. Following
the protest, he resigned from the task force, and Shaw appointed
Elletta Sangrey Callahan, an assistant professor of law and public
policy, to chair a reconfigured, fifteen-member Task Force on Student Rights and Responsibilities.

Callahan had been hired five years before and had been serving on the task force under Golden, but she knew little about SU's
administrative culture. She was surprised when Shaw summoned her
to his office to offer her the temporary chairperson's role and even
more struck as he spoke about the task force's purpose, how viscer-
ally pained he was talking about the survivors of sexual assault, and
his "priority to take care of the students and to make things right,"
she said.[8] Under Callahan, the task force proposed two significant
changes to the university's handling of sexual assault: It broadened
the definition to "nonconsensual sexual activity," which covered
everything from unwanted touching to rape, and it would not allow
alcohol as an excuse, recommendations that Shaw accepted. In July
1994, the university hired Anastasia Urtz, an attorney working
in Washington, DC, as director of judicial affairs. A new, special
judicial hearing board, composed of staff members and faculty and
advised by an attorney, was created to handle cases of nonconsensual sexual activity and other serious allegations of misconduct.

In December 1994, one incident elevated rape-reporting concerns from statistics to specific threat. A female student said she was
raped near the Quad around 1:15 a.m. Students learned about the
alleged rape only four days later in the *Daily Orange*.[9] The woman
reported the incident to SU's RAPE Center the same day, and coun-
selors there alerted SU security and called Syracuse city police. SU's
Department of Public Safety faxed a report of the incident and a
description of the attacker to deans and administrators. The people
who could most easily alert students—Golden's residence hall directors or even the *Daily Orange*—were not told.

Golden acknowledged to the *Post-Standard* that SU was required by the Campus Safety and Security Act of 1990 to notify
the campus of a potential danger in its midst and that campus
safety officers had faxed a report to administrators, but without

instructions, so nothing was done. *The Daily Orange* wrote a scathing editorial accusing the administration of a cover-up to protect its image. "You don't cover up a stalker," wrote Marc Bailey, the *Daily Orange* editor.

A few days later, the woman recanted her story to Syracuse police and was charged with filing a false report. The university's unresponsiveness to her initial report, however, highlighted a poorly run Office of Student Affairs.

Golden was also struggling with the Greek system. SU suspended six Greek organizations in the 1994–95 academic year for hazing and other violations, adopting a crackdown approach that had reduced the number of Greek organizations from fifty-two to forty in the previous five years. "The university is committed to realigning the Greek system regardless of the impact on the size of the Greek system," Golden told the *Daily Orange*.[10] Golden's hardline tactics so incensed several parents of fraternity members that Shaw had to step in as judicious communicator, explaining to parents why their sons' fraternity had been suspended.[11]

In December 1995, Golden resigned. Shaw replaced him with Barry L. Wells as interim vice president for student affairs and dean of student relations. A year later, Wells was appointed to the permanent position, making him the first African American vice president at SU. Wells brought commitment, thoroughness, and intensity to the job, in addition to a broad portfolio of job experiences. He came to SU in 1976, had been a director of academic advising and counseling services in the College of Arts and Sciences, associate director of admissions and financial aid, assistant director of student services for minority affairs, and coordinator for minority affairs. He had been associate dean (1993–95) and assistant dean (1985–93) of the College of Arts and Sciences.

Shaw had been criticized for keeping problematic top administrators longer than he should have and for offering departing administrators generous buyouts. Years later, he addressed the criticisms: "If I had a fault, it was probably that I took too long . . . to let somebody go," he said. "I guess I'm just a nice guy. It's hard. People's lives and careers are built into what they're doing. And you just have to be careful that you're making the right decision."[12]

Generous buyouts he defended with a manager's practicality: "If there's somebody that you'd like to see leave, it's better to give them the kind of package that they leave happy. They can either leave happy and get some kind of nice pay-out, or they can be publicly fired. And it's cheaper to pay them. Because [if they're fired] you're going to have lawsuits, stuff in the paper all the time, and it detracts from what you're trying to do. So generous payouts are very cost effective." He also noted that generous buyouts were not an option for him at the public institutions he ran.

Peace Officers

Crime on campus was a growing national concern in the early 1990s. The issue had been thrust into the national consciousness after the rape and murder of Jeanne Clery, a nineteen-year-old student in a Lehigh University residence hall in 1986. Clery's parents mounted a national crusade for campus safety, and media coverage highlighted other incidents. *People* magazine ran a cover story in December 1990 featuring accounts from date rape victims, and *USA Today* published a seven-part series on campus crime.

The federal Crime Awareness and Campus Security Act, or Clery Act, became law in November 1990. The new law required colleges and universities to gather crime statistics and make them available to the public by September 1, 1992.

When Shaw arrived on campus, he was shocked to find that SU's campus security force had virtually no police powers; they could not make arrests, and they could not even carry pepper spray. They had jurisdiction only on campus, and when a criminal incident occurred, they had to detain suspects, call 911, and wait for Syracuse Police Department (SPD) to come and make an arrest. They were "like security guards in a department store," Shaw said.[13] The campus security situation was unlike that at public universities at which he had worked before—in New York State, private organizations were not permitted to have police powers—and Shaw was determined to change it.

Relying on Syracuse police for security around campus had its own shortcomings and complications. In the fall of 1991, city police canceled a regular Marshall Street patrol after repeated student complaints about brutality.[14]

Establishing stronger police powers involved more than a university policy decision, however. It required new state legislation, new approvals from and a new working relationship with the Syracuse Police Department, and a sustained public relations campaign on campus. It took nearly all of Shaw's tenure to attain full peace officer status for SU's security force, under which they could make arrests and carry firearms.[15] When state legislation was finally passed allowing SU security to get full peace officer status, the legislation applied to all private colleges and universities in New York State.

There was a time—between 1964 and 1981—when SU's security personnel were deputized by Syracuse city police and had limited police powers. That ended when the state attorney general issued a legal opinion that local law enforcement did not have the authority to deputize individuals.[16] State universities, however, still had security with peace officer status, as did Cornell University, because it had a state college on its campus. Each state university campus could decide whether to let peace officers carry firearms, and SUNY ESF had decided against it.[17]

Lack of police powers negatively affected the morale of SU's security officers, who saw themselves as "rent-a-cops." That resentment was a contributing factor in security officers' attempt to unionize in 1990, an effort the university successfully resisted.[18]

In 1994, Shaw asked SU's Office of Government and Community Relations, under the direction of Eleanor Gallagher, to plan and execute a comprehensive effort to secure the approvals and support necessary for campus security officers to obtain peace officer status. SU's new director of state relations, Beth Rougeux, a "bulldog" on issues, began by lobbying state legislators.[19] State assemblyman Michael Bragman (D-Cicero) was majority leader and told Rougeux that he would not advance legislation to strengthen campus police powers unless police unions were behind it. One union concern was a potential loss of income—city police working a detail for a Dome event were paid time and a half. So Rougeux turned her attention to police union representatives. Two of her brothers were state troopers, which helped her understand police culture, she said. Negotiations over what would be allowed were long and challenging.[20]

In 1995, Governor George Pataki signed legislation that granted enhanced authority to public safety officers at private, independent college campuses that sought it. The gain was incremental but significant; it allowed campus security officers to carry nightsticks and pepper spray. They still could not pursue suspects off-campus, so new protocols between campus security and local police had to be established. To improve relations with the Syracuse city police, SU engaged them to provide the training required by the enhanced authority legislation, using a statewide curriculum.[21] State legislation directed that the local police chief appoint campus security officers but that power had to first be granted by the local municipality. Rougeux began lobbying Syracuse City Council members.

Meanwhile, opposition to enhanced police powers was voiced in debates at campus forums and in the pages of the *Daily Orange*. In the less-heated context of student surveys, however, a different opinion seemed to prevail. Two student polls, each with several hundred students participating, indicated student support for increased police powers, and the administration seized on the polls as proof of campus support for its security initiative.

In the eyes of Syracuse city police, SU's public safety officers remained minor players, and the university had to fight for every provision it gained. In 1999, SU worked out a new protocol, signed by Shaw and Syracuse police chief John Falge, under which city police and SU public safety officers would notify each other about any violent felony offense on campus or a report of a missing student.

A few months later, three armed men broke into a South Campus apartment, tied up and blindfolded three SU students, ransacked their apartment, and stole one of their cars. Campus public safety officers became aware of the incident only when they drove by and noticed SPD vehicles on the scene. The students were taken to SPD headquarters without SU's knowledge. The incident highlighted the need for better relations between the two agencies.

Then came 9/11 and a nationwide push for increased security in all aspects of American life. In a 2003 survey, some 90 percent of institutions with student populations of more than 15,000 had campus law enforcement departments with full police powers, including firearms.[22]

In October 2003, Governor Pataki signed a bill that enabled private institutions like SU to designate selected public safety officers as peace officers. Campus security could now make traffic stops, and their cars could be outfitted with lights and sirens. At SU, it would cost a half million dollars more for better-paid, better-trained, and better-equipped peace officers, who would, it was argued, be taking greater risks.

But before changes could be implemented, university community representatives needed to sign off. That happened at a University Senate meeting in February 2004, where a resolution was proposed to support the administration's plan to change some public safety personnel to peace officer status. One senator amended the resolution so that officers would not be armed with guns, but that amended resolution failed to pass. The senate ultimately voted to support the peace officer changes that included carrying firearms.

One final, opposing push came when Students against Firearm Enhancement (SAFE) and Students against Guns circulated petitions opposing the firearm provision, and some professors sent letters to trustees arguing that the increased presence of firearms on campus would make their use more likely. Those efforts proved fruitless.

Just a few months before Shaw would depart as chancellor, he achieved one of the first goals he had identified when he arrived at Syracuse: Fully trained and firearm-equipped peace officers would be patrolling campus by the fall of 2005.

Livingstock

May Day 1999 was a wake-up call for SU administrators. On May 1, house parties around the 700 block of Livingston Avenue, two blocks east of campus, morphed into a block party and spun into a riot. Street bonfires of brush, cardboard, and furniture flamed thirty feet in the air as more than 1,000 drunken students milled about.[23] Ninety police officers were called to the scene, some in riot gear. When police asked students to leave, some students hurled rocks and bottles at them and damaged a firetruck.

Campus security officers were at the scene, along with Vice Presidents Barry Wells and Eleanor Ware.[24] Ware called Shaw at his Skaneateles home and advised him to drive in to join Syracuse

Rowdy crowds of students and bonfires in the street characterized Living-stock, the postmortem moniker given a May 1999 festival on Livingston Avenue that grew out of control. The Post-Standard/Marla Brose.

mayor Roy Bernardi and city police chief Tim Foody, who had also been called. They watched until the riot quieted down around 1:15 a.m. Over time, the infamous night would be referred to in SU circles as "Livingstock," a conflation of the Livingston Avenue party with its riots and fires and those that took place two months later at the twentieth anniversary of Woodstock, in Rome, New York.[25]

Thirty-nine people were arrested, including ten on felony charges of first-degree rioting. Bernardi ordered a temporary ban on all city-issued permits for house parties until after the college semester ended. Twenty-one of those arrested were students at SU and SUNY ESF and were immediately suspended pending SU judicial hearings. At that time, SU was handling disciplinary procedures for SUNY ESF students, who followed the same code of conduct as SU students.

Shaw wanted action to be swift and strict, even though he had been advised that the suspensions could be overturned. "I don't care. We're going to do the right thing. We're going to be stern. This is going to be a teachable moment for the university community," he told Wells, his vice president of student affairs. Several suspended students were seniors scheduled to graduate May 15. Judicial hearings were arranged quicker than usual to accommodate those expecting to graduate. SU did lift all the suspensions just four days later, after a state Supreme Court judge overturned one SU student's suspension and temporarily barred the university from proceeding with a disciplinary hearing.

In the wake of the incident, a Mayday in every respect, the university needed to rethink the ways it addressed student drinking and mend its strained relations with neighbors and the city. Wells had seen the storm coming months before and had passed along to his staff reports of alcohol-fueled riots at universities across the nation.

Earlier that academic year, SU had taken measures to clamp down on student drug and alcohol abuse by toughening its code of conduct, making it a violation for an underage student on- or off-campus to be in the presence of alcohol. Alcohol consumption at SU played a role in 80 percent of all calls involving vandalism, harassment, and fights and in 90 percent of all sexual assault cases.

Enforcement of the stricter policy led to a one-year jump in alcohol-related violations, from 379 in 1997–98 to 917 in 1998–99.[26] Disorderly conduct cases also increased, from thirty-nine to eighty-one. Property damage cases rose from sixteen to forty-nine. Stricter rule enforcement was largely reactive, but Livingstock underscored the need for proactive strategies to reduce alcohol use. In August, the university distributed 1,000 packets of information to students living off-campus, and Shaw greeted incoming students with a frank warning about alcohol abuse. "There are some here who have battled addiction to alcohol or drugs and won," he said.[27] "There are others who will fall into that trap while they are here."

One strategy to address student partying, angry neighbors, and resentful city officials came with a neighborhood partnership concept that Shaw described to trustees in August. The university, the city of Syracuse, neighborhood associations, and residents would work together to improve the quality of life in the neighborhood immediately east of campus. City police and SU's public safety officers would coordinate weekend patrols of the neighborhood; the city would punish landlords who were not taking care of their properties and more strictly enforce underage drinking laws. SU would help pay for a city police unit to patrol the neighborhood on weekend nights, at least through the 1999–2000 school year.[28]

The university had considered paying for city police patrols in 1993 and dismissed it as being too expensive and a commitment without end. The estimated cost was one hundred thousand dollars a year. "Once in place, [it] will become an entitlement and not go away."[29]

The partnership was announced to the public at a media event staged at the Westcott Community Center. Afterward, Shaw and Bernardi walked through the neighborhood, joined by some forty city police officers, code enforcement officers, firefighters, and public works employees, who fanned out seeking code violations for everything from abandoned vehicles to garbage on the curb.

The following school year, the university reached out to off-campus students. At the semester's start, volunteers that included area homeowners, university officials, students, and business owners went door-to-door at houses rented to students, handing out welcome bags bearing the phrase, "Having a House Party/Don't Add Getting Arrested to Your Checklist!" Each bag contained information about tenants' rights, Syracuse city ordinances, SU's code of student conduct, emergency telephone numbers, and a voter registration form.

The police patrol made an impact. In November, 140 students from the neighborhood were disciplined for code of conduct violations; forty of those were arrested.[30] As months went by, fewer and fewer students were being cited for violations.

The university also began aggressively promoting weekend events, such as Late Night at the Gym, talent shows, and Syracuse Crunch Games. While efforts to counter alcohol and drug abuse are perennial undertakings at universities, Livingstock sharpened SU's focus on the issue.

Tennity Ice Skating Pavilion

The Marilyn and Bill Tennity Ice Skating Pavilion could not have come at a better time. The announcement for construction of the Olympic-sized skating rink on South Campus came the month after

Livingstock, although the Tennitys' $3.4 million gift had been in the works for years.

Marilyn Tennity was an SU alumna ('42) who had studied psychology. She was a native of Los Angeles but grew up on the East Coast and was the daughter of George D. Smith, who was the second chairman and CEO of United Parcel Service, Inc. (UPS) from 1962 to 1972, then a privately held company. The Tennitys lived in Santa Barbara and had become friends of the Shaws, who would stay with them on California trips. Mary Ann Shaw and Marilyn Tennity connected strongly. William Tennity, an alumnus of Rochester Institute of Technology (RIT), was a retired mechanical engineer.

SU's first ice rink was a recreational facility and not operated by the Department of Athletics. It was dedicated in 2000, and Shaw, who was not a skater, gamely took to the ice, supported by the arm of Bill Allyn, a trustee and longtime hockey player. Bill Tennity, beaming like a child, climbed aboard a Zamboni, nicknamed the "Bill T." Six months after opening, the ice rink had logged 14,000 visits.[31]

Smoking

In 1989, New York governor Mario Cuomo signed a law prohibiting smoking in public places. It would be the first smoking ban to affect SU, namely the Carrier Dome. The law had exceptions, however, that allowed smoking in private boxes of sports arenas like the Dome. Previously, Dome management had restricted smoking to certain gate areas. With the new state prohibition, Dome attendants issued fans smoking passes to step outside for their nicotine fix.

Smoking continued in the Dome in private boxes and in the press box, which was arguably public. One frequent press box visitor was hard-core cigarette smoker and athletic director, Jake Crouthamel.

In 1998, the university further reduced areas where smoking was allowed, prohibiting it in all residential dining facilities and residence halls, except in private living areas with the approval of all roommates. Smoking was also prohibited in all nonresidential, indoor locations on university-owned, operated, or controlled property. The only exceptions were designated "Smoking Permitted Areas."

The policy would be further tightened in 2000, when smoking was completely banned in residence halls. The Student Government

Association protested, sending Shaw a resolution stating that the SGA wanted the university to continue the existing policy, which permitted smoking in rooms with the consent of roommates. Shaw told SGA representatives that secondary smoke was the real issue, that thirty to forty other schools in the nation already prohibited smoking in residence halls, and that the new policy would stand.

Despite the university's restrictions against smoking on campus, the university continued to court tobacco companies for assistance with student internships. At the March 2002 trustee executive meeting, John Sellars, vice president for advancement, reported that his office had sponsored a successful student recruitment reception for Philip Morris, at which the company informed students about employment opportunities and intern positions. Plans were being made to make it an annual event, he said.

Remembrance Week

Memories of the thirty-five students who were killed in the Pan Am Flight 103 terrorist bombing of December 21, 1988, were still raw when Shaw began.

Under Eggers, measures were taken to heal the emotional wounds the tragedy left. A Place of Remembrance had been built in front of the Hall of Languages with a semicircular memorial wall that was the site of an annual service, and a separate Pan Am Flight 103 archive was established within the University Archives to preserve records and artifacts related to the tragedy. Two scholarship programs had begun—the Lockerbie Scholarship, which brought two students each year from that Scotland village where the plane had crashed, and the Remembrance Scholarship, a $5,000 award given to thirty-five accomplished SU seniors in memory of those who died in the bombing.[32] A fall convocation ceremony recognizing the scholars was held in Hendricks Chapel.

The Scottish Lockerbie Scholarship recipients had lived through the plane crash that killed eleven of their neighbors. The first Remembrance Scholars knew some of the victims or knew people who knew the victims, but for future scholars, personal knowledge of the victims would rarely be the case. The remembrance process had to evolve.

Around 1995, the scholars came to Judy O'Rourke, director of undergraduate studies and her boss, Ron Cavanagh, with a proposal to build a week of events and service work around the convocation and day of remembrance. "If we don't do something specific, this is just going to be a scholarship like any other," they told O'Rourke. "Remembering is not enough." Shaw liked the idea and provided roughly $3,000 to pay for whatever programming the students chose, bringing in speakers and screening films, for example.

In September 1995, the losses from the Pan Am Flight 103 tragedy were poignantly evoked when the mother of one of the victims brought her powerful sculpture exhibit *Dark Elegy* to SU's campus. Suse Lowenstein's twenty-one-year-old son, Alexander, an SU student at the time, was one of the 270 people who perished over Lockerbie, Scotland. Lowenstein's installation on the lawn between Lyman Hall and Bird Library comprised thirty-five larger-than-life figures of naked women in expressions of grief.[33] The creation began with Lowenstein's sculpture of herself, doubled over on her knees, clutching her abdomen. It was the posture she collapsed into upon learning of her son's death. Mothers of other victims were also represented. Some had posed for Lowenstein in her studio. The figures were on view September through March.

The Remembrance Scholarship program had begun in 1989 with more goodwill than money. Years later, the Fred L. Emerson Foundation, in Auburn, New York, offered a $500,000 challenge grant to build a Remembrance Scholarship endowment. Money came in slowly with small donations until Dick and Jean Thompson, of McLean, Virginia, stepped up with a $500,000 gift in 2000. Behind it was Dick and Jean's amazingly resonant story.

Both were SU alumni. C. (Catherine) Jean Terry ('66) married Richard "Dick" Thompson ('67) in 1974. Before then, Jean had endured two heartbreaking losses. The first came when she was an infant. Her father, First Lieutenant John F. Phelan, a young Army officer, died in Normandy, France, in World War II, before ever seeing his daughter. Jean grew up in Syracuse, attended SU as her mother had, and married a service member, Marine Corps Captain Richard Morin. They had a daughter. Before Morin had a chance to know his young daughter, he was killed in Vietnam.

Suse Lowenstein with some of her thirty-five figures of grief-stricken women on the lawn in front of Lyman Hall in the fall of 1995. Lowenstein's twenty-one-year-old son, Alexander, was one of 270 people who perished over Lockerbie, Scotland, when a terrorist bomb exploded in midair on Pan Am Flight 103 in December 1988. Courtesy of University Archives, Syracuse University Libraries.

So, with both Jean's father and husband having left home to serve in wars they never returned from, in 1974 she married a Vietnam veteran, Richard "Dick" Thompson, a 1967 graduate of the Maxwell School. Dick, an attorney who was vice president of government affairs for Bristol Myers Squibb, and later senior counsel at Patton Boggs, would become an SU trustee (2001) and chairman of the board (2011). Jean and Dick's Remembrance Scholarship gift was made in honor of the father Jean never knew, and the Thompsons became regular attendees at Remembrance Week events.

CHAPTER 6

Diversity

Upholding a Value

FROM THE START, Shaw affirmed diversity as one of SU's five core values. Syracuse had been founded as a coeducational institution in 1870 when few universities admitted women, and in some respects, the university had made noteworthy strides in that regard.

Robert Hill, SU's first director of affirmative action under Eggers and vice president of public relations under Shaw, had helped reconnect hundreds of disillusioned SU African American and Latino alumni through Coming Back Together reunions, which began in 1983 and are held every three years.[1] Prominent African American alumni, such as Dave Bing, Jim Brown, John Mackey, Billy Hunter, Suzanne De Passe, and Vanessa Williams, returned to SU for the triennial event to reconnect with each other and to meet and inspire current students.[2] Hill also helped SU develop a scholarship fund for African American and Latino students, raising $1.2 million through the Our Time Has Come campaign.

During Shaw's tenure, Coming Back Together evolved into a four-day event that included seminars for students about career and social issues.[3] In the years between campus reunions, African American and Latino alumni took Coming Back Together trips to the Bahamas, Aruba, South Africa, and Martha's Vineyard, a popular summer vacation destination for African Americans.[4]

One of the most symbolic and healing overtures toward African American alumni came in 1995, when SU held a tribute weekend for Jim Brown, honoring his induction into the College Football Hall of Fame forty years after he played for SU. Brown, who was a dean's

Robert Hill, SU's first director of affirmative action under Eggers and vice president of public relations under Shaw, helped reaffiliate hundreds of disillusioned African American and Latino alumni with SU through Coming Back Together reunions. Courtesy of University Archives, Syracuse University Libraries.

list philosophy major and an ROTC officer, was probably the best athlete at SU in the 1950s: an All-American in lacrosse and football who also played varsity basketball, until the lack of playing time prompted him to quit in 1955. Longtime Hall of Fame officials told *Post-Standard* columnist Sean Kirst that SU never tried too hard to push Brown's name for Hall of Fame recognition until Athletic Director Jake Crouthamel began what turned out to be a successful campaign for Brown.[5]

In day-to-day dealings on campus, Syracuse had much work to do to embrace diversity with a full range of racial, cultural, gender, and religious respect and equality. Although the university had been an early leader in admitting women, blacks, Jews, and other historically underrepresented groups, pockets of racism, sexism, anti-Semitism, and homophobia persisted. That legacy challenged the successful recruitment and retention of minority faculty and students and the engagement of minority alumni.

The challenge was not just to ensure fair and respectful treatment for minorities in the present. It involved overcoming mistrust about SU's sincerity in achieving its diversity goals and ensuring that it was actively building a critical mass of minority communities on campus in a way that minorities, especially faculty, felt comfortable.

In Shaw's first year, among tenured faculty, African Americans made up just 2.35 percent, Latinos 0.86 percent, and women 16 percent, numbers that were at odds with the student body's growing diversity, especially among women.[6] In 1992–93, women made up 49.9 percent of undergraduates and 49 percent of graduate students.

Shaw had a decent record on diversity issues: he had written about racial diversity on campuses as early as 1969 when he was a young dean at Towson State and continued while president of the University of Wisconsin system.[7] He had personally lobbied Congress members to end the military's discrimination against gays.

Shaw's first gesture toward gender equality was his insistence of decent pay for his wife, Mary Ann. It was more than personal. Shaw understood the power that such straightforward acts could have. Decades later, it can be hard to appreciate how important the symbolism of paying the chancellor's wife was for women at the university. It was the summer of 1991, and gender imbalance in the nation's institutions was on full display with the sexual harassment allegations against Supreme Court nominee Clarence Thomas. Thomas's hearings before an all-male Senate Judiciary Committee were widely televised. The full Senate voted to confirm Thomas in October, but the hearings had highlighted the dominance of men in that body. The following year, four new women were elected senators, bringing the total to six out of one hundred.

At SU, women and minority leaders continued their advocacy work. Shaw often met them halfway, while making some strategic and sometimes unpopular policy decisions of his own. An early Shaw policy initiative was a commitment in his restructuring budget to add $340,000 a year to strengthen faculty diversity and to expand the number of faculty in the African American Studies department.[8] Finding qualified minority faculty candidates was a challenge. Every faculty search plan required approval by the Office of Human Resources, and HR approval memos like this were routine:

> Your search plan has been approved. However, your school
> has an Affirmative Action goal to hire minorities, particularly

African Americans. Based on an algorithm developed by the federal government, the national availability of African Americans
who may have the requisite skills necessary to meet the qualifications of this position is approximately four percent. This search
provides an opportunity for you to achieve your goal. Every
effort should be made to identify and include qualified African
Americans in your search.[9]

Initially, progress was slow: By June 1995, only eleven women
and minority faculty had been hired, and Shaw insisted that cabinet
members provide him with analyses of the past year's hiring in their
areas and its impact on their unit's diversity.[10]

Other initiatives followed as he methodically addressed wom-
en's issues; among them were salary inequities, sexual harassment,
and the prevention of and response to sexual assault. Shaw began,
as he often did when facing an issue, by calling for an ad hoc faculty
committee, this one on women's concerns. The committee proposed
increasing the budget for Women's Studies and hiring faculty to specifically teach an introductory course.

Women's Studies was an interdisciplinary program with cross-
listed courses that were taught in various schools and departments.
The program had begun fitfully in the late 1970s and struggled to
get institutional support, with an administrative budget of only
$42,000 in 1991–92.[11] Women's studies was approved as a major
in 1992, and in 1994, the program received its first official budget
under the College of Arts and Sciences.[12] In 1991–92, roughly 1,187
undergraduates were enrolled in women's studies.[13]

Just as important as the program's academic focus on femi-
nist and gender studies issues, its network of faculty served as an
informal clearinghouse for those who had experienced harassment
and sexism on campus. Student complaints were often first aired to
trusted faculty in the Women's Studies program.

Shaw was reluctant at the start of his tenure to approve programs that involved a substantial or long-term financial commitment, like new faculty positions specifically for Women's Studies.
Instead, he funded two, eighteen-month consultant positions to
advise him on women's issues. They were filled by Diane Murphy,

professor of social work and director of Women's Studies, and Marie Provine, professor of political science. The two began January 1, 1993, and within four months had submitted a draft for SU's first sexual harassment policy.[14] The policy was an important start for the university in addressing sexual harassment, putting people with authority on notice that if a complaint was made about them by a subordinate, there would be no assumption on the part of university investigators that the relationship was welcome by the subordinate.

Murphy also assembled a history of women at SU, which she completed in 2004, a thorough and compelling chronology that exists only as a wall display in a ground-floor classroom of Eggers Hall.

Gays and Lesbians

In April 1991, students on more than one hundred campuses across the United States, including SU and the University of Wisconsin, took part in protests against a Department of Defense (DOD) policy that banned homosexuals from military service.[15] The DOD's policy of prohibiting ROTC programs from "knowingly enrolling or contracting homosexuals" conflicted with antidiscriminatory policies of many universities.

The protests had been building for years.[16] At the University of Wisconsin in Madison, students conducted a five-day sit-in outside Chancellor Donna Shalala's office, then moved to another room from which they were removed by police. Shaw, when Shalala's boss, had resisted students' demands to add a disclaimer in university publications saying the federally run ROTC program contradicted state and university laws banning discrimination because of sexual orientation.[17] He also overrode a UW–Madison faculty vote to ban the ROTC from campus.[18]

SU's University Senate had passed a resolution in February 1991, before Shaw arrived, calling for expelling the ROTC by 1994 unless the military accepted gay and lesbian members. Student protestors echoed the faculty position. The university formed a committee, chaired by Chris Witting, Board of Trustees chair, to consider the ROTC issue. Protestors' demands were coming at a difficult time for cash-strapped SU. The Army ROTC had been on campus since

1919, the Air Force ROTC since 1951. Student participation was declining in both, from 272 in 1987–88 to 161 in 1990–91. ROTC money paid for those students' tuitions and fees, an amount that totaled $876,082 in 1990–91. Removing the ROTC from campus would mean losing most of that revenue.

Witting's committee presented its recommendation to Shaw in August: the ROTC should stay on campus. The university's anti-discrimination policy *did* conflict with military policy, the committee acknowledged; the university would therefore lobby Congress and the military to change its policy. In September, Shaw sent letters to several members of Congress and to Dick Cheney, secretary of defense. "It is my intent to work toward increasing understanding and tolerance on this campus and in the society as a whole," Shaw wrote Cheney.[19]

SU's Lesbian and Gay Graduate Collective wrote Shaw, objecting to the university's continued support of ROTC programs, and Shaw responded considerately. "I believe that we have the same goal, but different methods of achieving it," he wrote. "Training future military officers on a college campus is preferable to leaving the task exclusively to the military. Exposing these young men and women to the diversity of people and ideas on this campus enlarges their view of the world. And that fact may have influence on DOD policy."[20]

In February 1994, the issue became muddled and somewhat muted with the DOD's institution of the "Don't Ask, Don't Tell" policy. The policy still barred openly gay, lesbian, or bisexual persons from military service but prohibited military personnel from discriminating against or harassing closeted homosexual or bisexual service members.

In an attempt to deter campuses from banning ROTC units, Congress in 1996 passed a law that denied federal grants, including research grants, to colleges and universities that prohibited the US armed forces from recruiting on campus or that failed to allow ROTC programs.[21]

SU kept up its fight. In 1998, the university filed an amicus curiae (friend of the court) brief with the American Council on Education challenging the US Armed Forces' "Don't Ask, Don't Tell" policy in the case of *Able v. United States*. The challenge, heard by the US Court of Appeals for the Second Circuit, was unsuccessful.

Changing the university's policies toward gays and lesbians was a more straightforward matter. In 1994, Shaw asked Joan Carpenter, vice president for human resources, to research and draw up a policy that would extend employee family and spousal benefits to same-sex domestic partners. He had been nudged in this direction by Eric Mower, a trustee. In early 1993, Mower sent Shaw a *New York Times* article about the University of Chicago and Stanford University giving gay partners the same benefits as married couples.[22] Few businesses or colleges offered such benefits in 1994. Apple, Microsoft, and HBO/Time Warner did. Enacting such a policy would put Syracuse in the company of Columbia, Cornell, Dartmouth, Harvard, Stanford, the University of Chicago, and Yale. None had experienced any significant increase in cost, Carpenter found.

Under the policy she drafted, SU's benefits would be offered to same-sex, not opposite-sex, domestic partners, because heterosexual couples had the legal opportunity to marry and if they decided not to it was by choice, the university's logic went; same-sex couples did not have this option. The full menu of benefits for spouses would be available to same-sex partners: health and life insurances, remitted tuition and tuition benefits for dependents, and access to the library and recreational facilities. Partners had to sign an affidavit that they had been in their domestic relationship for six months and comingled their money with something like a joint bank account, a shared lease, or mortgage.

Shaw discussed it with his cabinet and brought the matter to the University Senate, which endorsed it in February. He brought it to the Board of Trustees' Executive Committee in March. "I made it a business decision," he said. "The way I couched it, what percentage of our population is gay? Say between six and ten percent, probably ten. Do you really want to exclude ten percent of our population in the sense of getting the best and the brightest to do your work?"[23]

Vice Chancellor Vincow recalled an awkward silence before trustees voted to approve the measure. "You could see that Buzz was treading on dangerous waters with respect to the board," Vincow said. "He showed an enormous amount of courage."

Shaw bucked conventional norms again in 2001 when he announced that SU would no longer allow the Hiawatha Seaway Boy Scout Council to hold its annual Boypower Dinner in the Carrier Dome because scout policy banned openly homosexual troop leaders. It came down to a clash of policies, he told the *Post-Standard*. "The university policy clearly bans discrimination on the basis of sexual preference," he said. "The Boy Scout policy mandates exclusion on the basis of sexual preference. . . . There is a disconnect between our policy and their policy, and I'm not asking my board to change our policy and exclude gays."

The Boypower Dinner had been held in the Carrier Dome since 1984. It was the best-attended scout fund-raiser in the nation and the richest fund-raising dinner in Central New York.[24] Shaw had told Scout Council leaders about his decision the previous fall but waited to announce it in a letter to the council two days after a Boypower Dinner at which NBC's *Today Show* weatherman Al Roker was the main attraction. That dinner netted the council $395,000.[25]

Shaw had made his decision following a Supreme Court ruling the previous June, in which the Court ruled the Boy Scout policy toward gays was legal. Shaw had hoped the court's decision would be otherwise, and when it came, he felt compelled to act. He did not ask trustees if he could, because the action was consistent with university policy. He did consult with select people, among them, Bruce Carter, associate professor of psychology. Shaw asked Carter what he thought about banning the scouts from the Dome.[26] A storm of protest would follow the announcement, Carter told him. Shaw probed further: "Will anybody on campus be harmed by my decision?"

"No," Carter said. "Everything's going to be directed at you."

"Okay, fine. Then it's the right decision. That's my job."

Public outcry was vehement. Letters to the *Post-Standard* accused Shaw of being "politically correct," of not caring about family values. Homosexually active men do not make good role models for boys, one writer said. A *Post-Standard* editorial suggested the university was being hypocritically selective. "If [SU] doesn't ban the military, why ban the Scouts?"

Shaw was ever the pragmatist when deciding which diversity battles to fight. He embraced where he could the dramatic attitudinal shift that took place in the 1990s, as the nation became more "liquid, tolerant, nonjudgmental."[27] The popular television sitcom *Will and Grace* (1998–2006) normalized gay characters, *The Birdcage* (1996) portrayed gay men in stable, long-term relationships. Like much of the nation, the university became a more supportive place for gays and lesbians. Eight years after SU first granted employee benefits to same-sex domestic partners, thirty-two were registered with SU's human resources department, and eighteen subscribed to health insurance. In 2001, the University Senate approved the creation of a new office, the Lesbian, Gay, Bisexual, and Transgender Resource Center to serve students that identify as such. The office would report to the Division of Student Affairs.[28] Also, a year after Vermont became the first state to allow civil unions for gay couples in 2001, Hendricks Chapel adopted a policy to hold commitment ceremonies for gay and lesbian couples. The policy reconfirmed the chapel's "commitment to the University's core value of diversity."[29]

Women in Science and Engineering

For the first time in SU's history, the percentage of women within the student body surpassed the percentage of men—54 percent of students were women by 1997. The gender shift alarmed trustees, but SU was not alone.[30] Nationwide, the numbers of male college undergraduates declined from 58 percent in 1969 to 44 percent in 2000.[31] Fascinating theories existed to explain the phenomenon, from the higher percentages of boys than girls having disabilities and attention deficit disorder, to the lower percentage of boys graduating high school, but none of those definitively identified the root cause.

SU's science departments and engineering college had a dearth of women among their faculty, yet even in those formerly male-dominated fields, the number of female students increased substantially. The imbalance was highlighted in a study led by Cathryn Newton, chair of earth sciences, and Shobha Bhatia, chair of civil and environmental engineering: in the fall of 1997, 6 percent of faculty in engineering and computer sciences were women, while 26 percent of undergraduates were; in psychology, the disparity was even greater—19 percent of faculty were women, 71 percent of undergraduate majors were; in the other natural sciences and mathematics division, 8 percent of faculty were women, compared to 45 percent of students, depending on the major. To help reduce that disparity, Newton and Bhatia formed a chapter of Women in Science and Engineering (WISE), an international program that works to develop women faculty and students in the sciences, mathematics, and engineering. Under the program, Newton and Bhatia brought in high-profile female scientists and engineers to inspire students and developed mentorship programs to help female students successfully navigate the rigors of research.

*   *   *

Low-pay sweatshop production of clothing became an issue at SU and on campuses across the nation in the late 1990s, coming to broad public attention through a powerful and increasingly popular strategy: celebrity embarrassment. In 1996, Charles Kernaghan, a workers' rights activist, testified at a congressional hearing that a celebrity-sponsored clothing line sold at Walmart was being made by child laborers earning twenty-five cents per finished piece and working twenty-hour days in factories in Honduras.[32] The celebrity was Kathie Lee Gifford, a daytime TV talk show co-host. Gifford tearfully defended herself on her show, *Live! with Regis and Kathie Lee*, and later vowed to improve working conditions at factories that made her clothing.

Universities represented only about 2 percent of the clothing market, but they were big purchasers of collegiate-licensed apparel like sweatshirts and hats. Their collective buying power, sufficiently marshaled, could give them considerable leverage to affect working conditions. At Syracuse, the Student Environmental Action Coalition took up the issue. The sweatshop campus protest network was similar to the one that had pressured universities to divest from South African investments because of apartheid; in 1978, SU trustees had partially divested from stock in companies doing business in South Africa, prompted by student protests.[33]

To monitor working conditions in apparel factories, two national organizations formed, each trying to enlist universities as members.

The Fair Labor Association (FLA), a coalition of apparel makers, colleges, and the US Department of Labor, relied on companies to self-monitor working conditions and acted as a kind of accreditation group for the apparel industry. The Workers' Rights Consortium (WRC) monitored companies itself, attempting to uncover and address sweatshop abuses. SU joined the FLA in 1999, and the next year, students pressed Shaw to abandon it and join the WRC because, they said, the FLA was not independent enough. Shaw directed Peter Webber, director of auxiliary services and chairman of the university's Trademark Licensing Advisory Board, to study both organizations and make a recommendation.

Meanwhile, campus events kept pressure on the administration to join the WRC. On March 1, 2000, Kernaghan spoke at SU, brought to campus by the Student Coalition on Organized Labor and NYPIRG (New York Public Interest Research Group). Kernaghan was not directly affiliated with either the FLA or WRC, but his speech energized students around the sweatshop issue. Three weeks later, about a dozen SU students organized a "naked bike ride" around the Quad to protest SU's affiliation with sweatshops.[34] Protest signs were strategically placed over students' bodies. Campus security escorted away one male student for indecent exposure. The bike ride capped Sweatshop Awareness Week, during which nightly vigils were held to bring attention to the issue. Students issued a deadline for Shaw to join the WRC by April 1. More than a year went by before SU did.

In May 2001, Shaw approved Webber's recommendation to join the WRC. Webber liked the director, Scott Nova, and believed that the WRC's strategy of independent monitoring and university partnership could yield results. SU could have joined the WRC right away and gained students' approval, Shaw told Webber, but he wanted "to make a difference, not a point." Webber had convinced Shaw that the WRC was a solid organization with which SU could work. And it did in 2002, when SU helped the WRC intervene in a strike at the New Era Cap Co. in Derby, New York, outside of Buffalo, a company that made SU visored caps sold at the Dome and Syracuse University Bookstore.[35] Workers had been on strike for a year when Webber and Nova, meeting with New Era's CEO and labor attorneys, helped settle the strike in a few weeks.[36]

Minority Hiring

Shaw resisted student demands to set a fixed quota for hiring minorities, but behind the scenes he steadily pushed on various fronts to assist minority students and to hire more minority faculty and administrators. In 2003, SU joined a group of colleges and universities that submitted an amicus curiae brief to the US Supreme Court in support of the affirmative action programs at the University of Michigan. Two pending cases, *Grutter v. Bollinger* and *Gratz v. Bollinger*, challenged the University of Michigan's law school and undergraduate admissions programs, respectively. The Court upheld the affirmative action admissions policy of the law school and ruled against the undergraduate admissions policy that awarded points toward admission to underrepresented minorities.

As for hiring minority faculty, one of Shaw's key lieutenants was Howard Johnson, associate vice chancellor for academic affairs. An African American, Johnson came to Syracuse in 1973 as a professor with a dual appointment in mathematics and mathematics education. He was appointed associate vice chancellor in 1989 and dean of the Graduate School in 1995, replacing Robert Jensen, who had been named dean of the College of Arts and Sciences. As Graduate School dean, Johnson kept his associate vice chancellor title and his minority recruitment focus.

A big part of convincing minority faculty recruits to take jobs at Syracuse was assuring them they would be comfortable on campus. When they came for a visit, Johnson would gather African American and Latino employees from all stations—faculty and staff—to meet them and give recruits a sense of the community of which they would be a part. Finding and hiring experienced minority faculty was difficult—the candidate pool was small, the job market was vast, and lots of universities, many with far more financial resources, were trying to increase their percentage of minority faculty as well. "Let's say you found a really outstanding engineer," Shaw said. "If they are outstanding enough they are going to MIT or somewhere. Because there are just not that many in the [candidate] pool."[37]

Johnson looked to recruit bright graduate students who were working toward their doctorates. He partnered SU with the PhD Project, a diversity initiative sponsored by KPMG, the international accounting and professional consulting firm. The PhD Project helped fund and mentor African American and Latino students working toward their doctorates in business. In at least one instance, Johnson paid a stipend approved by Vice Chancellor Freund to a graduate student while he was working toward his PhD to lure him to SU. The student was Boyce Watkins who was at Ohio State and who joined the School of Management faculty in 2001 as assistant professor of finance.

In 2003, nearly 25 percent of SU's newest faculty included people from historically underrepresented groups, the university claimed in a report to the Middle States Commission on Higher Education. Additionally, the number of female tenured and tenure-track faculty members increased from 30 percent to over 33 percent between 1998 and 2003.[38]

Another diversity hiring initiative came when the Office of Human Resources reached out to dozens of community agencies in the city of Syracuse to match candidates from diverse backgrounds with SU staff positions. At a time when few minority job seekers were applying for SU staff positions, the Office of Human Resources, located in the Skytop Office Building, was all white, and minorities found it intimidating, recalled Neil Strodel, then associate vice president of human resources.[39] "We weren't friendly to the minority community."

Addressing this unwelcoming climate, Shaw devoted six of his *Buzzwords* employee newsletters in the spring of 2000 to the topic of diversity. Several years later, more than 1,500 staff were required to take diversity training, a university initiative that cost some $200,000 in consultant fees.[40]

Strodel also brought SU hiring managers to agencies in the city of Syracuse to meet diverse community leaders and to offer insights into how job seekers could best access the university's job network. The outreach yielded results and recognition. Largely because of its diversity hiring initiative, SU was recognized as an Employer of Choice in 2002 and 2003 by the Central New York Society for Human Resource Management.

Neil Strodel, vice president of human resources, launched diversity hiring initiatives for SU staff with Syracuse community organizations. Courtesy of University Archives, Syracuse University Libraries.

Racist and biased behavior persisted on campus, however, requiring ongoing consciousness-raising programs and quick administrative attention whenever incidents occurred. In February 2002, for instance, the *Daily Orange* printed a comic that depicted what appeared to be a black burglar breaking into a white person's home. The following day, students at a forum decried the cartoon as racist and insisted the university needed diversity initiatives for faculty, staff, and students, and in particular, the newspaper's staff. The university issued a statement condemning the cartoon.

Months later, on a May evening days before commencement, a white member of Sigma Alpha Epsilon fraternity went to a Crouse Avenue bar in blackface.[41] News of the incident spread quickly, and the next day some seventy-five students marched into the Tolley Administration Building and occupied the lower lobby, the stairs, and hallway outside Shaw's office. Students accused the university of failing to take action when incidents of racial bias occurred. They brought a list of twelve demands, including the suspension of the fraternity and its members and immediate expulsion of senior Aaron Levine, the student who appeared in blackface.[42]

At SU's 2002 commencement, students turned their backs to speaker Rudolph Giuliani, whose tenure as mayor of New York had been marked by charges of police brutality and racial profiling by members of the New York City Police Department. Courtesy of University Archives, Syracuse University Libraries.

Shaw met the group in the stairwell, asked who their leaders were, and brought the leaders into his office. Besides their demands, they were angry about the commencement speaker, former New York City mayor Rudolph Giuliani, who was to appear in three days. Giuliani was *Time* magazine's "Person of the Year" in 2001 for his resolute response to the September 11 terrorist attacks. Mayor Giuliani had championed crime reduction and law enforcement, but his tenure was marked by charges of police brutality and racial profiling by members of the New York City Police Department. The students and Shaw agreed that students could protest Giuliani at commencement as long as they did not disrupt the ceremony, and Shaw felt good about the meeting. "It was an important educational moment about civil disobedience," he said.

At commencement, when Giuliani approached the podium, several dozen students and some audience members stood and turned their backs to him, many raising wallets over their heads in memory of Amadou Diallo, an African immigrant who had been shot nineteen times by New York City police as he pulled a wallet from a pocket during a police stop.[43] Giuliani had been briefed ahead of time that the protest would happen and was "delighted that they were protesting," Shaw said.

Implementing diversity, or any of SU's other four core values across the university's academic enterprise, was one matter. Bringing those core values to bear on athletics—with its traditions, its competitive pressures, its devoted fans, and, at times, a harsh public spotlight—was a wholly different ball game. It required of Shaw determination and finesse, things any good athlete has in reserve.

Intercollegiate Athletics

A New Era

I F SHAW did not fully appreciate the unalloyed fervor of SU men's basketball fans, he had only to look through SU's news clipping file about the university's possible NCAA violations. Letters to the editor of the *Post Standard* reflected fans' indignation over the newspaper's investigative coverage of SU's third-ranked basketball program.

"Stories will harm SU, city, and paper."

"Unbelievable attack by a local paper."

SU basketball thrills sustained the city's spirit through long, bleak winters. On December 20–21, 1990, the paper published a report that alleged multiple violations of NCAA rules. If true, the report suggested, off the court the university's winning basketball program had spun out of control. The alleged violations ranged from grade-fixing to claims that sports boosters were paying players and providing them with discounted goods and services. Such improprieties had been happening for years, the newspaper alleged.

Eggers had promptly ordered the university to conduct its own investigation, with Lou Marcoccia, vice president of business and finance, overseeing it and the university's law firm, Bond, Schoeneck and King (BS&K), leading the probe. BS&K turned to the Michael Slive and Michael Glazier Sports Group in Kansas for assistance.[1] Glazier was a former NCAA investigator, and Slive a former Cornell athletic director and former executive director of the Pacific-10 Conference.

The Post-Standard was not the first to raise questions about the basketball program's integrity. In early 1990, *Raw Recruits*, a

book written by Alexander Wolff and Armand Keteyian, identified
a New York City agent named Rob Johnson who passed himself off
as an assistant SU coach in order to help the university recruit Con-
rad McCrae.[2] SU shrugged off that allegation until the newspaper
brought others to light.[3]

As Shaw assumed the chancellor's job, no issue was more urgent
to him than the academic restructuring that would steer SU through
its financial crisis. To sports fans across the country, nothing at SU
was more important than the NCAA-related investigation.

Whenever the university verified an allegation, it took action.
The most dramatic happened the evening of February 7, 1991, just
before a nationally televised game against Notre Dame, when the
university declared seven basketball players ineligible to play for violating NCAA rules.[4] Football players were going to fill out the team's
roster, but the seven basketball players were reinstated in time for
the game after SU told the NCAA about the violations and its proposed remedy: players would have to "pay" for the free services they
had received. Syracuse won, 70–68.

Besides the lawyer-driven investigation into violations, Eggers
had appointed a Faculty Oversight Committee (FOC) to work with
the legal team and to examine how players met academic expectations.[5] The FOC was chaired by David Bennett, a history professor
and chairman of the university's Athletic Policy Board. On paper,
SU already had plenty of people overseeing athletics: a faculty athletics representative, the Athletic Policy Board, a senate committee
on athletic policy, an athletic academic advisor, and a compliance
coordinator. The compliance coordinator title was held by Associate
Athletic Director Doris Soladay, and it was one of many responsibilities she had. But these individuals shared little information with
each other and had little or no enforcement power.

Bennett's committee determined that the athletic department
needed tighter oversight and recommended several actions that Shaw
implemented, chief among them that the FOC become permanent
and that a full-time compliance coordinator position be created.

Meanwhile, BS&K cast its investigative net wide, painstakingly
examining every intercollegiate sport. The completed investigation
involved 7,000 hours of work by attorneys and consultants, and 255

separate interviews of 155 witnesses. Some people named in news-paper accounts had refused to be interviewed by the university. The full report weighed in at 500 pages, with another 1,700 pages of exhibits.

In January 1992, Shaw reviewed BS&K's draft report with the trustees' Executive Committee and put the findings in perspective. There was no conspiracy of wrongdoing. No documentation of any-thing intentional. Some twenty violations were chicken feed: free meals to athletes at restaurants, invitations to homes for dinner, Christmas cards to players with $50 in them from booster and Syra-cuse car dealer Bill Rapp. "But chicken feed accumulates," Shaw said. "And we did have oversight/compliance problems."[6]

On February 17, the same day that Shaw released his university restructuring plan, SU printed a summary of its basketball investiga-tion in the *Syracuse Record*. Point by point it addressed allegations made by the *Post-Standard*. Of thirty-three newspaper allegations, eleven were NCAA violations, SU determined. The university's own investigation discovered another six. The summary did not mention violations found in other sports. Years later, basketball head coach Jim Boeheim would describe the violations as a sign of the times. "Back then college basketball was more Wild West than it is today."[7]

The report also summarized remedies, the most significant of which was the creation of a full-time position for a compliance direc-tor. In March 1992, SU hired John Hardt, thirty, a lawyer who had worked in the NCAA's compliance division.[8] Hardt would monitor compliance with regulations of the NCAA, the Big East Conference, and the university. He would monitor student-athletes' eligibil-ity status and financial aid packages and would implement a rules education program for players, coaches, staff, and boosters. Every coach involved in recruiting would soon be taking an annual NCAA certification exam for recruiters, and Hardt would prep them.[9] Hav-ing someone with Hardt's expertise would—the university hoped—mitigate NCAA penalties.

Eight months passed before the NCAA issued its decision, and when it came on October 1, it was harsh. SU's entire athletic pro-gram was placed on two years' probation for violations in men's and women's basketball, football, wrestling, and men's lacrosse. The men's basketball program was hardest hit, banned from postseason play in 1992–93 because of widespread recruiting violations. Syracuse had been to nine straight NCAA tournaments up to that point.

SU's lawyers tried to keep the men's basketball team eligible to play in the 1993 NCAA tournament by offering to donate $364,000 to charity—roughly the university's take from one year's tournament play. The NCAA said its bylaws would not permit such a deal. The NCAA basketball sanctions also reduced scholarships, off-campus recruiting visits by coaches, and expense-paid visits by recruits to Syracuse. Men's basketball would lose one scholarship in each of the 1993–94 and 1994–95 academic years.

The basketball program's violations were not the half of it. Wrestling and lacrosse both had exceeded their financial aid limits for several years. The lacrosse team had won the NCAA championship in three of those years—1988, 1989, and 1990; consequently, the NCAA reduced the number of scholarships each program could award beginning in 1993–94. Wrestling lost two and a half scholarships in each of four years, while lacrosse lost three scholarships in each of three years.

No penalties were assessed against football and women's basketball because of the limited nature of infractions by those programs. Shaw accepted the penalties but denied that SU's athletic department was uncontrolled. "This is not a maverick athletic program," he said.

Early in the investigation, SU had "disassociated" itself for three years from the agent and boosters who had granted players favors: Johnson, Rapp, restauranteur Fred Grimaldi, and Joseph and Cynthia Giannuzzi. Joseph Giannuzzi was president of SU's Hardwood Club, a 600-member sports booster organization that raised money to help defray recruiting expenses.[10] In February 1992, he was asked to step down as president and surrender the preferred seating privileges he and his wife enjoyed at games.[11]

Syracuse University paid BS&K at least $875,000[12] to investigate its athletic programs. The legal expense saved SU from more severe penalties, notably, a one-year ban from television for men's basketball, something that the NCAA had considered but decided against, citing the university's cooperation as a mitigating factor.[13]

When it was over, Shaw diplomatically explained the situation he inherited. "As the program grew and NCAA regulations became more complex, the system began to erode almost imperceptibly. We believed that it couldn't happen here. We believed that everything could be handled informally. We were wrong."[14]

Though banned from postseason NCAA or NIT play in 1993, SU was allowed to compete in the Big East tournament, in which they were blown out in the final game against Seton Hall, 103–70.

New York governor Mario Cuomo issued a public statement congratulating Shaw and Syracuse University on having the affair behind them. Shaw, who was practiced at bantering with politicians, saw an opportunity with Cuomo, a former pro baseball player who regularly played basketball with his staff.[15] Shaw wrote Cuomo thanking him for his kind words and added a postscript: "I hear that you sometimes engage in a little one-on-one 'hoops' in a rare free moment. How about a game soon? I'll be pleased to play on your court or mine. Of course, on mine I could offer an audience of 30,000-plus screaming fans, all on my side."[16]

*   *   *

With the NCAA investigation behind them, SU administrators were eager to restore their athletic program's tarnished reputation and to have a stretch of smooth sailing with no bad news. That was not to be. On the early morning of January 8, 1993, seven men's basketball players were involved in a highly publicized bar brawl. Michael Edwards, a senior guard, was charged with criminal mischief, a felony, for smashing the windows of the bar manager's Jeep. Teammate Anthony Harris lost three teeth. Six other cars near the bar also had their windows smashed, but no one was charged in connection with them.

At best, the incident would have been an embarrassment. Coming on the heels of NCAA penalties, however, the bar brawl, its circumstances, and the university's statements about it perpetuated the image of an out-of-control basketball program, as well as a rowdy, drunken culture up on "the hill."

The brawl occurred around 1:30 a.m. toward the end of a weekly five-dollar, all-you-can-drink beer night at Sutter's Mill and Mining

Co., a popular student bar in an alley off South Crouse Avenue. Harris, twenty, was underage. Two bouncers were arrested for assault, and it was not the first time Sutter's had had problems. The bar already faced numerous citations for serving underage patrons, and it closed for good a month after the incident.

Boeheim suspended Edwards for two games, and no other players were charged or publicly disciplined. Car owners with smashed windows wanted the university to pay for damages, but Crouthamel said SU would violate NCAA regulations if it paid for property damage caused by a student-athlete. Since no one had filed a complaint with the university, the university had no grounds for taking disciplinary action against any players, SU spokesman Robert Hill said. He did not help matters when he tried to downplay the incident: "People fighting in the street or in a barroom brawl, frankly, in these days and times, isn't shocking. It isn't good. But it isn't shocking."[17]

It was Boeheim who offered the most telling statement, when he told the *Post-Standard* that the basketball team had no rules regarding curfews or alcohol use.[18] Shaw noticed and directed Crouthamel to review SU's code of conduct for student-athletes.

Considering all that SU's athletic program had been through over the prior two years, Shaw's directive to Crouthamel was restrained and measured. The brawl and its aftermath "has shed light on the variable specificity from sport to sport in the expression of our code of conduct," Shaw wrote. "I do not want us to make a knee-jerk reaction that does not take the long-range implications of this process into account."[19]

Shaw told Crouthamel to compare SU's situation with that of other universities, particularly those with reputations for "highly competitive teams and for academic integrity as well as compliance with NCAA regulations," and to recommend ways to strengthen SU's student-athlete rules of conduct. In particular, Shaw wanted to know, should SU have specific rules for specific sports?

By July, a tougher code of conduct for student-athletes was in place. It called for a new, three-person committee to decide athletic penalties for players charged with felonies. Its members would be the athletic director, Crouthamel, the faculty athletic representative,

Bennett, and the chairman of the Senate Committee on Athletic Policy, Travis Lewin, a law professor. It specified action to be taken in the case of on- and off-campus sexual offenses involving an athlete; it established counseling and mentor programs for athletes; and it detailed the athletic department's policy on academics, sportsmanship, alcohol, smoking, and sexual harassment. It did not specify penalties for violations. Had the code been in place at the time of the bar brawl, Edwards, who was charged with a felony, would have been immediately suspended for 10 percent of the team's contests—at least three games—and his case would have been reviewed by the newly created committee.

The new code did not ban off-campus drinking by underage athletes or spell out penalties for underage drinking. The new policy would take some discipline out of coaches' hands, Crouthamel said, but would allow each coach to establish rules that were tougher than the code.[20]

*   *   *

The NCAA-imposed setbacks did not keep Orange teams down. In basketball, missing postseason play might have hurt recruiting, Boeheim acknowledged, but SU continued securing basketball talent like John Wallace and Lawrence Moten, who ensured solid winning records for the Orange.[21] The team was 23–7 in the 1993–94 season and made it as far as the Sweet Sixteen. In 1994–95, they had a run of fourteen straight wins, were ranked as high as sixth in the nation, and made it to the NCAA second round.

The 1995–96 team was led by and built around senior Wallace, a fiercely competitive team leader from Rochester, New York, who Boeheim expected to lose to the NBA draft in his junior year.[22] Donovan McNabb, SU's stellar quarterback, was also a member of that team but saw little playing time. The team outperformed everyone's expectations—it was ranked 42 in one early poll—and it took fans on the kind of joyride that Syracusans longed for. After losing the Big East championship game to Connecticut 85–67, the team headed to the NCAA tournament, where even Boeheim doubted the team would do well.[23] "They believed they were better than they were and sometimes that's as important as anything," he said.

SU's tournament victories were had with scrappy overtime play, thrilling last-minute baskets, and aggressive defense, and brought them to the championship game at the Meadowlands in New Jersey. They faced a powerhouse Kentucky team with eight future NBA players coached by Rick Pitino, the first assistant coach to work under Boeheim in 1976.

SU had a big fan contingent at the final game that included Governor George Pataki and Syracuse mayor Roy Bernardi, who joined the Shaws and other administrators. They watched SU hold its own all through the game, to be down by only two with four minutes left. With just over a minute remaining, senior Lazarus Sims, a terrific passer (sixth in the nation in assists) but playing with an injured wrist, drove toward the basket and passed low to Wallace. The ball was stolen, and Wallace aggressively went after it, securing his fifth foul, which took him out of the game. SU lost 76–67 in a heartbreaker that nonetheless made Orange fans proud. Wallace had scored a game-high twenty-nine points and hauled in ten rebounds before fouling out. SU shot 50 percent against the nation's best team and held Kentucky to 38 percent from the floor.

Boeheim continued leading teams to winning seasons and searching for the golden recruit. He found him in the fall of 2000 in Carmelo Anthony, then a junior at Towson Catholic High, in Baltimore. When Anthony arrived at SU as a 225-pound freshman in 2002, he was joined by Gerry McNamara, another freshman, from Scranton, Pennsylvania. The starting team was rounded out with Hakim Warrick, a six-eight forward, Craig Forth, and Kueth Duany, the team's only senior. Jeremy McNeil, Billy Edelin, and Josh Pace provided strong bench support. All season, against every opponent, Anthony was "the best player on the court," Boeheim said.[24] Connecticut defeated SU in the 2002–3 Big East championship, but the young team had the national championship in its sights.

SU made it to the Final Four for the third time in Boeheim's career. Only two players had prior NCAA tournament experience: Duany and McNeil. The Orangemen played near flawlessly in the semifinal game against Texas, winning 95–84. Anthony had thirty-three points—a record for a freshman in a Final Four game—and fourteen rebounds; McNamara scored nineteen points, Warrick

Freshman standout Carmelo Anthony led SU to its
first-ever national men's basketball championship
in 2003. Here he grabs a rebound against Valpa-
raiso University at the Carrier Dome, November 24,
2002. The Post-Standard/*Stephen D. Cannerelli.*

eighteen. The win put SU in the national championship game against
Kansas, which was favored by six to eight points at the Superdome
in New Orleans.

The lead-up to the championship game held Syracuse in its spell.
Orange was everywhere in the city, and Anthony, with his infectious
smile, projected absolute joy in his playing. One local coffee shop,
Freedom of Espresso, concocted a caramel espresso latte in honor
of the extraordinary freshman—"The Carmelo." Some 3,000 fans
traveled to New Orleans for the game, and at an SU pep rally there,
Shaw worked the crowd into a frenzy. Back in Syracuse, 11,000 fans
turned out at the Dome to watch the game on big screens.

Hakim Warrick blocking the last-chance shot of Kansas's Michael Lee to clinch the NCAA national men's basketball championship, April 7, 2003. The Post-Standard/*Stephen D. Cannerelli.*

SU opened with a strong and confident first half, in which McNamara sank six three-pointers that helped SU build a 53–42 halftime lead. Through the second half, SU held its lead, and with just under three minutes left, SU led 78–70. The lead shrank to 81–78 with twenty-four seconds left. Warrick was fouled and missed both shots. Kansas worked the ball around to Michael Lee, positioned for a three-pointer that would tie the game. Warrick, who had one foot in the paint when Lee received the ball, soared upward and blocked the shot, giving SU its first national men's basketball championship.

Warrick's block was the "biggest single play in Syracuse basketball history," Boeheim said.[25]

The win was a huge validation for Boeheim, who twice before had coached teams to the Final Four and left without the trophy, and who was said not to have the right stuff to win a championship. Anthony, all of eighteen years old, was named the tournament's Most Outstanding Player.

Back in Syracuse the team was greeted by 25,000 cheering fans at a Carrier Dome celebration. Two weeks later, Anthony announced he was leaving SU for the NBA draft, the first time an SU freshman would do so. Anthony was chosen third by the Denver Nuggets, in the same draft in which LeBron James was the first pick.

The Pasqualoni Era

In football, Paul Pasqualoni was head coach all through the Shaw years, a dramatic story in its own right. Pasqualoni had been defensive coordinator under former head coach Dick MacPherson and moved up when MacPherson left to be head coach for the New England Patriots.

Pasqualoni's first year as head coach was a strong one. With offensive coordinator George DeLeone, who brought the freeze option offense to SU, the team went 10–2 in 1991 and bested Ohio State in the Hall of Fame Bowl 24–17, a game in which sophomore quarterback Marvin Graves passed for two touchdowns, ran for one, and was named the game's Most Valuable Player (MVP).[26] The win gave SU a season-finish eleventh place in the AP poll. Pasqualoni talked confidently about being ranked in the top ten the following season, and some writers were speculating that SU might be in the running for a national championship.[27]

In 1992, SU finished its regular season 9–2, losing its last game in a suspenseful finish to first-place Miami, 16–10, before a capacity 50,000 crowd at the Carrier Dome. With forty-five seconds remaining, SU had brought the ball to the Hurricanes' twenty-one yard line. Graves was ill from exhaustion and heat yet stayed in the game. He rushed four yards on the next play, was sacked on the next two, then threw a last-chance pass to tight end Chris Gedney, who caught

Football coach Paul Pasqualoni. Here, in a game against Rutgers at the Dome on October 5, 1996, he challenges a referee's decision after a fumble that SU recovered was called back. The Post-Standard/*Nicholas Lisi.*

the ball and was tackled at the Hurricanes' three-yard line as the clock ran out.

Despite the devastating loss, 1992 was one of SU's best offensive seasons ever—it ranked in the top twenty nationally in scoring, rushing, and total offense. It ranked first in the Big East Conference in first downs and third-down conversions. The successful season's most telling statistic was its attendance record at the Dome—an average of 49,310 per game.

The Orangemen's record secured them a place in the New Year's Fiesta Bowl in Tempe, Arizona, where they beat No. 10 Colorado 26–22. SU ran up twenty points in the third quarter, including an electrifying kickoff return by Kirby Dar Dar, who took the ball in a reverse play that finished with a ninety-five-yard touchdown run.

Graves again won bowl game honors as offensive player of the game, and defensive guard Kevin Mitchell had eight tackles, two sacks, and two tackles for losses. Syracuse ended the season rated No. 6. It was the best two-year stretch the school had had since 1958 (No. 8) and 1959, its championship season. Pasqualoni seemed on his way to building his own storied legacy at SU.

In 1993, almost inexplicably, it came undone. The team went 6–4–1, lost four games by a combined total of 113 points, which included back-to-back losses to Miami (49–0) and West Virginia (43–0). It was the first time since 1947 that Syracuse had been blanked in two consecutive games. The year ended with no bowl invitation. Its defense was its weakest link. It had lost six capable seniors, and Dan Conley, a senior inside linebacker who Pasqualoni said was the "greatest he'd ever been around," sat out the first two games of the season with knee surgery. There were grumblings of Pasqualoni's program being too harsh, of coaches' micromanaging, and of complicated offensive strategies that had grown tired and ineffective. The 1994 season was more of the same, with SU ending the season 7–4, a second consecutive year with no bowl bid, and fans grumbling that SU's offense had become dull and predictable. On the brighter side, SU quarterback Kevin Mason, linebacker Dan Conley, and wide receiver Marvin Harrison were selected first-team All–Big East Conference by league coaches.

Football's fortunes changed in 1995 with the arrival of Donovan McNabb, who started the year as a redshirt freshman. Quick, elusive, and calm under pressure, he could dodge tacklers in the backfield and still get off passes that hit their target. One of his most memorable plays of the year, against West Virginia, was a bomb he threw to Harrison from the end zone for a school record ninety-six-yard touchdown.

In McNabb's first year, he completed 128 of 207 passes for 1,991 yards, sixteen touchdowns, and just six interceptions. He was the first freshmen quarterback elected to the Big East's first team all-star squad. Harrison was named to the Big East's first team all-star squad at two positions—wide receiver and return specialist.

The team finished the regular season 8–3, which earned them a trip to the Gator Bowl, where they defeated Clemson 41–0 on a

Quarterback Donovan McNabb's electrifying play led SU's football team to top-twenty rankings and four bowl appearances. The Post-Standard/ Frank Ordonez.

rainy Jacksonville field. SU had a 20–0 lead after the first quarter. McNabb, who would be named bowl MVP, threw for three touchdowns and ran for one more. Harrison, in his final game as a senior, suffered a broken thumb but continued playing, logging seven receptions for 173 yards and two touchdowns. Harrison, who by many accounts was the greatest wide receiver in the history of Syracuse football, ended his SU career holding nearly every university receiving record, averaging twenty yards over 135 career receptions, and was selected as a 1995 All-American, as was junior cornerback Kevin Abrams. SU finished ranked sixteenth in the nation with renewed aspirations for a national championship.

The start of the 1996 season was ugly—SU lost its first two games. The team found its balance, though, and won the next nine, finishing 9–2 and earning a spot in the Liberty Bowl, which it won against Colorado 30–17.

By the end of 1997, McNabb, a junior, had set a school record for touchdown passes (55) and was contemplating leaving SU early to turn pro. Then came the Fiesta Bowl against Kansas State, in which McNabb completed only 16 of 39 passes for 271 yards and two touchdowns. SU lost, 35–18, finishing the season with a 9–4 record.

McNabb stayed for his fourth year in 1998. The final regular-season game against Miami at the Carrier Dome provided a storybook finish. McNabb had three rushing touchdowns, including one that began as a quarterback draw and finished with a fifty-one-yard run to the end zone. With Syracuse winning 66–13, Pasqualoni let McNabb leave the game with eleven minutes left to a roaring ovation. The drubbing so thrilled and inspired SU fans that shortly after the game the New York State Lottery had to shut down the numbers in the game's score because it had sold out those numbers.

For the season, the team averaged 42.5 points a game, third in the nation. When SU was on its game, it could play with anyone in the country. With an 8–4 record, ranked No. 18 in the nation (6–1 in the Big East), it earned its third consecutive conference championship and a spot in the Orange Bowl against the University of Florida Gators (No. 7). In McNabb's final game, all Syracuse could manage in the 28–3 first half was a field goal. In the second half, SU continued its lackluster performance and lost 31–10.

*   *   *

Without McNabb in 1999, SU's football program seemed lost. The Orangemen's 1999 football season started successfully, but its second half was painful to watch. SU lost three out of four games, including a 62–0 drubbing by Virginia Tech and a 24–21 upset by Rutgers, which was 0–9 and a thirty-point underdog going into the game.

Fans' enthusiasm faded even faster than the team's fortunes. Armchair quarterbacks on radio talk shows, internet forums, and in letters to the editor were furious and called for Pasqualoni to be fired. Even trustees grumbled about the head coach. It was as if all that had gone before—SU's bowl games and Big East championships, its winning records, its drubbing of Miami the previous season—was meaningless and forgotten.

Fans were becoming less forgiving toward high-paid coaches. Pasqualoni had been SU's highest paid employee for several years, the press had reported, earning a total of $615,900 in the 1999–2000 season.[28] His salary was boosted by a new revenue source that would push coaches' salaries into the stratosphere—a corporate contract, this one with Nike. The apparel company was just beginning to market collegiate apparel. For having SU's football squad wear Nike-made shoes, hats, and rainsuits on the sidelines, Pasqualoni would be paid as much as $50,000 a year.[29]

Late in the season, when Shaw was asked by a reporter whether SU should fire Pasqualoni, he gave a reasoned, down-to-earth reply with a kicker at the end, a phrase for which he would be long remembered in Syracuse: "Look at your own personal life. You go to work some days, you really achieve at a level you're capable. Some days it's like having a career day, and some days you might as well have stayed at home. All of a sudden, you look at the football team, and they're never supposed to have one of those days? Let's join the human race and get a life."[30]

The next morning's front-page headline distilled Shaw's exhortation to a taunt. "Shaw to Angry Fans: 'Get a Life.'" Fans' frustration with Pasqualoni became ire toward Shaw, with season ticket holders canceling their subscriptions. "I resent being told to 'get a life,'" wrote a fan from Sackets Harbor. "We the fans are the ones who create the noise level that has made the Dome famous."

Shaw's utterance, combined with the team's sagging fortunes, hurt the athletic department's bottom line. Football revenue represented roughly half of the department's income. Football season ticket sales dropped from 36,000 in 1998 to 28,200 in 2001. At an average of $136 per ticket, that amounted to a loss of $1,060,800.[31]

"It stung us for two or three years," Pete Sala, then the Carrier Dome's assistant director of facilities operations, said of Shaw's statement. Shaw stood by his remark and said he made it to divert attention away from Pasqualoni. "I never felt bad one minute that I said it. I believed in Paul Pasqualoni. I wish I had supported him more with facilities. I believe he had the right values and was a good role model for the kids. And at that time he had a very good record. I believe he was getting the short stick."[32]

SU's football fans were coming to grips with a new reality in college football at Syracuse. The Dome was no longer the recruiting draw for athletes it had once been or the novel spectacle guaranteed to fill seats. SU had been financially frugal for a decade, taking money from the athletic program to support academics. Public universities with sparkling new weight rooms, locker rooms, sports medicine and rehab facilities, and huge new stadiums seating more than twice the 50,000-seat Dome were coming to dominate the sport. Ticket sales at every school provided revenue to support sports programs.

As the competition stiffened, so did scrutiny of Pasqualoni's football program and pressure to improve performance. In 2000, the team went 6–5 and was not invited to a bowl game. They did better than expected in 2001, making it to the Insight.com Bowl, where they crushed Kansas State 26–3. SU finished the season with a 10–3 record. But fans were looking for a national contender. In 2002, the team had its first losing season in sixteen years (4–8), and calls for Pasqualoni to be fired grew louder.

Shaw was under mounting public pressure to justify the university's decision to keep Pasqualoni. Ever the manager, he took a step back to consider how the coaching staff of every sport was assessed. He had Crouthamel require coaches to submit performance expectations for their team each year. At season's end, the coaches would be reviewed in light of how well they met those expectations. Crouthamel was a football man to the core and fought for Pasqualoni behind the scenes. He understood how much Pasqualoni had done with SU's limited resources, how the football landscape had changed, and what Pasqualoni was up against.

In December 2003, Shaw had Crouthamel issue a public statement that SU had evaluated Pasqualoni's performance and was confident in him.[33] In the same statement, Crouthamel encouraged fans to remain loyal and come to games—attendance was sliding. By 2003, average attendance was down 7,000 from a 1996 high of

48,000 per game. He acknowledged SU needed better training facilities, specifically an inside practice facility and a larger weight room.

*   *   *

The men's lacrosse team, which had come to dominate Division I play under Coach Roy Simmons Jr., continued its superiority, winning national championships in 1993, 1995, 2000, 2002, and 2004.

Its success was marred in late 1995 by more NCAA penalties after a second NCAA investigation. The penalties drove home the absolute necessity of complying with NCAA rules and the serious consequences that could come from violating them.

The second investigation began as the first had, with a newspaper story. This one claimed Nancy Simmons, the wife of Coach Simmons, had cosigned a car loan for lacrosse legend Paul Gait in 1989. Gait and his twin brother, Gary, from British Columbia, were three-time, first-team All-Americans. A six-month internal investigation revealed that Simmons did in fact cosign for the loan, enabling Paul Gait and his wife, Cathy, to buy a new 1989 Chevrolet Beretta for $9,015.50. Almost two years later, the NCAA determined that receiving the cosigned loan made Gait an ineligible player, and because he participated in the 1990 championship game, the NCAA stripped SU of its 1990 championship and ordered it to return the trophy.

Simmons's teams were already coping with penalties imposed after the first 1990–92 NCAA investigation, which cut three scholarships in each of three years—1993–94, 1994–95, and 1995–96. Even with three fewer scholarships, SU still won the May 1995 national championship game, its sixth.

Besides stripping SU of its 1990 championship, the NCAA Infractions Committee took away two lacrosse scholarships for 1996–97. However, SU successfully appealed, citing its own disciplinary actions: It would freeze the pay of its lacrosse coaches for two years and ban Simmons from recruiting trips for one year. The pay freeze affected Simmons and assistant coaches John Desko and Kevin Donahue.

In 1998, after taking his team on sixteen straight trips to the Final Four, Simmons retired. Desko became head coach and in 2000 won his first national championship with a convincing 13–7 victory

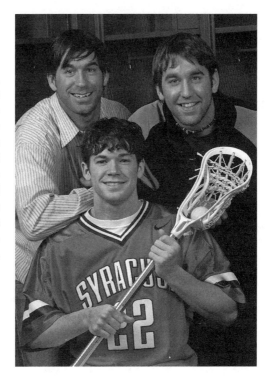

The Powell brothers, from Carthage, New York, created a family lacrosse dynasty at SU, leading the team to three national championships. Center, Michael Powell (2001–4); left, Casey (1995–98); right, Ryan (1997–2000). The Post-Standard/John Berry.

over Princeton. By 2004, he would take his teams to five national championship games, winning three.

As the twin Gait brothers had ruled the lacrosse field in the late 1980s, so the Powell brothers created a family lacrosse dynasty at SU at the cusp of the new century. Between 1995 and 2004, Casey, Ryan, and Michael Powell scored 440 goals, accounted for 428 assists, and helped lead SU to a won–lost record of 123–31 and three national championships. The Powells grew up in Carthage, a rural town in northern New York. At SU, each brother won a national title, each was a four-year All-American, though only Michael earned first-team recognition in each of his four seasons. Each Powell wore SU's coveted No. 22 jersey. Fittingly, the Powell dynasty ended in 2004 with a national championship, a 14–13 victory over Navy. Michael Powell was named the tournament's Most Outstanding Player for the second time.

Title IX

Nowhere at SU was the institutional status quo more disrupted by the gender equity push than in athletics. For decades, advances for women in athletics had been incremental and token. In 1970, the total budget for women's athletics was $3,500, up from $600 in 1959 and $200 in 1950. Then came Title IX, which stated that no person, on the basis of sex, should be excluded from participation in any education program or activity receiving federal funds.

Furthermore, Title IX required that female and male student-athletes receive equal treatment in every aspect of athletic programming: scholarship dollars proportional to their participation, practice and competitive facilities, publicity, and more. When Title IX went into effect in 1975, the women's athletics budget for five intercollegiate sports—volleyball, basketball, swimming, field hockey, and tennis—rose to $50,000.[34] A women's athletic department was created, with Doris Soladay as director. This was just the beginning. Universities receiving federal financial assistance were given three years to comply with the Title IX regulations. The NCAA fought it vigorously, claiming that the implementation of Title IX was illegal.[35]

Full compliance with Title IX was not just a challenge at Syracuse, where 70.4 percent of athletes were men and 29.6 percent were women. Men received 74.9 percent of scholarship dollars, women 25.1 percent. SU's compliance was "not out of line on average" with most other universities, Marcoccia told Shaw in 1992.[36] "The primary difficulty with Title IX compliance is caused by football," Marcoccia wrote.[37] With eighty-five male players on scholarship, football consumed the lion's share of the athletic budget. Something would have to change to bring athletic spending somewhere close to parity for men and women.

Gender equity demands were challenging the very foundation of SU's athletic legacy, and Crouthamel, SU's athletic director, was responsible for managing the transition. In 2003, Crouthamel, who arrived at Syracuse in the 1970s, reflected, "Everything has changed so dramatically. I was hired as the director of 'mens' athletics. It was us guys out here. Now we have twelve women's teams."[38]

INTERCOLLEGIATE ATHLETICS   131

Crouthamel played halfback for Dartmouth College and was the first player to be hired by the fledgling Dallas Cowboys in 1959.[39] He played a few preseason games and was cut, and moved to the New England Patriots of the American Football League, where he played in three games and recovered a fumble. That was the extent of his pro football career. He served two years in the Navy and returned to Dartmouth, where for seven years he was head football coach. He was named Syracuse's athletic director in the spring of 1978. Two years later, the Carrier Dome opened, renewing SU's football program and setting the stage for its men's basketball team to become a national power. Crouthamel was frugal and worked long hours fueled by coffee and Marlboro smoke. Even after a no-smoking policy was put in place at the Dome, he could often be seen puffing away in the front row of the press box.

A new era for women athletes at SU was announced at the October 1994 trustees' Executive Committee meeting, when Shaw said that the university would add three new women's sports—soccer, gymnastics, and lacrosse. The phased-in budgets for them would add $1.9 million to the athletic budget over eight years. Construction and renovation costs were estimated at $4.8 million, which would be funded from the Department of Athletics reserves.

The department would have to raise more money through donations and increased attendance at football and basketball events in order to increase its number of intercollegiate teams and the scholarships to populate them.[40] If it could not raise the money fast enough, the university would have to eliminate men's teams, but reconfiguring this would take several years. SU planned to add women's soccer in 1996 and women's lacrosse in 1997. Raising money was not a strength of Crouthamel, who was taciturn and self-effacing, not a schmoozer.

Women on SU's lacrosse club team did not want to wait years for intercollegiate privileges, especially scholarships. In 1995, eight members of the club team sued the university to establish an intercollegiate team.[41] The discrimination suit, filed in Federal District Court in Syracuse, asked a judge to elevate immediately women's lacrosse from club to varsity status. At the time of the lawsuit, SU offered eleven varsity sports for men and nine for women. Three hundred and sixty men were participating in intercollegiate sports, compared with 155 women.

Syracuse was now embroiled in the national fight over how quickly colleges had to comply with Title IX. Other universities were being sued, testing Title IX's strength. A House subcommittee would soon hold hearings about the impact of Title IX on men's sports. Meanwhile, women's teams at the Atlanta 1996 Olympic Games were raising the profile of women's sports. US women won more gold medals than ever, including golds for soccer, basketball, tennis, gymnastics, and the 100 meters. Their success was widely attributed to the maturing of collegiate programs started because of Title IX.

Two months after the lawsuit was filed, Crouthamel argued in a *Herald American* article that football should be considered differently than other sports at a university.[42] No other sport could match football's numbers—eighty-five scholarships and up to 120 male players on a team, he said. To have one female athlete for every football player was not right. Crouthamel was not alone with his argument: The College Football Association was proposing that football should be exempt from Title IX tests.

SU won the lawsuit in district court, a victory upheld on appeal.[43] Syracuse argued that because it had a history of expanding sports opportunities for women, it met gender-equity standards imposed by Title IX. It was the first time in any Title IX case that an institution had used the defense of having a history of "expanding opportunities" for women. As SU had planned before the lawsuit, it did field an intercollegiate women's lacrosse team, which played their first season in 1998.

The Title IX athletic budget restructuring was not over. In January 1997, SU announced it was cutting men's gymnastics and wrestling and adding women's softball. There was no place else to get the money, Shaw told the *Chronicle of Higher Education*.[44] He was not going to pay for it by raising tuition or reducing salaries, or by cutting the revenue-generating sports of football and men's basketball. He was not going to cut every sports team a little, weakening them all. "It is one of those unfortunate things you hate to do," Shaw said. "We have met the donor, and it is us."

Women's softball, which played its first season in 2000, required a new playing field, which SU estimated would cost between $750,000 and $1.2 million. Cutting wrestling and gymnastics would save the university roughly $700,000 a year. Hundreds of letters from alumni and parents of wrestlers and gymnasts came to Shaw and Crouthamel, expressing dismay over the cuts.[45] Some parents even wrote their representatives in Congress. A fund-raising campaign to save wrestling was started, but to pay the $450,000 a year that wrestling cost would take a wrestling endowment of $9–$10 million, Shaw told letter writers. No one saw wrestling supporters raising that kind of money.

Supporters devised a new strategy to save some semblance of both sports. A $2 million endowment could fund a nonscholarship, regional program, something like the club sports many women's teams had had. Wrestling and gymnastics supporters were given until June 2000 to raise $2 million for each sport. In the interim, the university would provide "bridge funds" to support scaled-down wrestling and gymnastics programs. If the goal was not met, wrestling and gymnastics would be done for good. And they were. Gymnastics' supporters quickly abandoned the strategy and saw their final season in 1997–98. SU wrestling's final season was 2000–2001.

SU hired coaches for their new women's teams—April Kater in soccer, Lisa Miller in lacrosse, and Mary Jo Firnbach in softball—a full year before their first seasons, giving them time to recruit, which paid dividends. In the women's lacrosse team's second season (12–4), it went to the NCAA's first-round playoffs, a feat it would repeat the next four seasons. The women's soccer team reached the second round of the NCAA playoffs in its third year (14–7–1). Women's basketball had been played at SU since 1971. In 1995–96 (14–14), it beat national powerhouse Connecticut (No. 2 ranked) 62–59.

*   *   *

Protections offered by the university's new sexual harassment policy were tested in 1997 when two women tennis players filed sexual harassment complaints about their varsity coach, Jessie Dwire. The two players, Kirsten Ericson and Dacia Kornechuk, accused Dwire of engaging in unnecessarily intimate body massages, unwanted sexual talk, and other improprieties. Both players quit the team after they complained to the university, and Dwire was suspended pending a hearing.

Dwire had a long and successful history as the women's tennis team's first coach, beginning in 1978. He led it to three Big East titles, saw the team ranked as high as No. 2 in the east, and produced two All-Americans. He was named the 1995 Big East coach of the year.

A hearing panel cleared Dwire of sexual harassment but found that statements he made in one instance violated the school's sexual harassment policy and in another violated its discrimination policy. The panel voted 3–2 to suspend Dwire for two years without pay. Neil Strodel, SU's associate vice president for human resources, however, accepted the recommendation of the panel's two dissenters and limited the suspension to three months.

The players and their families sued the university for $762 million, claiming that Dwire's behavior constituted sexual harassment and that the university intentionally discriminated against the players by first ignoring the charges and then giving a token penalty to Dwire.[46] After learning about the lawsuit, seven other women alleged that Dwire sexually harassed them as far back as 1978.[47]

Diane Murphy, the Women's Studies' director and a coauthor of the university's sexual harassment policy, stood by Ericson and Kornechuk, who had been students in her program. If called to testify, Murphy would be a "hostile witness" toward the university, she told Shaw. Days before the lawsuit was to go to trial in United States District Court in Manhattan, the university settled for an undisclosed amount. Two months later, Dwire resigned.

ACC Courtship

No sooner had SU won the men's basketball national championship than its big-time athletics programs faced an identity crisis—stay in the Big East or join the ACC (Atlantic Coast Conference). The ACC was trying to expand and had proposed Syracuse, with its high-profile national media stature, join it, along with the University of Miami and Boston College, two other Big East members. The decision would affect millions of dollars in future TV contracts and the viability of SU's entire athletic program.

Leaving the Big East would be like a divorce, especially for Crouthamel. He was one of its founders in 1979, together with the athletic directors of Providence, St. John's, and Georgetown, and he had a deep, personal loyalty to the conference. As one of the first college conferences to sign a TV contract with ESPN, the Big East helped bring SU basketball to a national audience.[48] Its annual championship series at Madison Square Garden gave SU Big Apple cachet. Even Boeheim credited the competitive conference for helping make his career.[49] "We were basically nobody until we got to the Big East," Boeheim wrote.[50]

Football was the driving force. The ACC was trying to build a more powerful football conference that could negotiate bigger television contracts. The big prize would be Miami, a national football power, which was led by President Donna Shalala, who was eager to leave the Big East. Miami was a geographic outlier, and travel costs to play conference games were high. Shalala had lobbied the ACC to invite SU and was personally lobbying Shaw through phone calls, urging SU to join.[51] With Syracuse, the ACC could secure a New York City audience and market.

The Big East had never been a powerful football conference; indeed, it did not begin sponsoring football until ten years after its founding. Not all basketball schools had football, and Notre Dame, with both football and basketball, chose not to have its football team be part of the Big East. The arrangements complicated the conference and weakened its unity.

All through the second half of 2003 the high-stakes drama of which schools would leave the Big East played out in the media. Eight US senators from states with Big East basketball teams wrote Shaw, Shalala, and Rev. William P. Leahy, the president of Boston College, pleading with them not to leave the conference.[52] The schools' departures, the senators hyperbolically wrote, "would undermine the integrity of intercollegiate athletics, be harmful to Title IX women's athletics programs, and send a troubling message to student-athletes across America."

Lobbying on all sides was intense. "Buzz kept putting us off," Shalala recalled. "I actually held out for him for a very long time. I almost screwed the whole thing up, because I was so loyal to

Syracuse, the opportunity to get them in. We wanted another private university in the ACC." But if SU stayed behind while other schools departed the Big East, its revenues could well decline. Days before an ACC delegation visited SU in June, the trustees authorized Shaw to determine what was best and to pay the Big East and/or the ACC whatever money was necessary to change league affiliation.

After the ACC delegation visited SU, all signs indicated that ACC officials would approve SU's move, with Shaw and Crouthamel feeling so confident about it they were gearing up to announce it. However, days later, the ACC withdrew its offer to Syracuse and invited Virginia Tech. The Big East mounted a last-minute effort to entice Miami to stay, offering it a guarantee of $45 million over five years and a supplemental fund to help with travel costs.[53] In the end, Miami and Virginia Tech accepted the ACC's offer, and in October, Boston College also left for the ACC, a move that blindsided SU and that Crouthamel took as a personal snub—Boston College had vouched to remain part of the Big East.

With three football schools departing, the Big East needed new football members. Under NCAA bylaws, a conference required eight members for its schools to be eligible for a bid to the Bowl Championship Series, which was worth $12–$14 million annually for the Big East. In November, the Big East added Cincinnati, Louisville, and South Florida for all sports, and DePaul and Marquette for all sports except football.

Big East play continued for Syracuse, but the conference had lost some of its luster and had a cobbled feel to it. The reconfigured conference likely brought SU less revenue than the ACC would have and fewer blue-chip student-athlete recruits. The next chancellor would face a major decision about which athletic conference SU should affiliate with, Shaw wrote in his transition notes.

CHAPTER 8

New Entrepreneurism

Commerce on Campus

WHILE SHAW'S DETERMINATION to restrain tuition increases and hold down enrollment reduced SU's income, other areas of the university could generate more revenue if approached creatively. Large tuition increases were a thing of the past, and early on Shaw made clear to cabinet members what that meant: A 1 percent change in tuition was worth $1.4 million in a given year.[1] He encouraged administrators to think entrepreneurially, to grow revenue where they could.

Auxiliary Services provided nearly 25 percent of the university's revenue and offered potential for revenue growth.[2] The category involved most anything that was not academics or athletics: housing, food services, Drumlins (which included sports and banquet facilities and a travel agency), the bookstore, licensing revenue from clothing, and any other revenue generator that could be added to the mix. It was overseen by Peter Webber, director of auxiliary services, who had begun working at SU in 1971 as a graduate assistant when he was earning his MBA. Webber enthusiastically embraced Shaw's entrepreneurial push. He was also Shaw's tennis doubles partner and arranged games for them to play three times a week, so the two spoke frequently, and Shaw encouraged Webber to try things.

Initially, just like the rest of the university, Auxiliary Services' revenue suffered from fewer students who were paying for housing and meals. In Shaw's first year, auxiliary revenues were projected to drop $600,000. From Webber's perspective, no potential income-generating initiative was too small to ignore. For example, a Clinique cosmetics counter he brought into the bookstore turned out to be surprisingly profitable, he said.

Another income-generating category was academic auxiliaries: the Division of International Programs Abroad (DIPA) and University College. Both held growth potential that did not require increasing the number of fully matriculating students on campus.

International students, who usually paid the full cost of attending SU, were seen as another undeveloped market that could boost tuition revenue at a time when the university was reducing overall enrollment and increasing financial aid.

Colleges were required to cover more of their own costs, a new pressure for most deans. While expectations were not the same for all colleges—some were expected to make money, some to break even, some to lose a lot less—many deans, some for the very first time, formed advisory committees of successful alumni and experts in related fields to raise their college profile and build donor networks. For the Maxwell School's first advisory board, Dean John Palmer brought in David Maxwell, the president and CEO of Fannie Mae (Federal National Mortgage Association); Frank Carlucci, who had been secretary of defense, national security advisor, and deputy director of the CIA; and Elliot Richardson, who had held four different cabinet positions under two presidents, most notably attorney general under Richard Nixon. Advisory board members, in addition to whatever donations and tangible advice they offered, brought prestige to the school and helped provide leads and introductions to others in high levels of government.

Shaw nurtured the entrepreneurial spirit with discreet and strategic financial bonuses that rewarded, incentivized, and retained key faculty, administrators, and staff members—among them computer technicians during the massive 1990s conversion from mainframes—when he felt such morale boosts were important.

An early entrepreneurial initiative in Auxiliary Services came in 1992 when SU spent $370,000 to convert Kimmel Hall cafeteria to a food court serving eight different franchise food brands, among them Burger King, Pizza Hut, and Dunkin Donuts. Students could use their SUpercard, the debit account portion of their meal plan, to pay for purchases. Anyone, affiliated or not with SU, could come and pay cash. Merchants on South Crouse Avenue and Marshall Street were irate. Ted Dellas, owner of the Varsity, a restaurant, complained in a letter to Shaw that the university, as a tax-exempt not-for-profit, competed unfairly with venders in the Crouse–Marshall neighborhood. How could private businesses survive?

Serving franchise-name food catered to students' tastes and increased auxiliary revenue. Webber was pleasantly surprised when, through doughnuts, he learned the revenue power of brand names.[3] Kimmel's doughnut kiosk first opened without Dunkin Donut signs. When signs went up months later, doughnut sales increased nearly "900 percent."

SU's law firm, Bond, Schoeneck and King, explained to merchants that the food court was really nothing new—branded foods were sold under licensing agreements, similar to SU's agreement with Coca Cola, through which the university bought the franchised foods, which were prepared and sold by SU employees. As for complaints that anyone could use the food court, the law firm cited a 1979 court case that had been decided in the university's favor, allowing the public to shop in the bookstore.[4]

When Shaw finally met with members of the Crouse–Marshall Business Association a year later, he received an earful. Business was down, they told him. Shaw floated a proposal: What if the area received a facelift? Something like Armory Square, in downtown Syracuse, where street and facade improvements and a beefed-up police presence had made that neighborhood a commercial destination. Crouse and Marshall, two city streets on SU's campus perimeter, were the university's closest commercial district, and they had a run-down, bedraggled look, with cracked sidewalks, bent parking meters, congested parking, and a crazy web of utility lines. Improving those streets could help the businesses and enhance a major gateway to campus, Shaw said. Figuring out how to pay for it would be the challenge.

SU was already working on a cooperative service agreement with the city of Syracuse regarding University Place and College Place, streets that ran in front of the Science and Technology Building and the Hall of Languages. The streets were closed during the day to public traffic for a two-year trial that started in Eggers's last year. When the agreement was finalized in 1994, the city conveyed ownership of College Place and portions of Euclid Avenue, University Place, University Avenue, and South Crouse Avenue to the university, for which the university paid the city $250,000 a year, with increases for inflation, for twenty years. The university maintained the streets, curbing, and sidewalks, and removed snow. The city agreed to allocate the money the university paid to neighborhood betterment initiatives near the university.[5]

The financing solution for Crouse Avenue and Marshall Street eventually came through politics. US representative James Walsh, who represented Syracuse, had worked his way up to become a member of the Appropriations Committee and chair of several subcommittees, including Housing and Urban Development (HUD). The chairs of the appropriations subcommittees were known as the House's "Cardinals of Spending," and Tom Walsh, then SU's director of federal relations and no relation to the congressman, recognized the opportunities within HUD. He brought them to Eleanor Ware (formerly Gallagher), his boss on the government relations side, and together they sought Shaw's approval to craft strategies for projects for which Representative Walsh could get funding. The two-year Crouse–Marshall Street improvement was the first HUD project that SU's federal relations team completed with Walsh.

Helping the SU team to get all the ducks in line for federal grants to the city were Irwin Davis, the Metropolitan Development Association's president and CEO, and David Mankiewicz, president of the University Hill Corporation. Walsh secured $1.85 million through HUD for the first phase of the street improvement project in 2000 that buried utility lines and widened Marshall Street by four feet to allow for diagonal parking. The next year, Walsh secured $1.93 million from HUD for a second phase that buried more utility lines on Crouse, installed brick pavers on Marshall Street and its sidewalks, and added street furniture and landscaping.

In 1998, the university addressed another neighborhood concern when it purchased the low-occupancy Marshall Square Mall for $4.5 million. The purchase expanded the campus's reach and gave the university more control over a key piece of real estate. By 1999, the university had raised occupancy to 94 percent, earning

The nearly $4 million renovation of Marshall Street in 2000, funded with federal grants, expanded and vastly improved the look of the campus perimeter and helped improve relations with retail store owners. Courtesy of University Archives, Syracuse University Libraries.

enough rental income that the mall more than paid for itself and enabled much-needed facade improvements.

The collective changes vastly improved the look of the Crouse–Marshall area, attracted new merchants like Starbucks, and earned the appreciation of formerly disgruntled merchants, so much so that Gallagher's office was able to push through City Hall approval for both a business improvement district and a special lighting district.[6]

Sheraton

Around the corner from Marshall Street was another project in need of attention, the Sheraton University Inn and Conference Center. The hotel had opened with great fanfare in 1985—Mayor Lee Alexander cut a ribbon before 350 guests who sipped Dom Perignon and nibbled chocolate-covered strawberries.[7] John J. Ginley, an SU alumnus and architect, was the principal behind the development team of University Avenue Properties, Inc., the hotel's proud owners.

The privately owned Sheraton Hotel was run down and on the verge of bankruptcy when Syracuse University purchased it in 2000 for $11 million. Courtesy of Steve Sartori.

The Sheraton was a valuable amenity so close to campus, with its conference room and restaurant, its 231 guest rooms and suites that hosted alumni, parents, and trustees. SU owned the land, which it leased to the hotel's partners for a minimum of $132,000 a year for fifty years. Between 1986 and 1991, however, the partners paid nothing to SU. Nor did they pay city taxes or build a fund for renovations. By 1999, the hotel facilities had so deteriorated that the Sheraton chain was going to cancel its franchise agreement. The partners had restructured financing three times at that point and needed to restructure again. They owed the university $1.5 million and were on the verge of bankruptcy.

Trustees urged Shaw to do something to save the hotel. "I don't have the staff or the time to make anything happen over there," Shaw said. "It's going to take a lot of money and a lot of work and we don't run hotels." Trustees persisted, so Shaw directed Lou Marcoccia to look at it. Working with consultants, Marcoccia came up with several scenarios, ranging from converting the hotel to student

Lou Marcoccia, senior vice president of business, finance, and administration services, orchestrated SU's purchase of the Sheraton Hotel and successfully turned around its fortune. Courtesy of University Archives, Syracuse University Libraries.

housing to moving the newly created College of Human Services and Health Professions (a merger of the School of Social Work and the Colleges of Human Development and Nursing) to the hotel to moving the bookstore there from the Schine Center.

The decision was to keep it as a hotel, and the university formed a private, limited liability company, the Sheraton Hotel & Conference Center, LLC, with Marcoccia as president. SU lent the LLC $11 million from its endowment, which was paid to University Avenue Properties, Inc. and University Inn Project Partnership in order to acquire the mortgage from Bankers Trust Company, plus another $5 million for renovations. The new trustee chair, Joe Lampe, a hotelier himself, helped negotiate the deal. The hotel would maintain the same tax agreement with the city of Syracuse, which included an anachronistic state-authorized property tax break for a twenty-six person bomb shelter in the hotel's parking garage.[8]

As the LLC's president, Marcoccia benefited from a bonus structure that tied his salary to the hotel's performance. When renovations were complete, he renamed the hotel's restaurant Rachel's, in honor of his daughter. Two years later, in 2002, Marcoccia obtained a better loan from JP Morgan Chase Bank, and the LLC paid off its endowment loan. By 2003, the Sheraton's employee morale, occupancy rate, and customer service had substantially improved, and it was netting the university some $500,000 a year.[9]

Dome Events

The Carrier Dome, which opened in 1980, was a revenue boon to SU's Department of Athletics. Dome event proceeds during the Eggers years contributed $10 million to an athletic department reserve, which Shaw tapped to help pay for restructuring changes—academic scholarships—and later, facility improvements to accommodate more women athletes under Title IX requirements.

Athletic Director Jake Crouthamel was the Dome's first managing director, a job he kept until after the NCAA investigation. Part of SU's settlement with the NCAA was that Crouthamel would no longer oversee the Dome, a responsibility that officially went to Patrick Campbell.

The Dome remained Crouthamel's preoccupation—it had to. It fed athletics' revenue stream and had an annual $100,000 fee to pay the city of Syracuse. The bill was the result of a tax dispute settlement under Eggers. In exchange for the Dome being exempt from property tax, the university paid the city a minimum of $100,000 annually, more if the university's seventy-five-cent surcharge on nonathletic events exceeded that. Nonathletic events raised as much as 12 percent of the Dome's operating budget.[10] So Crouthamel was forever looking for revenue opportunities: the Moscow Circus, the World Tour of Figure Skating Champions, a two-day convention of the Promise Keepers (an Evangelical Christian organization for men), and championship games for high school football, lacrosse, and field hockey.

Within the broad universe of public events, two were specifically prohibited at the Dome: professional wrestling and Grateful Dead concerts.[11] That did not stop Crouthamel from repeatedly trying to bring such events though.

The wrestling prohibition stemmed from Eggers's personal dislike of fighting sports.[12] The Dome had held just one boxing match, in 1981, at which Sugar Ray Leonard retained his world welterweight crown against Larry Bonds. The Dome had never held wrestling. The Grateful Dead ban came after their only concert at the Dome in 1984 (see appendix E).

When Shaw indicated the athletic budget would be cut, Crouthamel asked him about hosting wrestling. Since the Onondaga County War Memorial was undergoing renovations starting in April 1992 and would be out of commission for a year, why not move its pro wrestling events to the Dome, Crouthamel suggested. Months earlier, the War Memorial had sold out a bout between Hulk Hogan and Paul "Mr. Wonderful" Orndorf.[13] Shaw, new on the scene, polled his administrators.

Marcoccia argued against pro wrestling, saying that it would convey the image that the university was "solely dollar driven." Furthermore, Marcoccia wrote, "people who attend War Memorial–type events would have little or no affinity for S.U. We do not need the atmosphere of those type events on our campus."[14] The pro wrestling ban continued, although Crouthamel made another bid in 1994 to host a World Wrestling Federation (WWF) extravaganza. Shaw responded with a version of Eggers's sentiment. "I'm not sure what it does for our image, but I know it isn't good. Unless strong, persuasive arguments to the contrary, I'd rather not."[15] The Grateful Dead ban was soon unnecessary. The band broke up in 1995, shortly after its lead guitarist and main songwriter, Jerry Garcia, died.

The Shaws took a personal interest in the success of Dome events, especially basketball games, even suggesting to Crouthamel "lively" songs to be played over the Dome's sound system. The list included Bill Haley's "Rock Around the Clock," Elvis's "Hound Dog," Little Richard's "Tutti Fruiti," and Ray Charles's "What'd I Say." "The above is guaranteed to rock the Dome, reviving old times, inspiring the boomers and totally confusing those under 25," Shaw wrote.[16]

International Study

International students had been attending SU since the late 1960s in increasing numbers. In 1992, full- and part-time students from eighty-eight countries accounted for 2.8 percent of SU's undergraduate population and 27.8 percent of the graduate population. More than half came from three countries: Taiwan, People's Republic of China, and South Korea.[17] Tom Cummings, dean of admissions, traveled to Asia for three weeks in 1995, exploring ways to boost Asian student enrollment. He returned convinced that recruiting only from Syracuse would not be successful, and he proposed to Vincow that SU station a representative in Asia.[18] He even had a person in mind: Brian Connolly, an SU alum ('83) and a former aide of US senator Patrick Moynihan. Vincow approved.

At age thirty-four, Connolly set up shop in a shared office in Hong Kong in February 1996. The only other American university with a student recruitment office in Asia was Boston University. For six years, at an annual cost of roughly $200,000, Connolly served as SU's utility man in Asia. Two or three times a year, he traveled to education fairs in Tokyo, Seoul, Taipei, Bangkok, Singapore, and other cities. He visited schools, contacted alumni, and followed up on requests from the Development Office. He helped organize two trips to Asia by the Shaws, trustees, and alumni.

The late 1990s turned out to be a difficult time for Asian recruitment, and the number of new undergraduate students (freshmen and transfers) coming from there actually declined from seventy-one to sixty between 1995 and 1997.[19] After a decade of unprecedented economic growth, Asia was hit with a recession in 1997, with a series of currency devaluations.[20] Some Asian stocks fell by as much as 70 percent, and inflation in Hong Kong averaged between 7 and 9 percent. The situation so challenged some Asian students that the university offered them financial counseling, no-interest loans, and tuition deferment to help them continue at SU. Not many took up the university's offer; as of March 1998, the university had spent $27,000 helping twenty-eight students, with many more receiving financial counseling. In some cases, students who were funded by their governments were called home.

Connolly returned to the United States at the end of 2002, and SU did not replace him. Student numbers had not increased as dramatically as administrators had hoped. Competition was increasing from places like Britain and Australia, and from Singapore and Hong Kong, which were expanding their university systems.[21] Connolly had laid important groundwork for SU. As the internet became a more reliable tool for recruitment and admissions, the number of Asian students at SU would steadily increase.

Back in Syracuse, support services for international students received a major boost in 1999 from a woman who knew firsthand what it was like to struggle in a foreign country: Lillian Slutzker donated $1.9 million to SU's Office of International Services.

Lillian was the widow of Emanuel "Manny" Slutzker, who in 1949 opened Manny's—a school supply, university T-shirt, and paraphernalia store on Marshall Street. Lillian Slutzker was a Hungarian Jew who fled Nazi Germany in 1939 and met her husband when he was a US Army Medical Corps medic in England.[22] Manny's remained a fixture on Marshall Street even after Slutzker sold the business in 1995. She had run it on her own since the mid-1970s, when her husband suffered several heart attacks and became ill with Alzheimer's disease. After her gift, SU renamed its Office of International Services, at the corner of Walnut Place and Waverly Avenue, the Lillian and Emanuel Slutzker Center for International Services.

The Slutzker Center gift was not the first time Lillian Slutzker supported the university. In 1997, she donated $600,000 to endow two lacrosse scholarships. The Slutzkers were close friends with former SU lacrosse coach Roy Simmons Jr. and his wife.

*   *   *

DIPA, SU's long-established study abroad program, had become a moneymaker for the university and was closely watched by administrators. In 1991, for every fifty students DIPA enrolled, the university netted some $224,000 in profit.[23] What set it apart was its far-flung cosmopolitan centers in Florence, Madrid, Strasbourg, London, Hong Kong, and Harare, Zimbabwe, enchanting trustees. Joe Lampe, trustee chair, who liked to travel to European DIPA centers to explore SU real estate opportunities, boasted that SU's Madrid center had its own, SU-named bus stop.[24]

SU first began sending students abroad in 1919 when SU's medical students traveled to China. The program evolved to become the stand-alone Division for International Programs Abroad, and it regularly attracted more students from outside SU than it did from within. Its high-quality reputation for teaching, programming, and accommodations helped grow its enrollment. During Eggers's tenure, its program in Florence was cited in the *New York Times* as "the Cadillac" of study abroad programs.[25] The year after SU's Pan Am flight 103 bombing, in which thirty-five DIPA students were killed in a flight home from London, DIPA had a record enrollment: 1,694.

DIPA was also distinctly complex among university divisions, with six locations on three continents, each with its own language, culture, currency and exchange rate, real estate, and employment laws.[26] It operated like an international business, buying currency futures as a hedge against devaluation, owning and leasing real estate, and hiring security contractors to protect students and faculty. In London, because British law does not recognize universities as not-for-profit, SU established DIPA London as a charitable trust to avoid value-added and corporate taxes.[27]

Enrollment began declining in 1990–91 and continued until 1995–96, when it reached a low of 1,139.[28] Administrators attributed the decline to anxieties about terrorism—the Desert Storm war with Iraq took place in early 1991—as well as increased competition from other programs costing less.[29]

DIPA was led by Nirelle Galson, a worldly director who spoke six languages and was uniquely suited to manage the program successfully all through the Shaw years. As a Jewish child, she had been imprisoned with her family in the former Yugoslavia and after release fled with her mother to Italy, the two of them disguised as the child and wife of the Muslim Turkish man who escorted them out. Her father, she learned, had been shot by Germans. She attended schools in Italy, Israel, and England, twice running away from religious schools in which she had been placed. After marrying Allen Galson, she moved to Syracuse, earned a BS degree in human development in 1971, and shortly after began working at University College as assistant director of undergraduate study degree programs. She joined DIPA in 1976 as assistant director and advanced to director in 1979.

DIPA's Zimbabwe program began in 1993 at the urging of African American Studies professors Bruce Hare and Horace Campbell. SU purchased a building in Harare for $179,000 in 1995 and made Campbell its resident director.[30] By 2001, some 381 students had studied at the Harare center, but shortly after, SU closed the center for good. Zimbabwe's political and economic instability, which had challenged the program from the beginning, ultimately made the operation too unsafe.

In 2001, DIPA settled into its first permanent home in Syracuse when it purchased the fraternity house at 106 Walnut Place from the Chi Corporation of Alpha Omicron Pi for $525,000.

Study abroad became a signature feature of Vice Chancellor Freund's academic plan. She encouraged campus academic programs to build study aboard into their requirements. She was also focused on boosting SU's retention rate, and SU students who studied abroad had one of the highest graduation rates of any cohort—95 percent.

In 2002, *U.S. News & World Report* ranked SU's study abroad program, which was later renamed SU Abroad, number 5 in the nation.

University College

University College (UC), like DIPA, was a profit center for SU. Because it had no faculty of its own, it "borrowed" them from other SU colleges, paying them extra, or "overload." That enabled it to have a more freewheeling approach and to offer classes—usually to nontraditional part-time students—that capitalized on market opportunities.

UC was overseen by Thomas Cummings, who was also vice president of enrollment management. When Cummings came to SU in 1965 as an administrator at UC, the college had over 5,500 degree-seeking, part-time undergraduate students. Enrollment declined through the 1980s and 1990s as fewer adults pursued degrees part-time and as competition from state and other local colleges increased. In the mid-1990s, UC's enrollment hovered around 3,000. Still, in 1993–94, UC had revenues of $20 million, most of which went to SU's general operating expenses, a point that deeply frustrated deans whose faculty were generating the revenue and who wanted their colleges to be credited for it. "We were in a war with the deans constantly over this," said Cummings. The revenue distribution issue with UC was never fully resolved during Shaw's time.

By the same token, UC, with more flexibility and access to nontraditional students, could help other colleges launch programs for working professionals using faculty, say, from the Maxwell School. UC would pay half their salary, while Maxwell paid the other half. If the program thrived, the home school might take full responsibility for it, as Maxwell did with its National Security Studies program led by Director Bill Smullen.

In 1998, the university sold UC's downtown Syracuse location—Peck Hall, Reid Hall, and an adjacent parking facility—and UC moved to 700 University Avenue. The sale price of $475,000 paid for renovations in its new home.[31] At the same time, UC merged with Summer Sessions into the Division of Continuing Education and Summer Sessions (DCESS), reducing some administrative expenses.

In 2001, UC offered its first-ever degree program, a bachelor of professional studies, which offered professional working people credits for their work experience.[32] Combined with new offerings of noncredit certifications through things like its Center for Business Information Technologies, UC continued offering alternatives to full-time matriculation at SU while capturing nontraditional students—and their revenue—that the main campus could not get.

CHAPTER 9
Work Environment
Building Community

SUIQ

One of Shaw's very first initiatives came from the world of manufacturing. Total Quality Management (TQM) was an approach to management that had been shown to improve quality output, customer satisfaction, and profits for businesses and to break down communication barriers between departments. Other economic sectors were adopting TQM. The city of Madison, Wisconsin, used it to speed up repairs of municipal vehicles. When Michael Williamson, an assistant to Madison's mayor, was hired by Donna Shalala, chancellor of the University of Wisconsin–Madison, Williamson encouraged her to bring TQM to campus. They used it to speed the processing time of graduate applications, which helped them secure top graduate students before other schools. Institutions like Penn State and RIT were using it, and the American Association for Higher Education had started an Academic Quality Consortium so universities could exchange information about TQM.

Shaw had met Williamson in Wisconsin, had seen what TQM had done for Madison—the city and the campus—and believed TQM could help SU. In his second month at SU, Shaw had Eleanor Gallagher bring Williamson to Syracuse to introduce the program to his cabinet. Quality was like sex, Williamson told cabinet members: Everyone is for it, everyone thinks they can do it by following natural inclinations, and when problems arise, most blame them on someone else's poor performance.

Separately from Williamson's efforts, consultants who had been hired to analyze SU's administrative operations had noted that the Financial Aid and the Bursar's Office tended to give students the runaround. The Bursar's Office even closed during lunch hour, when many students were free to do business. Shaw referred to this kind of poor service and "less than courteous treatment" as the "Syracuse Syndrome."

TQM was not unknown at SU. Before Shaw stepped on campus, John Sala, physical plant director, had implemented a Quality Service Program that introduced "a continuous process that exceeds the expectations of the customer." Shaw wanted the entire university to adopt such a program, and so he included it in the restructuring process as one of the 33 Initiatives, asking Gallagher to oversee it, both of them well aware that there would be resistance to thinking about students as customers. And there was. Some people came to training "kicking and screaming," said Ann Donahue, a human resources staffer who became director of training.

To get help from those who had been successful with TQM, Shaw recruited Corning, Inc., just as the University of Wisconsin–Madison had recruited Proctor and Gamble. Corning's vice chairman was SU alumnus Richard Dulude ('54, mechanical engineering), who was also an SU trustee. David Luther ('58 business) was Corning's senior vice president in charge of quality. Corning would share its TQM training materials with SU.

Implementing SU's TQM initiative would take most of Shaw's tenure and profoundly impact the university. Staff and administrators were still praising the program twenty years later, saying that it laid the groundwork for improved delivery of services to students and created a sense of teamwork within and across departments that reduced turf battles.

Shaw and his cabinet members were trained first by Williamson. Vice presidents and directors were trained next, followed by academic deans; 120 team leaders would train some 3,000 employees. As each new train-the-trainer program began, Shaw attended it to emphasize the importance of the work. To make the program its own, SU developed its own name and logo: SUIQ, or Syracuse University Improving Quality.

Trainings were held at Drumlins and lasted more than a week, covering such things as interpersonal skills and how to conduct meetings efficiently. Once trained, divisions established Quality Councils and Corrective Action Teams that met regularly to self-evaluate. By early 1994, SUIQ still had not been fully rolled out, and administrators were debating whether faculty should undergo training. Most faculty wanted nothing to do with a corporate-based training program: They had students, not customers. Some faculty expressed concern that an emphasis on serving students would lead to indulging students.[1] Cathryn Newton, who as dean of the College of Arts and Sciences sat through SUIQ videos, remembered them as "mind-numbing . . . stultifying." David May, executive director of communications planning, weighed in that faculty should not be forced to take the training; they should be considered "internal customers."[2] The decision was made that, although deans were required to participate in SUIQ, faculty were not. Yet, the cultural shift that SUIQ brought about by bridging divisions and departments trickled down to faculty and complemented their own "student-centered" focus, according to many participants. Across the university, the overall experience for staff and students generally improved. "[SUIQ] enabled me to develop relationships in the academic community—first through the deans and then through the faculty—that would pretty much have been impossible without that kind of work," said David Smith, dean of admissions. "Trust came just discussing and arguing about things."[3]

One key principle of SUIQ was not to instinctively blame an employee if quality or outcomes were poor. "If you've got intelligent, hardworking people and yet the results are problematic—the problem is not with the people, it's with the system that the people are working in," said Michael Flusche, associate vice chancellor for academic affairs. "So, let's look at that system and see what we can change, what we can improve."[4]

In hindsight, Shaw said SUIQ made quality improvement "much more complicated than it should have been," but as it eventually became more streamlined, its principles became part of new employee orientation and were presented in less than a day.

In 1997, Shaw approved an employee recognition program that would honor employees, everyone from faculty to staff to bargaining unit members. Joan Carpenter, vice president for human resources, had drawn up a proposal for the program in 1994.[5] The cost was roughly $90,000 a year for a dinner, a luncheon (for employees with fewer service years), and gifts—the bigger the milestone, the bigger the gift. Those with forty-five years of service (there was one at the time) could choose from a $420 gift offering. A different event, a special dinner, was held to acknowledge teams of employees who most improved service. Team members would receive US savings bonds or a sculpture designed by a student or faculty member.

Shaw had identified caring as one of SU's core values, and the collective effect of these initiatives created a culture of acknowledgment that took hold from top to bottom. Beth Rougeux, SU's director of state relations, recalled receptions for state representatives before football and basketball games at the Dome's Club 44. Before a reception ended, Shaw would thank the staff that had served them and invite guests to do so as well. Staff recognition was a hallmark of events hosted by the Shaws.

Since 1979, select faculty had been recognized each year through the Chancellor's Citation, an acknowledgment of exceptional contributions in academic achievement. With Shaw's push to incentivize performance through recognition and acknowledgment, the Chancellor's Citation celebration became bigger, with a more formal dinner attended by past recipients. A new category was added that recognized outstanding contributions to the university's academic programs. In 1997, the first year of that category, Rosanna Grassi, associate dean for student affairs in the Newhouse School, and June Quackenbush, manager of student computing services, received that citation. It came with no monetary award, but it was a highly respected recognition, with each designee receiving a substantial piece of art produced for the occasion by an SU art professor.

Buzzwords

As SUIQ's training of 3,000 staff kicked into high gear in December 1995, Shaw began supporting the training with a monthly newsletter to university employees called *Buzzwords*. The one-page newsletter was simple, direct, positive, and affirming. The masthead included a small caricature of an executive typing at a computer and the tagline, "Thoughts on SUIQ from Chancellor Kenneth A. Shaw." Each issue focused on a topic that was clearly identified in the center of the page.

Written, or dictated, with Shaw's folksy candor, polished by his assistant Kathryn Lee, the newsletter had the feel and effect of Franklin Roosevelt's fireside chats. Twenty years later, employees from that era were still keeping favorite *Buzzwords* over their desk.

Shaw published it monthly at first, then less frequently. Some years, only one or two issues would be published. He continued it right through the end of his tenure, squarely addressing issues that went far beyond SUIQ, like diversity, SU's institutional subsidy of athletics, and merit pay for high-performing employees.

The Strike

As much as SUIQ improved communications between many staff and managers, relations between organized labor and SU's management were at a low point. On August 31, 1998, 630 members of SEIU Local 200A, which represented physical plant, food service, and library workers, went on strike. They launched SU's first strike in twenty-six years just as the semester was beginning and some 2,900 freshmen were getting their first impressions of the university.

Each day, workers picketed at fourteen locations around the campus perimeter, including sites near the chancellor's house and outside the library. Strike news dominated the *Daily Orange*'s front pages, with escalating rhetoric polarizing the campus. Faculty who supported striking workers refused to teach classes or held teach-ins at picket sites. Shaw threatened to dock the pay of faculty who refused to teach. Some students handed out union flyers. Others complained about being awoken by picketers' chants at 5 a.m. and how the strike was disrupting their education.

Underlying the contractual issues were management's disregard for organized labor and the union's distrust of management.[6] SU's director of labor relations, Vince Scicchitano, took a hard, take-it-or-leave-it line in negotiations, and it was Scicchitano's last labor negotiation for SU. "It was more about respect than anything else," said Jack Walker, a union representative.[7]

The union's contract had expired June 30, and shortly after the university began preparing for a strike. Auxiliary Services supervisors built an inventory of flash-frozen meals, easily thawed and served in dining halls. During the strike, supervisors scrambled to maintain dorms, dining halls, and athletic facilities, getting help from office staff, students, and temporary food service workers. Some worked sixteen-hour days to keep dining halls and the Dome running smoothly.[8] On the Monday the strike began, the university released the first of a series of daily newsletters, *Negotiation News, SU Working toward a Settlement*, which tried to counter union claims of unfairness and to pressure union members to settle.

The strike tested Neil Strodel, SU's associate vice president of human resources (HR). He had been hired to head HR nearly two years before by Eleanor Gallagher, who had become vice president for human services and government relations following Joan Carpenter's retirement. Strodel had been head of HR at Syracuse China and Goulds Pumps, and he arrived at SU to find a "formulaic" approach to HR issues and a deep rift between labor and management that led to the strike. "He (Shaw) didn't see it. He wasn't told about it," said Strodel. "Nobody in the higher-ups understood how we got there or why. They just wanted it to go away."[9]

The strike was settled after only a week, on Sunday, September 6. Striking workers did not gain much on paper—they lost a week's pay and agreed to a three-year contract: Physical plant and food service employees would receive percentage pay increases of 2.5, 3, and 3. Library service workers' wages, which lagged behind those of counterparts at other institutions, received percentage increases of 6, 4, and 4. On the administrative side, Shaw distributed bonuses to administrators who had helped minimize strike disruption.[10]

The strike profoundly improved labor relations and not just for union workers. It brought to Shaw's attention the issue of low pay for many university employees and created impetus to change relations with the union. Almost immediately after the strike, Strodel brought in a labor mediator from Cornell University to meet monthly with union officials to discuss issues. "We didn't want to wait until we get to the bargaining table and have another strike," Strodel said.

Relations improved so much that, before SU hired Jack Matson as SU's director of staff relations and recruitment in 2000, SEIU members were consulted about whether to hire him. "That had never happened before," said Coert Bonthius, SEIU Local 200A representative.

A fair-wage initiative was one issue discussed, and union representatives pointed out that SU's low pay conflicted with its values. "If you're a university and you say you believe in equal justice, how can you pay your people so low?" Strodel recalled union representatives saying.[11] In 2001, Shaw announced that the university would hike wages nearly 40 percent for SU's lowest-paid, nonunion staff—nearly 800 technical, clerical, and temporary employees. Starting pay for many had been minimum wage, $5.15 an hour in New York State. Under the new plan, the lowest starting wage would be $7.75 per hour effective July 1, 2001, $8.50 in 2002, and $9.01 in 2003. Shaw paid for it by reducing a planned 4 percent salary increase for all other staff to 3.9 percent.

Although the fair-wage initiative did not directly affect union members, it set the stage for improved negotiations. For its 2001 contract, SEIU negotiated wage increases of 3.25 percent the first year and 3 percent in each of the next two years.[12] The number of wage steps—which incrementally raise pay—was reduced from eight to six for physical plant workers and from eight to five for library workers.

The Storm

The day following the strike's conclusion was Labor Day, and union members were scheduled to have the day off. However, Central New York awoke to a scene of devastation on Labor Day, September 7, 1998, and union members were called in to campus.

Just after 1 a.m., a derecho—a series of fierce, fast-moving thunderstorms with straight-line winds—began moving through the area, striking with tornado-level wind gusts of up to 115 mph. Blowing out of the west, the storm damaged hundreds of buildings and tens of thousands of trees in Central New York. More than 200,000 people lost power, which was not fully restored until the following week. At the New York State Fair, which had to shut down,

Skytop Apartments suffered severe damage in the 1998 Labor Day storm.
Courtesy of University Archives, Syracuse University Libraries.

two people were killed. New York State declared the community a disaster area and federal aid was sought. Hundreds of work crews, including utility squads and National Guard troops, worked around the clock to overcome mounting problems.

On campus, stunned work crews and others spent the morning—a holiday when no classes were scheduled—assessing the damage, a process that would take most of the day. At noon, the university news service issued a press release advising students that classes were expected to be held the following day, but at 5 p.m., as a clearer picture of the damage emerged, the university announced that Tuesday classes would be canceled. Hundreds of trees were splintered or uprooted across campus. Dozens of windows were damaged in residence halls, dining centers, and academic buildings. Floor-to-ceiling windows were blown in at Brockway Dining Center. Two sets of speakers fell from the Carrier Dome roof.

The greatest damage occurred on South Campus, where roofs on ten of thirty-five Slocum Heights apartment buildings sheared off. The entire South Campus was without electricity. An apartment unit on Winding Ridge Road was damaged when winds caused a wall to collapse. Amazingly, for all of the damage, only two minor storm-related injuries were reported on campus.

The university provided immediate shelter for about 140 students at Archibald Gymnasium and eventually relocated some 570 students and their families to the Hotel Syracuse and another thirty-four to the Syracuse Marriott during the weeks that repairs were being made to South Campus. Buses were provided to transport students between hotels and campus.

During the week when many Central New Yorkers were without power, the university's food services provided 10,000 meals for off-campus students and nearby residents. Cornell University sent an eight-person grounds crew, along with a portable generator to power refrigeration equipment at the SU Commissary and tree removal equipment. The university established an emergency loan fund for students to replace personal items and books damaged by the storm. Students, faculty, and staff helped with cleanup efforts. One SU staff person who volunteered remembered Mary Ann Shaw showing up with cookies and drinks.

The Saturday following the storm, many homes in Syracuse were still without power. SU opened Manley Field House to televise publicly its second football game of the season, against the University of Michigan in Ann Arbor. The game was broadcast on two large-screen televisions for the first 3,500 fans who wanted to watch the game. There was no admission or parking charge.

Storm damage repairs totaled $5 million. SU's cost was just $100,000 after insurance payments and $141,000 it received from the Federal Emergency Management Agency (FEMA).[13]

September 1998 had been a hard month—first the strike, then the storm. Shaw was relieved and appreciative for those who had made difficult circumstances manageable. He thanked "our union colleagues who came back to work early" and issued an extra day off to all staff for the holiday many of them missed.

A few years later, union organizing among graduate assistants raised concerns among SU administrators. The Office of Human Resources formed a communications team, which included the dean of the Graduate School as well as contacts in each school and college. The team mailed letters to each graduate student, posted articles in the *Record*, and successfully discouraged graduate assistants from joining a union.[14]

Westcott Neighborhood

Syracuse University had a long-standing, interdependent relationship with the bohemian residential neighborhood to the east commonly known as Westcott. Over decades, any number of SU employees had lived there, and landlords provided student housing that the university did not have to build or care for.[15] Half of the 2,100 residences in the seventy-five-block area were rentals, and in the best of times its high population density brought challenges—absentee landlords, a shortage of parking, and conflicts between students and permanent residents. Restructuring's employee cuts and an enrollment decline threatened to throw the neighborhood even more out of balance, some faculty and administrators feared.[16]

Some were concerned that, with the university's lower enrollment, landlords would not get the high rental income they were counting on and would let properties deteriorate or would further change floor plans of single family houses to add apartments.[17] Moreover, high-cost rentals had driven up real estate prices, making the area unattractive for prospective home buyers who would likely have to pay extra to reconvert a home to its original floor plan.

The university wanted to stabilize the neighborhood by attracting owner-occupants back. In Shaw's third year, he directed SU's Real Estate Office to investigate ways to do that. The result was the East Neighborhood Guaranteed Mortgage Program, first offered to full-time employees in 1994.

With no down payment, employees could get 100 percent financing to purchase single- or two-family homes within the east neighborhood. SU would guarantee mortgages with participating banks (Chase, Fleet, Key, OnBank, and Marine Midland), and borrowers would save the cost of private mortgage insurance typically required under conventional financing. The program was modeled after one that the University of Pennsylvania had started in 1967.

SU expanded the program in 1999 to include the Outer Comstock neighborhood (contiguous to Manley Field House and the
University's Skytop properties) and, in 2000, to include properties
built or rehabilitated under the Syracuse Neighborhood Initiative.[18]
Since university bylaws prohibited loans to trustees, faculty, and
staff, the Board of Trustees had to change its bylaws to allow the
loans. By 2000, seventy-two SU employees had taken advantage of
the program.

Dome Roof

Syracuse's "blizzard of the century" came March 13–15, 1993.
Thirty-five inches of wet, heavy snow fell in twenty-four hours, with
a total of 42.4 inches over three days. Under the snow's weight, the
Carrier Dome's air-supported roof became compromised and had to
be carefully deflated, and it was not the first time.

It took a Herculean effort by SU maintenance workers to protect
the 6.5 acre Dome roof during big snowstorms. In terms of logistics,
execution, and risk, it dwarfed every other endeavor on campus. Six
to eight times each winter, when weather forecasters predicted a big
storm, the university called in its twenty-person snow removal team
to climb to the Dome's Teflon-coated fabric roof to prevent catas-
trophe.[19] Heavy snow risked forming depressions in the roof where
melted water would pond, tearing fabric from cables or bursting the
fabric, causing the roof to uncontrollably deflate, buried under tons
of snow.

The snow removal team worked against time and the elements
like forest fire fighters, outfitted with boots, rainsuits, gloves, hats,
and a plastic shovel. They hauled firehoses nearly fourteen stories up
(roughly 165 feet) to blast 140-degree water on the snow. Harnessed
in against freezing wind, they tried to prevent a snow base from
building up that would give more snow a place to stick.[20] When wet
snow depth reached eighteen inches or pushed the roof down twenty
feet, they had to retreat to prepare for deflation.

Inside the Dome, the same workers raced to dismantle and cover
the basketball court and take down seating and the large curtain
partitioning the Dome. The deflating roof held a potential avalanche

The Carrier Dome, intentionally deflated after a heavy snowstorm to prevent the snow's weight from tearing the Teflon-coated fabric roof. Courtesy of University Archives, Syracuse University Libraries.

of snow and water, and high winds threatened to catch the fabric and twist cables. Once the roof was deflated in a controlled way, the worst threat was past and workers would clamber over the draped roof fabric, opening six-inch drain plugs so melted snow drained into the stadium. Vacuuming and squeegeeing took days.

When Shaw read a description of what it took to protect the Dome's roof in snowstorms, he wrote Marcoccia: "I want to be sure that the roof workers are well-paid. They are doing us a great service. Also, please tell me how much insurance we provide for them."[21]

As much as the Dome's roof had become a landmark for the university and the city of Syracuse, it needed close monitoring and regular replacement. In 1992, Pete Sala, the Dome's operations manager, secured an estimate of $7.5 million to replace the roof. Shaw was already tapping into the athletic department's reserve fund, which Eggers had created in part to pay for roof replacement. Significant money would need to come from somewhere else, and the 1993 blizzard prompted the university to contemplate a funding source used when the Dome was built: New York State.[22] The university updated its case for the Dome's positive impact on local and regional economic development and began lobbying state representatives.

By 1997, replacement costs had doubled to $13.3 million for a roof, with another $700,000 for design and bidding. SU obtained two $350,000 member items for the design phase from Senator John DeFrancisco and Assemblyman Michael Bragman. Both member items came through the Department of Economic Development. Work was scheduled for 1999. Additional money needed for the roof itself had not yet been secured. SU was seeking $6.3 million from the state's Community Enhancement Facility fund, which would involve commitments of one-third each ($2.1 million) from the governor's office, the state senate, and the state assembly.

The Dome had become a critical part of the Central New York economy. It had an estimated economic impact exceeding $60 million over seventeen years; SU had paid state and local tax revenues of some $12.5 million. Besides the national attention and revenue that came from SU sporting events, the Dome had become "a center of community service and civic pride . . . a mecca for amateur and high school athletics."[23] Without proper replacement, costly emergency repair, with all the disruption it would cause, would be "only a matter of time," the university said in its briefing statement to state officials.

SU and the city of Syracuse had another Dome improvement on their wish list: a $6.1 million, multilevel annex on the Dome's west end that would add a media interview room to seat 300, as well as additional restrooms and concessions facilities. Syracuse mayor Roy Bernardi was pushing for SU to host the NCAA men's basketball Final Four tournament. A large media room was the one thing the Dome did not have that the NCAA required. (In 2000, the Carrier Dome would host the NCAA Division I men's Eastern Regional semifinals.)

Governor George Pataki was the first to commit. In the summer of 1997, he indicated his office would provide $2.1 million if the Senate and Assembly did. A year later, neither had. The legislative houses were controlled by two men, Republican senator Joseph Bruno and Democratic assembly speaker Sheldon "Shelly" Silver.

With letters and phone calls, Shaw pressed local representatives DeFrancisco and Bragman to lobby their leaders for the funding.

Beth Rougeux worked with legislative staffers to monitor negotiations. In June, she was getting indications that the Senate would fund its share of the project, but she had heard nothing from the Assembly. Shaw called Bragman, who said he was "very optimistic" that Assembly funding would come through. August came and still no Assembly commitment.

On Monday, August 31, SU's SEIU Local 200A went on strike. The following Saturday morning, Assembly Speaker Silver called Shaw at home and asked how strike negotiations were going. Union support was critical for any Democrat. Silver mentioned nothing about the Dome, Shaw said, but ultimately, not a penny came from the Assembly. Some staffers cited its rejection as the only time they saw Shaw angry. "I didn't like it, but that's life," Shaw said years later. "We got two-thirds of what we wanted and that was better than nothing."

The Dome's new roof installation was completed in 1999. Performed by BirdAir engineering of Buffalo, the job cost $14 million—$4.9 million paid by the state, $6.1 million in tax-exempt financing, and donations of roughly $3 million. The work, which included a new sound system, was marred by falls of two workers, one of whom died. On June 8, 1999, a forty-one-year-old construction worker, Bryan A. Bowman, of Phoenix, fell sixty feet to his death while working on the roof replacement project.[24] Bowman was wearing a safety harness but was not tethered to a safety line when he slipped and fell through a seam between two Teflon-coated fiberglass roof panels. A few weeks later, another worker fell some fifty feet when he stepped on an unmarked metal hatch that covered a utility shaft. Dave Paduana, forty, of Syracuse, broke numerous bones after landing on a concrete floor.[25]

Perhaps nowhere more than with Shaw's management of the workplace were the small-town values he assimilated early on, in Edwardsville, Illinois, so on display. The progressive LeClaire community where his grandfather and aunt had worked and the brass works where his father had been a union member gave him empathy for workers at all levels once he became aware of their needs and helped him understand the benefits that came when employees were treated with respect. He had seen, too, the costs of confrontations between employees and management and did what he could at SU to avoid them. Decades after leaving the blue-collar city of his childhood, Shaw would say of his father, Kenneth W. Shaw, "When they took a strike he went on strike. And in Madison County (Illinois) there were strikes a lot."

CHAPTER 10
Reassessment
Adjusting Course

F OUR YEARS INTO HIS TENURE, Shaw needed to make more budget cuts. Increased financial aid, which initially had been funded with money from reserves, had to be sustained. In November 1995, he announced $6 million more in university-wide cuts over three years. Fifty more staff would be cut, and another twenty-five faculty would depart through supported resignations.

Despite this need for a second round of cuts, a certain stability had been achieved, in large part through the five-year, rolling budget planning Shaw instituted, which allowed for negatives along the way as long as the budget met its targets five years out.[1] Income and expenses were more predictably constant, with tuition increases of 5 percent, room and board increases of 4 percent, and salary increases of 3 percent.

The university had changed substantially. Formerly weak schools were boosting enrollment and improving their bottom line, and academic quality was improving. Research had been hurt. Schools, departments, and faculty competed for money and students in ways that had not existed before, heightening tensions. Offsetting this was Shaw's openness about budgeting, which enabled deans and faculty to understand they were in this together and, through restructuring's changes, were being spared a worse fate.

Reviewing the magnitude of changes that occurred so quickly, I am indebted to Donald Haviland, who in 1999 analyzed the effects of SU's restructuring for his doctoral dissertation at SU's School of Education. Some of his findings are incorporated below.[2]

Student Enrollment and Quality

SU became smaller. From a high of 12,577 undergraduates in 1989, it was steadily enrolling about 10,200 undergraduates. Incoming classes (freshmen and transfer students) were steady at 2,900, down from 3,200 in Eggers's last years. For each one hundred new students the university did not get each year, roughly $5 million in revenue was lost.[3]

The enrollment drop was deliberate and enabled SU to raise its admissions standards and improve the overall quality of its student body. In 1991–92, when SU admitted 89 percent of applicants, entering students' SAT scores averaged in the sixty-eighth percentile on the verbal and math tests.[4] Seven years later, they averaged seventy-first and sixty-ninth in math. While the improvement appears modest, given the fierce competition among universities for students during the 1990s, especially with the expansion of public universities, the increases were significant, Haviland observed.

Student quality varied by school and, as reflected by SAT percentile rankings, increased in all schools except nursing, where the verbal percentile dropped from fifty-eight to forty-seven, and math dropped from sixty to forty-seven. The College of Nursing's declines further supported Eggers's Ad Hoc Advisory Committee's view from four years earlier that the school could not hold its own and should, at the very least, be consolidated with some combination of human development, education, and social work.

Financial Aid and Minority Students

While enrollment declined and budgets were being reduced, financial aid for undergraduates nearly doubled, from $24 million to $44 million between 1992–93 and 1997–98.[5] Financial aid's full cost was not paid from the regular budget until 1997–98. The discount rate, the total cost of financial aid divided by gross tuition income, rose significantly under Shaw, from 15.3 percent his first year to 38.2 percent in 1997–98. Meanwhile, tuition increases, which had been as high as 12.4 percent under Eggers (in 1989–90), were held between 5.0 and 6.6 percent during Shaw's first seven years.

The matrix of factors used to determine the amount of financial aid that would improve student quality, school by school (often one student at a time), were overseen by David Smith, dean of admissions and financial aid. When prospective students had multiple college offers, the financial aid offered to them was often the deciding factor for choosing Syracuse. "You had to estimate what you needed to do to influence the behavior of people," Smith said. "And it was all based on one very simple premise: it takes decades to change your image, but you can change your price in a heartbeat."[6]

In an ongoing attempt to improve the quality of incoming students and to compete with what other colleges could offer, in the fall of 1999, Admissions increased the amounts of its merit scholarship awards (given to top students regardless of financial need) to a maximum of $10,000 yearly. In 2002, the maximum was hiked to $12,000. Further tweaking the admissions program, blue-chip prospects of engineering and arts and sciences could receive an extra $4,000, or a total of $16,000. Engineering simply needed bodies, as year after year it was not meeting enrollment targets. At the College of Arts and Sciences, the university's largest college, the quality of students had a major impact on public opinion about the quality and competitiveness of the entire university.[7]

A milestone in student quality and number of applications was achieved in 2003 when SU had a waitlist for the first time.[8] Putting a student on a waitlist deferred the university's determination about their admission until after a given date, when the first round of admitted students indicated whether they were coming to SU. The waitlist was an enrollment strategy adopted in addition to the alternate offer strategy. Students placed on waitlists were often qualified at the lower end of admissibility and often did not wish to be considered for an alternate offer. The waitlist demand continued the following year for arts and sciences, Whitman, Newhouse, music, and drama.

Efforts to improve the numbers of minority students were not as successful. The percentage of minorities (African American, Asian American, Latino, and "others") enrolling as freshmen remained constant through 2004, averaging 20 percent of total enrollment, slightly lagging minority growth nationally.[9]

Faculty and Staff

The faculty in the late 1990s was fewer in number, younger, and in some areas, more diverse. The departure of high-paid, senior faculty had been crucial to restructuring's financial success.

By 1996, SU's overall number of employees had declined by 557, or –13 percent, which was more than the university's –9.5 percent enrollment drop. Employee cuts were generally distributed evenly: –15.1 percent of full-time instructional faculty; –6.5 percent of adjunct and part-time faculty; –8.6 percent of academic staff; –13.8 percent of nonacademic staff. Some schools lost a significant portion of faculty. Arts and sciences lost –12 percent of its full-time instructional faculty (those with tenure, on a tenure track, or not on a tenure track) between 1991–92 and 1996–97. Education lost –26 percent. Engineering and computer science lost –43 percent.

Shaw came to a university heavily dominated by white, male faculty, and he allocated $340,000 to increase diversity among faculty and new faculty hires in the African American Studies department. Improvements in the percentage of minority faculty were slow in coming. Between 1990–91 and 1997–98, the percentage of women increased from 23 percent to 29 percent, African American faculty increased from 2.9 percent to 5.3 percent, and Latino faculty rose from 1.7 percent to 2.9 percent.

Diversity hiring varied greatly by department. A Maxwell professor told Haviland, "My department needed to have women but didn't beat the bushes for them and didn't change our job qualifications for them, which is one thing you can do."[10] In the spring of 1998, the Department of Chemistry had no tenured women on its faculty and only one on a tenure track.

Teaching and Learning

Shaw provided incentives for students and faculty to improve grades and strengthen teaching. For undergraduate students, there were new freshmen seminars, summer orientations, and opportunities to work with faculty in research. For faculty, the Meredith Professorship was launched in 1995 to reward outstanding teaching. The first Meredith recipients were William Coplin, of public affairs, Linda

Alcoff, associate professor of philosophy, and Bill Glavin, chair of the magazine department at the Newhouse School. (See also chapter 2, pp. 38–39, for a description of Meredith Professorships.) Meredith Professors were obliged to share their skills and insights with other faculty.

A similar recognition program created in 1995 was the William P. Tolley Distinguished Teaching Professorship in the Humanities, named for former chancellor William Pearson Tolley, who died in 1996. It offered a bonus of $24,000 for three years to a tenured professor in the humanities who would work to strengthen instruction. David Miller, professor of religion, was the first recipient.

The Gateway Luncheon series was started to improve teaching. Professors who were selected as Gateway Fellows—usually those who taught a large enrollment class—would lead lunchtime workshops on a teaching issue or strategy, such as breaking big classes into teams of students. Additionally, small competitive grants ranging between $3,000 and $5,000 were issued to faculty to design syllabi or support systems to improve learning. Out of these grants came lasting features at the university, such as books in the Martin Luther King Jr. Library and the curriculum of the Lesbian, Gay, Bisexual, and Transgender (LGBT) Studies program.

The emphasis on teaching and learning affected who was hired. Some extraordinary scholars did not get jobs, or did not accept jobs, after seeing what was expected of them. "For example, a mumbler, or a person who cannot communicate well . . . won't get a job," Vincow told Haviland.[11]

Student perceptions about academic quality and faculty commitment to teaching improved, according to a 1997 report of enrolled and prospective students by the firm Clark, Martire & Bartolomeo, Inc. (see appendix F). Students still felt they were being taught too often by graduate research assistants and not enough in small classes. However, most important for student recruitment efforts, more students were willing to speak proudly about SU to others. The views of minority students were another matter. While 28 percent of Caucasians gave "Happiness at SU" an excellent rating, only 13 percent of African Americans concurred and only 17 percent of Latinos.

Library

As the digital age dawned, Syracuse University Library was at the frontline of computer use within the university. Its computer clusters provided some of the first university computer access to students and faculty, and the library provided the gateway for online searches. When students or faculty needed to research material, they made their request to online librarians, who would search databases, many of which were on CD-ROMs, and print out an index of material, for a fee.

Syracuse University was a national repository for a major database of journals and articles called ERIC (Educational Resources Information Center), which was overseen by the federal Department of Education. In the late 1980s and 1990s, there were thirteen differently themed ERIC databases at universities across the nation, and the one dealing with information and technology was housed at SU. Further advancing computer use, the library, together with the School of Information Studies, assembled a campus-wide program, Beyond the Walls, that introduced faculty to the potential of collaboration through the internet.

All of this was foreign, disruptive, and confusing to many. Digital materials were an expensive new cost, and no one knew if or when they would replace printed materials. Jobs at the library were constantly being redefined. "We weren't sure how much of a flash in the pan all this stuff was," said Pamela McLaughlin, then the library's electronic resources coordinator. Some librarians struggled as they "just could not get the hang of how to interact with these things and produce a result that made sense to them," she said.[12]

Shaw's restructuring cuts added to the library's pressure. David Stam, director of libraries, had come to SU in 1986 when there was no hint of impending cuts or a shift in focus away from research. Stam had been director of research libraries at the New York Public Library and had been hired to build the library's research capabilities. Shaw cut the library budget by $840,590, implemented over four years.

Shaw did allow for annual 5 percent increases for library acquisitions, but the increase was swallowed up by the new costs of digital materials and the inflation of periodicals, which was averaging three times the consumer price index.[13] In 1985–86, the library held 23,027 serials (publications issued in successive parts intended to be continued indefinitely); in 1995–96, it held 16,278. "You talk to some of the physicists and other science people, and they would say that the heart of the section is being canceled," a librarian told Haviland.

In 2000, as library services became further digitized, the university offered a buyout for librarians and associate librarians, modeled after the faculty's supported resignation program. The resignations meant more responsibilities for those remaining: Where one librarian once served as liaison for several departments, that librarian might now have responsibility for an entire school or several schools.[14]

Toward the end of Shaw's tenure, the Carnegie Library was slated for improvements, but they were put off. Carnegie's foyer had been converted to classrooms during the Eggers years, so that its front entrance was closed—people had to enter from the side—giving the general impression that the whole library was closed.

Research and Faculty Relations

As long as anyone working at Syracuse University could remember, it had prided itself on being a research institution. For many faculty, research was their identity, so the grief and distress felt by some after cuts that shrunk research-heavy departments were profound. Shaw had cut away a part of them. However, while SU's research identity was hard-earned, it was getting shaky by 1991.

Tolley expanded research programs during the 1940s and 1950s, striking partnerships with General Electric (whose electronics division was headquartered in Syracuse), with IBM in Endicott and Poughkeepsie, and with the Department of Defense. By the late 1950s, Syracuse ranked twelfth nationally among universities for the amount of sponsored research money coming to it.[15]

In 1966, Syracuse joined the Association of American Universities (AAU), the nation's premiere association of research universities. From the start, SU's affiliation with the AAU was a stretch. Research funding is a key criterion for AAU membership, and SU had sold its medical school—typically a funnel for research dollars—to the state in 1950. SU's research identity was affirmed in 1973 when the

Carnegie Foundation for the Advancement of Teaching listed SU among its top classification of research universities.

Eggers's ambition to raise SU to "the next tier of excellence" was expensive—top research faculty had to be well paid. SU's off-campus master's programs for electrical engineering and computer science helped subsidize research through the 1960s, 1970s, and early 1980s. When GE and IBM cut jobs in the late 1980s, however, lucrative off-campus programs dried up and undergraduate tuition made up the difference. Meanwhile, research competition among universities had increased dramatically, especially at well-funded state systems.

The soul-searching examination of SU undertaken by Eggers's 1991 Ad Hoc Advisory Committee questioned the high cost of research at SU and even whether SU should have been accepted into the AAU in the first place. "Our error in being included [in the AAU] was a tribute to the rhetorical power of Chancellor Tolley to get us in," Palmer said.

Research spending declined during Shaw's first six years and greatly shifted between schools.[16] Engineering's research spending dropped by more than half, Maxwell's more than doubled, and information studies' nearly tripled, the latter two capitalizing on their relationships with government agencies.[17] Overall, cutting research programs and investing in undergraduate education was essential for SU's survival, Shaw determined.

Nationally, the need to emphasize undergraduate learning was becoming a popular cause. Undergraduates were being neglected at major research universities, a 1998 Carnegie Foundation report found, an argument Shaw had been making about SU.[18] The report positively cited Syracuse for its Future Professoriate Program, which trained graduate students to teach. Shaw could not have asked for a better endorsement of his restructuring strategy. SU's overall decline in research spending, though, threatened its standing in the AAU.

Restructuring cuts had also confirmed some faculty's impressions that Shaw was not an academic but a business manager, that he did not understand or care about high-level study or research.[19] Further antagonizing some faculty was a social component—Shaw, unlike Eggers, a former economics professor at SU, did not mingle and chat up faculty at parties. Shaw even cut back on one of their favorite summer gatherings—a three-day retreat at the Minnow-brook Conference Center in Blue Mountain Lake. Under Eggers, department chairs, deans, and sometimes Athletic Director Jake Crouthamel—as many as fifty people—would hash over issues at the lodge. Informal conversations over cocktails fostered a collegiality and sense of cohesion that disappeared under Shaw, some felt.

Retreats under Shaw were shorter, smaller, more work-focused, and closer to home—at Stella Maris Retreat House in Skaneateles or at the Sheraton Hotel and Conference Center. Sprawling gatherings of mixed groups were not efficient, in Shaw's view. "I never felt that having such a wide range of backgrounds and people led to honest talk," Shaw said.

His guardedness around social interactions with faculty helped maintain leadership mystique, he had found. As a young college administrator, Shaw had watched Illinois State University president Robert Bone attend faculty functions nearly every night. "It didn't help him, after a while," Shaw said. "No matter how well you stay up with current events, music, everything, you don't know very much. What you know is what you do. So you're at a dinner, and they want to talk about Emerson. You got nothing to say. There's no pay-off."[20]

Retention

To improve student retention (staying at a school through gradua-tion), the university had turned to the ideas of Vincent Tinto, one of the nation's leading experts on student retention and an SU faculty member at the School of Education. In his book *Leaving College*, Tinto advocated strengthening students' residential experience, pro-viding more on-campus employment opportunities, and increasing student–faculty interaction.[21] Schools with the highest retention rates were the ones that set the highest standards for their students and supported student learning with programs outside traditional classroom settings, Tinto found.

SU had begun such initiatives in 1991 with the Freshman Forum, a semester-long program in which a senior faculty mem-ber would acquaint a small group of freshmen with SU's offerings, its expectations, and skills for living independently. Students would meet weekly with the faculty member, sometimes sharing dinner at their house, or attending a Syracuse Stage event, visiting a museum, or even spending a weekend at a state park. There were summer bridge programs for incoming students who needed help transitioning from high school, closer tracking of students' progress, more proactive advising, and exit interviews with graduating students.

Getting Tinto's ideas across to faculty was a challenge, however, and Vincow went at it by teaching portions of Tinto's book to deans at their weekly meetings and by encouraging them to pass along the strategies. Retention rates did improve, from 65 percent in 1991 to 70 percent in 1998. Even with the improvement, in 2001, SU still lagged behind nearly all of its twelve peer colleges (appendix G). More troubling was that only 40 percent of minority students (blacks and Latinos) graduated in six years.[22]

The reasons were hard to get at and harder to address successfully, and the university devoted considerable resources to both. Racial tensions in the United States were still high, and students entering SU in the early twenty-first century had had their worldview shaped by scenes of the Rodney King riots and the trial of O. J. Simpson.[23] Horace Smith, an African American who had been associate director of the Higher Education Opportunity Program (HEOP)—which used state funding to provide programs for students from disadvantaged backgrounds—was named associate vice president overseeing the Office of Student Support and Retention. That office would initiate programs to help retention. The Center for the Support of Teaching and Learning would monitor the retention office's progress.

In 2003, the university instituted a $120 annual co-curricular fee for all undergraduate students, providing the university with an additional $1.3 million.[24] The co-curricular fee was in addition to a $104 student activity fee—its funds were administered by the Student Association, and the student activity fee could only be increased by a student referendum; repeated attempts to increase it had been unsuccessful.

Money collected through the co-curricular fee would be administered by the Division of Student Affairs, and in several instances, it supported programs already funded by the student activity fee: Light Work, some club sports, and student activities staff. But co-curricular fee revenue also helped launch new programs: diversity programs, an outdoor recreation program, an office to help off-campus students, and a program to cultivate emerging student leaders. Funding also went to enhance educational programs in residence halls.

Middle States Accreditation

Conveniently, SU came due for an accreditation review by the Middle States Commission on Higher Education in the late 1990s, after many of the university's improvement initiatives were taking hold.[25] The review of the evaluation team, led by John DiBiaggio, president of Tufts University, was generally glowing. The team found at SU "a general sense of hopefulness, a belief that Syracuse is a much different and improved place compared with just a few short years ago."

The team's report highlighted weaknesses that had also been identified in a university-wide review of Shaw two years earlier—that fund-raising was weak and that research had slid.[26] Improving both would dominate the administrative agenda for the next six years. Additionally, the committee recommended raising faculty salaries, correcting minority and gender imbalances among faculty, and enriching residence hall and recreational experiences—such as expanded gym facilities hours—to help retention and reduce alcohol use.

SU's years of steady improvement were heartening but had taken their toll on faculty and deans. After what seemed like countless committees, task forces, reports, and constant change, a sort of restructuring fatigue had set in.[27] Advances in student quality and retention were stalling or sliding. Faculty were yearning just to teach and stay the courses they were on.

Following the Middle States report, SU stepped up its faculty innovation program by starting the Vision Fund. In 1998, Shaw allocated up to $1 million a year to support the Vision Fund, a competitive grant program that encouraged faculty and academic departments to improve instruction through innovative partnerships. In the Vision Fund's first year, twenty-one grants were awarded, eleven of them at the maximum amount of $30,000.[28]

One of the first grants was for an Urban Design Center created by the School of Architecture and the Center for Public and Community Service to work with neighborhood projects on the city of Syracuse's west side. Another was a proposal from Beth Prieve, in the School of Education, to expand the work of SU's Gebbie Speech-Language-Hearing Clinic (established in 1972 for low-income and minority children).

Thanks to strong investment returns and successfully closing in on its $300 million capital campaign goal, the university's finances were on a growth trajectory, which led Shaw to become moderately more aggressive with investments. In 1998, trustees agreed to shift $160 million from a conservative Plant Fund reserve to higher risk/higher return endowment funds.[29] In 1999, Standard & Poor's upgraded the university's bond rating (for $231 million in outstanding bonds) from A to A+. The rating agency cited SU's "successful implementation of fiscal and academic restructuring between 1990 and 1998, which has led to an enhanced financial profile and improved academic standards." Buoyed by the improved financial outlook, Shaw was looking for someone to launch still more initiatives to boost research and improve student quality and facilities.

In May 1999, Deborah Freund was appointed vice chancellor for academic affairs and provost to fill the spot vacated by Vincow at his retirement.[30] Freund, the first woman to hold that position at SU, brought a dramatically different style of management and personal interaction. She was as energetic and vivacious as Vincow was disciplined and analytic. She was creative and interdisciplinary. Her experiences in academia and public health economics would help her relate to the university's professional and academic components.

She came to SU from Indiana University Bloomington, where she had been vice chancellor for academic affairs and before that chair of the health sciences and administration faculty. The daughter of a prominent New York City surgeon, Freund grew up in the Upper East Side of New York City, which would be a fund-raising advantage given her connections with associates of successful alumni in New York. She studied classics at Washington University in St. Louis, earned dual master's degrees in applied economics and

Deborah Freund, hired in 1999, was Syracuse University's first woman vice chancellor. Courtesy of University Archives, Syracuse University Libraries.

public health (medical care administration), and a doctorate focusing on health economics from the University of Michigan.

Freund brought urgency to Shaw's new focus on improving research. She knew SU's membership with the AAU was in possible jeopardy and learned that some of SU's top research faculty were demoralized and looking elsewhere for work. She pushed Shaw to create another academic plan that would strengthen research, improve student retention, and secure SU's membership in the AAU. Shaw reluctantly agreed.[31]

But before that academic plan was completed, Freund would oversee a merger that presaged the plan as well as the difficulties it would encounter. Three autonomous programs—Social Work, Nursing, and Human Development—would become one, the College of Human Services and Health Professions (HSHP).[32] William Pollard, who had been dean of the School of Social Work since 1989, was named dean of the new college, which officially opened July 1, 2001. The merged schools, each of which had its own decades-long history, occupied eight locations across campus, making it difficult for faculty to work together as part of a unified college. There were power struggles among faculty that made interdisciplinary work difficult, Pollard told trustees in November 2001.[33] Tenured nursing faculty were offered jobs in fields related to their specialties, but SU would no longer offer undergraduate and graduate degree programs in nursing. (See further discussion of the nursing program in chapter 12.)

Significantly, the merger put the idea of interdisciplinary collaboration between colleges and schools into play. Just as many faculty were adjusting to the first restructuring changes, SU would assemble a new academic plan, a process that would involve dozens of meetings with students and faculty and even draw in alumni participation through surveys.

Freund released her ambitious new academic plan, called A-SPIRE (A Strategic Partnership for Innovative Research and Education), in May 2001. The "spire" acronym was a lofty allusion to the tendency of colleges and departments to isolate from one another. A-SPIRE addressed SU's sagging research status with a call for doubling the amount of sponsored research money coming to the university, raising millions of dollars to fund one hundred new endowed professorships, and creating a new faculty position—"professor of practice"—to attract cutting-edge professionals who were not tenure track. The overall A-SPIRE Plan was supported by a financial commitment of $5 million per year for ten years.[34]

On the student side, it called for expanding the number of learning communities in residence halls—where students with similar interests and majors lived near each other, could study together, and sometimes take classes in the residence hall—all to improve academics and reduce alcohol and drug use. It also called for having all students participate in public service or a "community-based learning experience" before they graduated. In addition, the plan proposed a grand redesign that would establish four topical, interdisciplinary areas of research partnership to highlight SU's greatest strengths. While the proposed partnerships would not merge any more colleges, they would call for unprecedented cooperation across colleges. The four interdisciplinary areas were information management and technology; environmental systems and quality; collaborative design; and citizenship and governance.

Blending programs and schools was not a new idea. The 1991 Ad Hoc Advisory Committee had recommended merging the School of Information Studies with the School of Management, the College of Nursing with the School of Social Work, and the School of Architecture with the College of Visual and Performing Arts. A-SPIRE took the blending idea to a new level. The most straightforward partnership, elements of which were already in place, was citizenship and social transformation. It would draw faculty from the College of Arts and Sciences, the College of Law, and the Maxwell School, schools that were already working together. Others, like environmental systems and quality, would involve entities that had never worked together: SUNY ESF, SUNY Upstate Medical University, College of Engineering and Computer Science, Maxwell School, College of Arts and Sciences, and School of Architecture. Structural obstacles and resistance were considerable; there were few incentives for schools or faculty to cooperate, and little of A-SPIRE's blending happened.[35] But A-SPIRE strongly identified the university's strengths and areas in which to invest. In that regard, it supported the need for more academic buildings. Behind the scenes, a push was on to find donors and public funding to address SU's space shortage, which was critical. In the higher education "arms race" for big and well-equipped facilities, SU was lagging behind.

Making Space

A Space Planning Advisory Committee, formed in 1998 and chaired by Michael Flusche, associate vice chancellor, had identified $200 million in new buildings and renovations, with construction taking five to seven years. To approach the average amount of space per student offered by a comparison group of research universities—among them, Boston College, Notre Dame, and Cornell—SU would need to add more than a million square feet, according to Dober, Lidsky, Craig and Associates, the academic space planning firm that Flusche's committee had hired. Flusche's committee was recommending SU add 400,000 square feet of new construction and renovate another 350,000 square feet. Proposed construction included a significant addition to the north side of Bird Library facing Waverly Avenue, an expansion on the Center for Science and Technology for

Barry Wells, vice president for student affairs, worked closely with Vice Chancellor Freund to develop student learning communities in residence halls. Courtesy of University Archives, Syracuse University Libraries.

Life Sciences (biology and chemistry), an expanded or new School of Management building, an expanded Newhouse School, and possibly a new building for the College of Human Services and Health Professions. The new construction and improvements were needed to "recruit the caliber of students and faculty that SU needs to advance in national standings," the space committee said.

*   *   *

Several other elements of A-SPIRE took hold, most important, the work to improve student retention. SU was losing students at both extremes of performance: successful students who were not challenged as well as struggling students. Retention was addressed on a number of fronts, among them, making it easier for students to take courses outside their major or to study abroad for shorter lengths of time. Additionally, Freund joined forces with Barry Wells, vice president for student affairs, to create more programs that supported academic learning outside of classrooms.

Wells started at Syracuse in 1976 on the student affairs side as a counselor and the first coordinator of the Office of Minority

Affairs. He had moved to the academic side and worked his way up to associate dean in the College of Arts and Sciences before Shaw appointed him to lead student affairs. Wells brought a welcomed energy, focus, and thoroughness to the Division of Student Affairs, and with Freund's emphasis on retention, he expanded the number of learning communities in residence halls. As many as fifteen learning communities were created, including ones for management students, women in science and engineering, multicultural living, citizenship education, and substance-free living. In 2002, SU's learning communities were ranked twelfth in the country in *U.S. News & World Report*.[36]

Freund's retention plan aimed to increase the six-year graduation rate to 80 percent in five years and to 85 percent in ten years. By 2003, the graduation rate had improved to 79 percent; the gap in the drop-out rate between Caucasian and African American students had narrowed from 23 percent to 6 percent.[37]

R AISING ENOUGH MONEY to compete in the big leagues of
academic and research universities has been a perennial issue
for Syracuse University. SU's relatively low endowment—a pool
of invested money that generates income—has affected everything
from the quality of students and professors to enrollment numbers,
from the condition of physics labs to the performance of its athletic teams. The disparity between SU's aspirations and its means to
achieve was highlighted late in Shaw's term, when trustees proposed
hiring a Nobel Laureate in the sciences to elevate the university's
research and academic status.

Then-Vice Chancellor Deborah Freund dutifully looked into it.
Bringing a Nobel Laureate to Syracuse would cost $50 million to
start and another $7 million annually, she estimated. Besides need-
ing to offer a significant salary and provide first-class space and
equipment, SU would have to hire eight faculty colleagues in the
Nobel Laureate's specialty area, a staff of twelve postdoctoral students, twelve technicians, an administrative assistant, and two clerical staff. Getting twenty top-notch graduate students to work with
the professor would mean providing them full tuition plus stipends.
There were "virtually no examples of Nobel faculty moving from
higher- to lower-ranked schools," Freund reported. Tuition-depen-
dent Syracuse was not going to hire a Nobel Laureate anytime soon.

SU's history of alumni giving, fund-raising, and investing is
as complex and varied as the history of its colleges and schools.
It is a story of outsized personalities and half-baked strategies, of
accountants' meticulousness and caution, of grandiose events, of

unexpected developments, crushing disappointments, and impressive successes.

Chancellor William Tolley (1942–69) was an expansionist, a shrewd opportunist, and a fearless fund-raiser. During his twenty-seven years as chancellor, he added nearly 1,000 acres to SU's landholdings and erected forty-seven new buildings, at a cost of more than $70 million.[1] He seized a historic opportunity of serving veterans returning from World War II. In just five years, he more than tripled enrollment.[2] He went to New York City, reaching out to wealthy business owners, some affiliated with SU, some not, but sharing an interest in learning. In New York, Tolley persuaded Samuel I. Newhouse to construct the first of two buildings for the School of Journalism.

In March 1961, Tolley told his board that in nine years, by 1970—the university's 100th anniversary—SU would raise $76 million[3] ($464 million in 2017 dollars). The endowment would get just $5 million of that ($31 million in 2017 dollars). Tolley's fund-raising prowess and GI Bill tuition proceeds funded SU's expansion, enlarging its footprint, but he left behind a small endowment.

Tolley's short-term successor, John Corbally (1969–71), never got fund-raising off the ground. His term was marked by antiwar and Black Power protests, student strikes, canceled classes, and a boycott by black football players before he abruptly left to become chancellor of the University of Illinois system.[4]

Chancellor Eggers (1971–91) had an aversion to asking for cash. A $35 million Second Century Campaign, announced in February 1973, did not meet its goal. Another $35 million campaign, launched in 1977 to replace existing buildings, was successful.[5] To renew his development team, Eggers brought in Lance Baker, a former high school superintendent (Jamesville–Dewitt) whom Eggers had first hired as president of SU's Utica College in 1980. Eggers made Baker vice president of development in 1987, just as his final fund-raising push, the $100 million Campaign for Syracuse, was beginning. By 1989, that campaign met its goal, raising $103 million, and trustees committed to continue the campaign to bring in another $60 million, a goal met in June 1991. Generally, alumni had little habit or expectation of giving. Apart from sports, they were rarely encouraged to be a part of the institution and resented being contacted only for donations. The university acknowledged its fund-raising problem in a briefing book assembled for candidates to replace Eggers. Endowment per student ranked SU 120th in the nation, while its enrollment placed it sixth among private universities.

When Shaw took over, SU's endowment was $165 million, and he wondered about the possibility of doubling it in five years.[6] Every aspect of the university's fund-raising needed work, starting with the Board of Trustees. For help, Shaw had a special ally—Mary Ann Shaw.

The Board

Even more than its faculty in 1991, SU's Board of Trustees reflected the power paradigm of mid-twentieth-century America. Its membership and leaders were older, mainly white men who lived and worked in Central New York. Since the early 1960s, an unbroken succession of Syracuse-area business leaders had served as board chairman: Gordon Hoople (1963–67), a Syracuse physician; Dwight Winkelman (1967–70), chair of D. W. Winkelman Co., Inc. of Syracuse, an internationally known heavy construction firm; Royal O'Day (1970–75), chair of Marine Midland Bank; Melvin Holm (1975–81), chair of Carrier Corporation; Chris Witting (1981–92), chair of Crouse-Hinds; and H. Douglas Barclay (1992–98), a powerful former state senator and attorney. Robert Allen, who succeeded Holm at Carrier, became chair of SU's budget committee. When major corporations were headquartered in Syracuse, they were major donors to the university. By the late 1980s, however, Syracuse was losing its corporate headquarters. Carrier had been purchased by United Technologies Corporation in 1987, Crouse-Hinds was bought in 1981 by Cooper Industries.

The board's geographically limited leadership was criticized at a June 1992 trustee meeting by Chester P. Soling ('54), a New York City–based architect and real estate developer, and trustees agreed to increase the board's geographic diversity.

Meanwhile, the Shaws began working to engage trustees and alumni to a far greater extent. Semiannual board meetings were opportunities for dinners at the chancellor's house and were greatly expanded upon by Mary Ann, who saw to seating arrangements, strategically positioning board members with administrators seeking their support for a program or with academics who would excite their interests, all the while keeping sight lines open between the head table and her university contacts seated among the guests. Scholarship students, who served food and provided musical entertainment, would be ready to chat with board members about their study programs. During multiday meetings, Mary Ann organized events for board members' spouses.

The Shaws hosted board members and financially successful alumni at athletic events. Alumni relations staff researched attendees' backgrounds, which the Shaws then studied, and cabinet officers were asked to attend the pregame events to assist with entertaining duties. Mary Ann mingled with guests at the pregame events and in the chancellor's box while Buzz would take several others into the stands, sometimes entertaining them at football games by running down to the sidelines to do push-ups with cheerleaders when SU scored.[7]

Trustee meeting formats changed. Shaw had his administrators submit reports that were distributed before meetings, so presentations were shorter and more substantive discussions could take place. Trustees who chaired committees were encouraged to become more engaged, to ask questions of administrators reporting to them, and to lead discussions on relevant topics.

The financial requirement for being a board member was clearly established for the first time—a $1 million gift was the minimum. Exceptions were made for celebrities or members who would help diversify the board. Getting $1 million gift commitments from trustees created an incentive to make the board larger. Barclay, trustee chair from 1992 to 1998 and a board member until he was appointed ambassador to El Salvador in 2003, objected to the million dollar buy-in. It attracted people who might not otherwise qualify in terms of expertise and experience. "Now you've got a lot of people involved and they all want to be influential," he said.[8]

From 1991 to 2004, the voting board's size grew from thirty-nine to fifty-one. The number of women increased from three to nine. The percentage of Syracuse-area trustees remained the same, 33 percent. The permanent Executive Committee, which formerly had seven people all from Syracuse, drew four from Syracuse and three from elsewhere, most notably, Joseph Lampe. When Barclay's term ended as chair, Lampe, a trustee since 1987, became SU's first trustee chairman from west of the Mississippi. With Shaw's interest in having a more activist board, Lampe, energetic, driven, and demanding, was a perfect fit.

A Syracuse native who grew up in Gloversville, New York, Lampe graduated from Syracuse University in 1953 with a bachelor's degree in speech and dramatic arts and, in 1955, earned his law degree. Soon after graduating, he headed west, getting involved in real estate and hotel development in Los Angeles and Scottsdale, Arizona. Lampe's cosmopolitan ease with travel and his familiarity with successful alumni and business people across the country brought a new geographic diversity to the board. He was proud of and fascinated with SU's Division of International Programs Abroad (DIPA), pushed for some of the first organized trustee trips to SU's foreign study centers, and became personally involved in negotiating SU's foreign real estate transactions. So frequently did he commute to SU meetings from across the country that he kept a set of clothes at the campus's Sheraton Hotel.

New York City, Overture

New York City had the largest concentration of wealthy SU alumni anywhere in the nation. Shaw visited there his first December and met with alumni on the Metropolitan Advisory Board, a group organized to enhance the university's presence in greater New York. He returned enthusiastic about fund-raising potential and encouraged Baker to increase SU's visibility in New York by undertaking "substantive projects" that would showcase SU's academic strengths, like those at Maxwell or Newhouse.

One New York alumnus who had come to Shaw's attention was Donald Schupak ('64), an investment banker, deal maker, and a media-savvy attorney. Schupak had welcomed Shaw in November with a letter proposing to link New York City schools—especially its new, small, alternative high schools—with faculty at the Maxwell School. With major budget cuts looming, the university was slow to commit to a new partnership with anyone.

On January 25, 1993, the *New York Times* printed a lengthy article that presented the partnership between SU and the city's proposed High School for Leadership and Public Service as a fait accompli.[9] The story's main source was Schupak, whose portrait accompanied it. Faculty from the Maxwell School would help shape the high school's curriculum, and SU alumni nearby would mentor the students. Those who excelled would get full scholarships to SU. The school would open at the site of the old Stuyvesant High School in Manhattan, a fourteen-story high-rise on Trinity Place. The school would be "a factory for enfranchisement for an entire generation . . . of unmotivated students," Schupak told the *Times*.

Baker had been working on the idea with Thomas Sheldon, an old friend he had put in charge of Lubin House, SU's Manhattan headquarters. Sheldon's background was similar to Baker's: he had been a school superintendent and preceded Baker as president of Utica College. He had also worked as New York State deputy commissioner of education. Their education backgrounds helped the two men work out the unusual agreement between the New York City Schools chancellor's office and SU.

Shortly after the Schupak article, Mary Ann Shaw brought some twenty alumnae together at Lubin House to explore how they would like to get involved with SU. Jane Present ('56), owner of a travel agency, mentioned the high school partnership she had read about in the *Times*. That was an endeavor worth supporting, she said.

The high school opened in September 1993 with 123 ninth-grade students. Professor Bill Coplin served as the SU/Maxwell School advisor, and high school students would intern at public service agencies around the city. In 1994, SU began sending Maxwell students to intern at the high school, and they essentially taught Coplin's freshmen public policy course.

Meanwhile, Present helped organize the Friends of the High School for Leadership and Public Service, Inc., which incorporated in 1996 to raise money to support the high school and to provide SU alumni mentors for high school students. As its first president, Present was a dynamo, whether she was securing a piano from Lincoln Center, free tickets for students to the New York City Ballet, or breakfast for 600 students and staff at the Regent Wall Street Hotel to celebrate the school's tenth anniversary. "There's a Yiddish expression called *farhandlen*, and it means to negotiate. I'd go in and twirl my hair and say, 'But these kids . . . ' and every time a need arose, we figured out a way," she said. Present met her husband, Daniel H. Present, a gastroenterologist, at SU. They later created a fund that sponsors an author each year in the Raymond Carver Reading Series. Both received George Arents Awards, SU's highest alumni honor.

Alumni who made up the Friends organization established SU scholarships for High School for Leadership and Public Service graduates. Some, like Present, have maintained friendships with high school alumni long after they graduated from SU.

Commitment to Learning

By the spring of 1993, academic restructuring was well underway, enabling Shaw to turn the university's focus toward fund-raising. In May, trustees endorsed a seven-year, $300 million Commitment to Learning campaign. The campaign was meant to fund new restructuring initiatives more than it was to build the endowment. One-third of the money would go toward scholarships ($100 million). The remainder would be distributed to support faculty ($45 million), academic programs ($100 million), academic facilities ($25 million), and unrestricted support ($30 million). Trustee Marvin Lender ('63), whose family owned Lender's Bagels, would serve as campaign chairman. After graduating from SU with a degree in political science, Lender helped grow the family bagel bakery in New Haven, Connecticut, from six workers to a 700-employee operation with three manufacturing sites that produced frozen, prepackaged bagels. The company was sold to Kraft Foods in 1984.

The fund-raising/endowment need had presented itself directly to Shaw earlier in the spring when more than forty students, angry about the announced 6.5 percent tuition and 4.75 percent room and board increases marched to the Tolley Administration building.[10] Why could not SU discount its tuition 50 percent, like Rice University, in Houston, one student asked Shaw. Rice, with 4,100 students, had an endowment of $1.2 billion, or $305,284 per student. If

Syracuse, with an $11,580-per-student endowment, were to match Rice's ratio, its $231.7 million endowment would need to grow to more than $5 billion, Shaw explained.

At November's trustee meeting, Shaw presented more sobering endowment-per-student comparisons: Northwestern, $81,137; Vanderbilt, $73,058; Cornell, $51,164; Boston College, $28,689; Georgetown, $27,732. In light of such comparisons, the $300 million campaign amounted to a scramble just to stay in the game.

The campaign brought with it a push for each college to have its own development office. The schools and colleges in the best financial shape—Maxwell, Newhouse, Law, Architecture, Arts and Sciences—already did. Barbara Wessel, who joined the Development Office in 1989 to focus on upstate New York, became senior director of college-based development.

Within the Commitment to Learning campaign, the College of Law conducted its own $7.5 million campaign. Part of the money went toward the $12.5 million construction of Winifred MacNaughton Hall, and renovation of E. I. White Hall. MacNaughton Hall was occupied in 1998. It was named for the wife of Donald MacNaughton ('39, Law '48), who was president and CEO of Prudential Insurance Company of America. The MacNaughtons' sons, Donald (Law '68) and David (Law '77) were also graduates of SU.

The Commitment to Learning wrapped up in December 2000. Some 46,000 alumni contributed, and sixty-eight new, named scholarships were created. To celebrate publicly, Shaw and Baker rode in a limousine to the Sheraton Hotel and Conference Center accompanied by a Brinks armored vehicle carrying an oversized $360 million check.

Courtship of a Literary Lion

William Safire was one of the most respected American political commentators of the late twentieth century. A speechwriter for President Richard Nixon and Vice President Spiro Agnew, a linguist, bibliophile, and conservative-libertarian columnist for the *New York Times*, Safire attended Syracuse University in the 1950s and dropped out after two years. Prominent alumni are often courted in particular ways over long periods of time, and SU's courtship of

William Safire, a Pulitzer Prize winner who attended SU in the 1950s, helped open doors to many prominent, influential, and affluent SU alumni. Pictured here with Shaw. Courtesy of University Archives, Syracuse University Libraries.

Safire is noteworthy for its duration and for the way it opened doors to other major donors.

Safire received an honorary degree from SU in 1977 and spoke at commencement the following year. Through the early 1980s, Eggers visited him in New York and Washington, DC, where Safire worked as a *New York Times* columnist.[11] Eggers asked for Safire's help to connect with Morton Janklow ('50), an SU alum, literary agent, and close friend of Safire. In 1987, SU raised $1 million for a Safire professorship in the English department. When Eggers retired in June 1991, Safire presided over a tribute for the chancellor. Then, in 1993, Safire donated his book collection to SU, along with $100,000 from the Dana Foundation, on whose board Safire served.

The money went toward construction of the Safire Reading Room in Bird Library.[12] The 1,427 volumes in Safire's book collection—more than half of them (734) Civil War books—would fill the shelves.[13]

Safire was elected to SU's Board of Trustees in May 1994. The Safire Room was to be completed that November in time for the trustee meeting, when the university would officially open the room and hold a dinner honoring Safire. Safire didn't want a special dinner, he told David Stam, University Librarian.[14]

Despite Safire's reluctance to be feted, SU's Development Office saw a potential event with Safire that tapped his powerful network of wealthy SU alumni as too valuable an opportunity to let pass. In January 1995, Thomas Walsh, a development officer in Washington, visited Safire and told him as much; Safire agreed. Walsh encouraged Safire to have his literary agent, Janklow, take the lead creating a guest list. By summer, both Shaws were planning and negotiating details with Janklow. For one, who would invite Donald Newhouse? He had been a trustee since 1991 but had not been to campus in years, even though he visited Syracuse to check on his newspaper holdings.[15] The invitation should be made by Shaw, it was decided.

When Thursday, November 2, 1995, came, a tightly orchestrated, day-long Safire celebration unfolded flawlessly. An SU-chartered plane flew guests from LaGuardia Airport, a first for an SU donor event. There was continental breakfast at the chancellor's house, a motor tour of campus, lunch in the Safire Room, and dinner (quail and vegetable terrine) at the chancellor's house. In between, guests participated in panel discussions to which were also invited trustees and their spouses, as well as select groups of alumni, students, and deans.[16] Afterward, letters of praise came to Shaw from featured guests, most notably, Donald Newhouse, who had been shown the impact the Newhouse School had on thousands of students. "We gave him a wonderful day," said Walsh. The event was so successful and engaging that it became a template for others in New York City, leading to some of the biggest gifts of the Shaw era.

New York City, Act I

When Chancellor William Tolley opened SU's doors to GIs in the 1940s, tripling enrollment, he also welcomed a different constituency that was facing quota obstacles elsewhere—Jewish students. SU, like many universities, had restricted admission of Jews and discriminated against them throughout the early twentieth century. Jews were housed apart from Christians at SU from 1927 to 1931. Fraternities and sororities openly admitted they would not admit Jews or Catholics, historian Greene wrote.[17] Tolley's welcoming admissions policy changed lives for thousands of students, one of whom was Robert Menschel. In turn, Menschel's gratitude changed SU. His story of engagement reflects that of a generation of Jewish students who, as alumni, profoundly impacted the university.

Menschel attended the Bronx High School of Science (commonly known as Science), a specialized school for math and science students that has graduated more Nobel Laureates and Pulitzer Prize winners than any high school in the United States. Menschel's classmate at Science, and for a time at Syracuse, was Safire, who won the Pulitzer in 1978.[18] SU was Menschel's second choice. He wanted to attend the University of Pennsylvania, an Ivy League school with a strict Jewish quota, where he was put on a waiting list.[19] As an SU freshmen, he shared a room in a two-story, prefab dorm at Collendale, off East Colvin Street, with two GIs who were as different as could be from Menschel, and he remembers them putting their fists through walls when angry.[20]

Menschel found a boomtown spirit at postwar SU that he happily exploited. At registration, if he did not like his assigned courses, he would tear up the computer punch card and work his way into classes he wanted at Maxwell, public communications, business administration, and even graduate courses. "You had to go for the best," he said. "That's where I first learned that."

After graduating with a bachelor's degree in finance ('51) from the School of Management, Menschel joined Goldman Sachs, became a partner, founded Goldman's institutional department—investing money for foundations and universities—and would serve on SU's Investment and Endowment Committee. In 1981, he became an SU trustee.

Menschel's lifelong interest in photography led him to take a special interest in Light Work and its entrepreneurial director Jeffrey Hoone. Light Work was an unusual entity at SU.[21] Operating out of Watson Hall on Waverly Avenue, it began in 1973 as an artist-run nonprofit to support photographers, both students and community members, and fell under supervision of the Division of Student Affairs. Light Work raised all of its operating and program funds, and Hoone, ever on the lookout for funding, reached out to Menschel, who appreciated Hoone's international vision and big ambitions for Light Work.

In 1985, Menschel donated $250,000 for the Robert B. Menschel Photography Gallery on the top floor of the new Schine Student Center, which would be curated by Light Work. Menschel's giving was mostly quiet, steady, and strategic. He looked for ways his gifts could help raise SU's quality and put the university on a bigger stage. He led an initiative to establish the Chair in Modern Letters, named in honor of his former SU roommate, Safire. He made gifts to support the Humanities Distinguished Teaching Professorship, the Honors Program, and the Maxwell School campaign of the early 1990s. He was disappointed in SU's investment strategy, which he found too conservative and lacking initiative to engage alumni in New York City. "It was an upstate university that had an upstate mentality," he said.

A few years later, Menschel donated $2 million toward a $3.2 million renovation of Light Work's facilities, which were newly named the Robert B. Menschel Media Center. Menschel drew into the project New York City architect Richard Meier, who helped with architect Michael Wolniak's ('78) design, and Sol LeWitt ('49), a major figure in late twentieth-century art, who also attended SU during the GI Bulge. LeWitt designed the wall drawing just inside the Media Center's entrance.

Menschel had been donating annual, six-figure sums to the university for years. In 1998, he added another gift, stipulating that the university use it to bolster its New York City presence. By the end of 1998, little had changed. Menschel was frustrated and let Shaw know it. To address Menschel's concerns, Shaw tapped Walsh, who had dual reporting lines to Eleanor Gallagher and Lance Baker and was responsible for both the university's federal relations and development operations in Washington, DC. The Shaws had grown to know Walsh working with him in DC, where Shaw would attend meetings of the AAU or Sallie Mae, whose board he was on, while Walsh would set up lunches or cocktails between alumni, Mary Ann, and himself. "Mary Ann brought something different," said Walsh. "This wasn't just tea with the chancellor's wife. This was a part of the executive organization of the institution." For top donor prospects, Walsh would bring Shaw in. By January 1999, the stature of Walsh's role and his responsibilities in development would surpass his rank in the dual DC job. He moved 100 percent into the Development Office and became assistant vice president for development and public affairs in New York, with Lubin House staff reporting to him. The move was atypical for Shaw. He had maintained a hands-off relationship with Baker's advancement and development staff for eight years. Now, as Baker was wrapping up his Campaign for Syracuse and preparing to retire, Shaw felt compelled to act on New York. "I think [Shaw] was a little embarrassed that nothing had been done," said Walsh. "He had egg on his face. He had cultivated a relationship with [Menschel]. And this is what ends up happening?"[22]

Understanding the stakes involved, Shaw committed to being in New York three to four days a month to meet with whomever Walsh suggested. At the same time, Walsh ramped up the approach he had used with the Safire Room dedication to the standards of the world's financial and cultural capital. New York alumni would see the university in ways they had never seen it before, and the Shaws would develop relationships that would set the course for SU in the twenty-first century.

New York City, Act II

New York City was not an easy place for Shaw. Native New Yorkers would reflect he had a "deer-in-the-headlights" look when he first came to the city and would ask cab drivers to slow down. His droll, matter-of-fact manner was at odds with the brusque intensity and self-conscious style of so many New Yorkers. However, his plain-spoken unpretentiousness and self-assurance, which connected him so well with people in Syracuse, won over people in New York, too.

As much as New York challenged Shaw, Walsh was at home there. He started life in Passaic, New Jersey, and when he was eight, he moved with his family to Grand Island, New York, outside of Buffalo. An SU graduate theater major ('84), he worked in New York as a dramaturge for Arthur Storch, the founder of Syracuse Stage and chair of SU's Department of Drama (1974–92). Walsh brought to development an understanding of the city and a sense for the dramatic, and he set out to engage SU's most prominent, A-list alumni—the likes of Menschel, Donald Newhouse, and Marty Whitman—with high-profile SU events that would persuade others to get involved. "New York is a top-down driven town," Walsh said. "There's millions of people there. But if you've got six of the right ones, just about anything can happen."

By fall, the New York strategy was hitting its stride. Between September 1999 and March 2000, Shaw was in New York thirteen days, averaging three contacts per day, usually with male prospects. Mary Ann was in New York sixteen days, averaging four contacts per day with female prospects. In addition, one high-profile event after another was drawing attention to SU from the worlds of art, finance, media, and culture. The Shaws would continue this strategy right through their final years at SU.

On October 25, 1999, Shaw awarded an Arents award for musical theater to Lynn Ahrens ('70), who had recently won a 1998 Tony for the lyrics of the Broadway musical *Ragtime*. She received her award at a dinner for seventy at the Pierpont Morgan Library in Manhattan, an event sponsored by Menschel. SU musical theater students performed a medley of Ahrens's songs. It was the first time since the award's beginning in 1939 that an Arents had been given off-campus. Over the next few years, Shaw would distribute a number of Arents awards at events across the country. Two days after the Ahrens event, Menschel hosted a luncheon at Goldman Sachs for potential donors for the soon-to-be-built School of Management building. George Burman, the school's dean, updated eighteen alumni about plans for the school's emerging fund-raising campaign.

On November 9, at the Museum of Television and Radio, the university presented a panel titled "Syracuse University: Where They Learned to Lead an Industry." More than 200 people listened as Edward Bleier ('51) moderated a panel that included Ken Auletta

('77), Fred Dressier ('63), Morton Janklow ('50), Robert Miron ('59), John Sykes ('77), as well as University trustees Joyce Hergenhan ('63), Martin Bandier ('62), and Arielle Tepper ('94).

Meanwhile, Lubin House became more public and prominent as a second-floor room was designated a full-time gallery open to the public. Until then, Lubin House had been exclusively for SU-related visitors.[23] Well-publicized and high-profile exhibits of artists such as Milton Avery and photographer Gordon Parks, a noted African American photographer and filmmaker, were displayed.[24] In 2003, the gallery got a major upgrade through a gift from Louise ('44) and Bernard Palitz, with an inaugural exhibit of works by William Blake.

SU/celebrity synergy reached a high point with a dinner honoring Ken Auletta, a journalist and media critic for the *New Yorker*, part of the Condé Nast magazine empire owned by the Newhouse family. Auletta earned a master's degree in political science from the Maxwell School in 1965. Joint invitations from the Shaws and Donald and Susan Newhouse went out to 237 people and their guests, a who's who list of New York–based political, television, and literary celebrities. Among them were Mario Cuomo, Michael Bloomberg, Ted Koppel, Nora Ephron, David Hallberstam, Charlie Rose, Walter Isaacson, David Remnick, Vanessa Williams, Peter Jennings, Mike Wallace, Tom Brokaw, Aaron Sorkin, Gerry Stiller and Anne Meara, Joyce Carol Oates, Bill Safire, as well as a host of SU alumni, deans, administrators, and trustees. On June 6, 2000, before a room full of glitterati at the New York Public Library Trustee Room, Shaw presented Auletta with the Chancellor's Medal. Celebrating the reason they were all there, Susan Newhouse wore a gown of orange—SU's signature color. Like the Arents for Ahrens, Auletta's Chancellor's Medal was the first given in New York.

One year later, Donald and Susan Newhouse would again lend their prominent names, and more, to a George Arents Award event. The invitation from the Shaws and Newhouses was for an event on the top floor of the Condé Nast Building at 4 Times Square. The recipient was the building's designer, architect Bruce Fowle ('60). The forty-eight-story building had opened in January 2000 as one of the first green-design skyscrapers in the United States. Cocktails

were served in the building's mechanical room, amid the environ-
mentally friendly gas-fired absorption chillers. Afterward, Fowle
wrote a note to Shaw: "I haven't felt so 'orange' and so proud since
the 1959 football season!"[25] For the first time in its history, Syracuse
University's development program in New York City was firing on
all cylinders.

Baker was winding down his university relations post when,
in August 2000, the university appointed John Sellars, a former
minister and accountant, to replace him. Sellars came from Michigan Tech, a small, public research university in the state's Upper
Peninsula, where he had been the senior vice president of advancement and marketing.[26] Prior to his college development work, he
had worked as an accountant and a minister for the Community
of Christ Church, a small offshoot of the Church of Jesus Christ of
Latter-Day Saints. As the new senior vice president for institutional
advancement, Sellars would oversee all aspects of the newly named
Division of Institutional Advancement, including operations in New
York City, taking over a staff of 150 and a budget of more than
$10 million.[27] Sellars had been recommended by Shaw's old mentor,
James Fisher, who served as consultant for the search committee and
recommended Sellars as "first-rate."[28]

In an unusual arrangement, Shaw kept Walsh in New York and
promoted him to vice president of leadership gifts, ensuring that
Walsh would continue working with SU's top donor prospects, most
of whom lived in New York City. Shaw did not want to interrupt
Walsh's momentum in New York and intended to optimize the talents of both men.[29] But the arrangement created a structural tension
between Sellars and Walsh that worsened over time. Methodical,
organized, and thorough, Sellars was more linear in his development
approach than Walsh and, like Shaw, a Midwesterner and not at
home in New York City. "Let's face it, John is not a New York City
boy, and I am not either," Shaw said.

Sellars was tasked with increasing annual giving and laying
the groundwork for the next capital campaign. To sweep through
alumni records and identify alumni donor prospects, he turned to
the New York–based consulting firm Marts and Lundy, which had

worked with Baker on the Commitment to Learning campaign. By August 2001, the firm had identified more than 10,000 new top prospects, highlighting the wealthiest 2,000 with the greatest potential for giving. Of those, nearly half—863—were from New York City and Nassau and Suffolk Counties. On the West Coast, 161 were from the Los Angeles, Long Beach area. The rest were scattered around the Northeast.

Sellars's formulaic approach was reflected in his monthly reports to the trustees' Executive Committee, printed on day-glow orange or pink paper and always beginning with the Development Office's mission statement. He organized the printing of an alumni directory and launched the Quad's "Orange Grove" paver campaign in front of Bowne Hall.

Roughly two and a half years into his job, Sellars told Shaw that the new capital campaign, slated to begin in 2003, had to be postponed another two years. Eleven staff members had left the advancement office, and while he had hired five new ones, he was having a hard time getting more. It was a national problem, he said. Sellars was also having trouble getting deans to cooperate with him, especially those who for years had been conducting their own school-based fund-raising.

Sellars did set the stage for the next fund-raising campaign, for which neither he nor Shaw would be around. He established better tracking systems for monitoring the performance of development staff and more regular contacts with major donor prospects. "If John was disappointed by anything it was that he felt he could do more in New York City and Tom thought that was his place," said Shaw. "If there was criticism of John, I think it came from certain New York City donors."[30]

Before leaving the chancellorship, Shaw ensured that Walsh would maintain a prominent role in the university's Development Office. At a trustee Executive Committee meeting in March 2003, Shaw introduced a deferred compensation agreement for Walsh that provided incentives for him to stay on through the Cantor transition and an additional incentive to stay on staff until 2010. Trustees unanimously approved the agreement.

In so many areas of development and fund-raising, Shaw furthered and expanded upon what had been in place: relationships were being built, projects and programs were being discussed, big donors were beginning to commit, and trustees were expected to give generously. Together with strong investment gains through most of the 1990s, it seemed as if Shaw's goal of "doubling our endowment and reserves" could be achieved.[31] The market would fall, though, and then came 9/11.

CHAPTER 12

9/11

Retrenchment

SEPTEMBER 11, 2001—a day that stunned and changed the world, no less impacted SU. Before that dark Tuesday, Syracuse University's development program in New York City was achieving success in ways it never had before. Plans for $180 million in new and renovated buildings were progressing, which would rely in part on endowment money that had grown substantially over ten years. At least $50 million in endowment money had been assigned to academic initiatives. All this slowed or was temporarily halted as the stock market dove after 9/11, slashing SU's endowment and forcing administrators to scale back plans and search for where they could cut expenses.

In New York City, two blocks south of the World Trade Center, students at SU's partner school, the High School for Leadership and Public Service, at 90 Trinity Place, had to be evacuated. The engine of the second plane that struck the South Tower landed on the school's roof. School personnel led students from the fourteen-story building to Battery Park, where most were put on ferries to Staten Island or New Jersey. In the 9/11 aftermath, the school was used as a morgue.

More than anything, though, the shock, scale, and emotional trauma of 9/11 was hard to comprehend. Four airliners hijacked by nineteen al-Qaeda terrorists crashed in the eastern United States, killing 2,996 people and injuring more than 6,000. Two planes crashed into the North and South Towers of the World Trade Center complex. An hour and forty-two minutes after the first crash, both 110-story towers collapsed. SU lost more than twenty alumni. At least sixteen students lost close relatives and friends, and one student lost a parent.[1]

The immediate campus reaction unfolded over days and was marked not just by a reeling sense of shock but by a sense of déjà vu for those who had been around SU more than a dozen years. It was December 21, 1988, when an onboard bomb exploded during Pan Am 103's flight from England, killing thirty-five students returning from a semester of study abroad. All 259 passengers and crew members on that flight were killed, as were eleven residents of Lockerbie, Scotland, where the plane crashed. The Pan Am bombing had given the university community an institutional memory of what to do in the face of sudden tragedy. On 9/11, a crisis management team that had been forged in the aftermath of the Pan Am episode shifted into gear.

The core twelve-member crisis management team was co-chaired by Judy O'Rourke, director of undergraduate studies, and Mary Jo Custer, director of student affairs and associate to the vice president for student affairs. O'Rourke had been at the center of the university's Pam Am Flight 103 response. By noon on 9/11, the team's numbers had grown to seventy, with multiple subcommittees that created plans for Shaw's cabinet to review (see appendix H). Kevin Morrow, executive director of the Office of News Services, and his team fashioned the university's official responses to the terrorist attacks and daily campus emails with updates about events and developments.

Their first decision was to continue to hold classes, which were seen as a natural, structured gathering place for students and faculty to support one another. At 3 p.m., a university-wide assembly was held at Hendricks Chapel. Every seat was filled, people stood along walls upstairs and down, and concern and grief were palpable. For the next two days, Shaw held briefings at the chapel to update the campus on what had been learned and what new programs and services were being offered. "I felt it was necessary for people to know I was there for them, and to know what I was thinking," Shaw said.[2]

Kimmel Food Court and the Schine Student Center remained open all night for students to watch television or just to be together. Students used AOL Instant Messenger for personal updates. (Facebook

On the afternoon of September 11, 2001, the SU community filled every corner of Hendricks Chapel for an impromptu memorial service. Courtesy of University Archives, Syracuse University Libraries.

was not launched until 2004.) Counseling was offered. Phone banks were set up so that anxious students could contact their families, though most students had cell phones.

People sought action to move beyond their feelings of helplessness and grief. At an on-campus blood drive in Maxwell Hall, thousands tried to give blood, swamping the staff; there was capacity for only 106. Hundreds more donated blood at a downtown drive days later, and campus blood drives continued through the semester. A shirt and sock drive for World Trade Center rescue workers filled a seventeen-foot truck that took the goods downstate. The Student Government Association laid bedsheets in the Quad on which hundreds of students, faculty, and staff recorded their thoughts. On September 20, Shaw, together with SUNY Upstate Medical University president Gregory L. Eastwood and SUNY ESF president Cornelius B. Murphy Jr., led hundreds in a march from the Quad to Clinton Square in downtown Syracuse for a community memorial event, We Stand Together: A Gathering of Hope and Healing. A campus memorial service for the twenty alumni and sixteen parents and loved ones who died in the attacks was held on October 8.

SU's football game scheduled for September 15 against East Carolina was rescheduled for September 29, and other sporting events—women's volleyball and soccer, cross country, and field hockey—also had their September 15 events canceled.

The following week, SU's September 22 game at the Carrier Dome against Auburn University was played as scheduled and became a symbolic and cathartic event, broadcast nationally on ESPN. A crowd of 43,403 spectators, the largest sports crowd in the state since September 11, patiently endured enhanced security screenings at the Dome's entrance and waved small American flags that had been placed on each seat as they listened to Governor George Pataki address the terrorist attack. "While those evil criminals have been able to break our hearts, they haven't been able to break our spirit," he said. "The American people are stronger and stand more unified than ever before."[3] SU defeated the Auburn Tigers 31–14.

The attacks generated near hysteric suspicion toward Muslims nationwide, something that President George W. Bush had spoken out against in a speech six days after the attack.[4] Attempting to allay fears on campus, the Graduate Muslim Student Organization held weekly information events on Islamic culture and traditions. The university's Graduate Student Organization designated a week in November as Islamic Recognition Week to promote dialogue about the culture. David Rubin, Newhouse dean, chaired a University Forum initiative that scheduled weekly events with faculty discussing topics relevant after the attacks: "An Overview of the Taliban"; "The US and the Muslim World—How We See Each Other"; "US Foreign Policy in the Middle East: Is This the Key to Peace?" and more. Out of those forum discussions would evolve a new undergraduate major in religion and society that examines the ways religion interacts with other aspects of public affairs, such as politics, diplomacy, law, and business.[5]

On October 9, the University Lectures series kicked off.[6] Planned as a series long before 9/11, the first lecture began with former US Senate majority leader George Mitchell, at the time the US special envoy to Northern Ireland, who spoke about peace initiatives.

Three weeks after the 9/11 attacks, on October 2, Shaw gave his State of the University address, originally scheduled for September 13. It was the most personal and heartfelt speech he gave at Syracuse. He stressed the importance of connecting with and supporting one another, of tolerance, and of finding healthy ways to cope in stressful times. "Pray, meditate, and appreciate the sanctity of life," he said. "Tomorrow is never promised." He spoke of the university as a place where the search for truth can be pursued without fear of reprisal, and he warned against drawing absolute conclusions based on the attack. "Let's not forget that humankind's most egregious offenses have been committed by people who were sure they were right. From the Inquisition to the Nazi Holocaust to the attacks of September 11, we can see the destruction created by zealotry."[7]

Financially, 9/11 was a blow to SU, as it was to the entire country. The most pressing concern was SU's 13 percent endowment portfolio losses and the implications those would have on expansion plans. The country's recession had been well underway before the attacks. The internet bubble had burst, bringing the Dow Jones Industrial Average from a high of 11,722 on January 14, 2000, to a low of 9,796 on March 7, 2000. The 9/11 attacks drove the Dow to 8,920, and threats of war kept it sliding until it bottomed out on October 9 at 7,286—a 37.8 percent decline from its peak. Just as SU was planning to invest part of its endowment in a bolstered academic plan (A-SPIRE), along with new buildings and renovations, that endowment was shrinking. Since July, its endowment, now at $611 million, had decreased by $97 million, or 13.7 percent.

The economic pinch and the fear around it persisted into the next year, when Shaw noted that a reduced endowment distribution would mean projected budget deficits for five of the next six years, and he braced trustees for worse possibilities: a continued recession, a further drop in the stock market, and cuts in federal aid, all of which could prompt another restructuring exercise.[8] Those were the worst-case scenarios, and contingency plans had to be made. Nevertheless, he renewed commitment to invest in the academic and space plans, but only after pausing. The university would not borrow more money until the economy stabilized, Shaw told trustees in

November 2001.[9] Meanwhile, the School of Management project and the nearby parking garage would continue to go forward.

SU would cut where it could. Already, the university was decreasing the number of doctoral programs. Four faculty positions in the sociology PhD program had been eliminated. Twenty-one doctoral programs in the School of Education were reduced to six. The university would invest strategically where it made most sense. There would be more pain, Shaw told trustees. "We will not, I repeat, will not utilize the extra dollars you've made available to maintain everyone's budget at the present level." The academic plan and space plan were the university's top priorities. Something would have to give. In the search for weaknesses to prune away, one school and one affiliated auxiliary were identified—Nursing and Syracuse University Press.

Nursing

SU's College of Nursing had been a target for closure from the start of Shaw's tenure. It was a hard decision to make. It had a proud tradition—founded during World War II, it was retained when SU's medical school was transferred to the state system in 1950. The College of Nursing offered the only baccalaureate nursing degree in the Syracuse area and offered master's degrees as well. However, it was small and expensive for the university to operate. In 1991, nursing was the only college for which the university met full financial aid for all students. Its enrollment that year of 138 had dropped to one-third of its 1980 enrollment, due in large part to the growth of nearby hospital-based nursing programs.

Eggers's Ad Hoc Advisory Committee suggested nursing be consolidated with the social work and human development programs. The committee's assessment of nursing was blunt: "A fundamental problem appears to be that an insufficient number of prospective undergraduate students in Nursing are willing to pay for four years of private university costs." The committee also noted that "nursing faculty do not have a strong record of scholarship."[10]

Grace Chickadonz, the college's dean, tried mightily to turn the program around and grow enrollment with existing staff. She had come to SU in 1987, recruited as dean from the Medical College of

Ohio in Toledo. Shortly after arriving, she was "shocked" to find the lack of regard among influential people on campus for SU's nursing program. "They wanted Syracuse to be Cornell, and Cornell didn't have nursing," she said.[11] In 1993, the college formed the Center for Nursing and Health Care to develop innovative health care approaches. Presumably, the focus on innovation would strengthen the college's reputation and attract research funding. Enrollment did grow—by 1996, undergraduate enrollment had risen to 368, an increase of 166 percent.

The following year, however, enrollment dropped. The "quality of our programs has declined," Chickadonz complained to Vincow, saying that faculty were overworked and morale was low. Attempting to boost graduate student enrollment, she pushed to develop new campus and online programs. Chief among them was the Family Nurse Practitioner program, into which SU accepted sixty-six students in 1997. The state Education Department had not yet approved it and had warned the college not to launch it without certification. Nevertheless, it began offering the program in September, and Chickadonz was anxious about its status with the state. "We must gain this approval in order to keep the students who are already enrolled and to recruit new ones," she wrote Vincow. "We will have a public relations nightmare on our hands if we do not achieve this." Months later, Chickadonz's worst fears came to pass. As the spring 1998 semester wound down, the college informed Family Nurse Practitioner students that the program for which they were just completing their first year was not certified and that none of the credit hours they had accrued would count toward a degree.[12]

The state had not approved the program because of low licensing test scores of undergraduates and because there were too few faculty to teach the specialty.[13] Some students sued. The public relations nightmare played out in courts, which killed enrollment. In 1999, SU paid a total of $1.1 million to thirty current and former graduate students, compensating them for tuition and other costs.[14] Thirteen others rejected the settlement and sued for at least $13 million.

In September 1998, Chickadonz resigned as dean to begin a "study leave." That same month, Vincow announced that he would step down at the end of the academic year. SU offered to reimburse

students for the tuition they paid for courses that would not transfer to another school. Cecilia Mulvey, who had served as associate
dean, was put in place as nursing's interim dean.

September 11, 2001, and its economic aftermath was nursing's
death knell, but the college's final expiration took time. When Freund
first identified the program as a possible source of cost reduction in
her November 2001 report to trustees, every option—from reinven-
tion to closure to new mergers and partnerships—was being considered. Freund had asked SUNY Upstate Medical University president
Gregory Eastwood if Upstate would like to absorb SU's College of
Nursing. The medical university was not interested.

One of Freund's first tasks when she arrived on campus was to
resolve the nursing program mess, and she had quickly merged it
with the College of Human Development and the School of Social
Work into the College for Human Services and Health Professions
(HSHP). The merger fit her overall A-SPIRE Plan for collaboration
across disciplines. Trustees approved the merger plan in April 2000,
William Pollard was named dean, and HSHP officially opened on
July 1, 2001. While the merged HSHP made sense in theory, it faced
a good deal of obstacles. Many faculty were not interested in working together as one college, which was spread across campus in eight
different spaces.[15] Meanwhile, the nursing program's enrollment was
dwindling, and its Family Nurse Practitioner problems and resulting
litigation had damaged the college's reputation and hindered recruitment. In 2000, *U.S. News & World Report* had ranked SU's nursing graduate program No. 103. By 2002, graduate enrollment had
declined to such an extent that the college admitted no graduate
students that fall.[16]

Administrators began formulating a closure rationale that
would be acceptable to the university community. Closing would
save about $1 million a year that would be used to add sections to
popular courses that university students were being closed out of, a
move that would help overall student retention. SU's nursing program had a hard time competing with those at public universities,
Freund noted. A New York State resident could earn a bachelor's
degree in nursing at SUNY Binghamton for an annual tuition of
$4,549, as opposed to SU's annual tuition of $21,954.

Furthermore, nursing's alumni and faculty did not bring much money to the university. Gifts from nursing alumni in 2002 totaled $44,089, less than one-half of 1 percent of the $27,270,658 in gifts all schools and colleges recorded for the year. Similarly, nursing faculty brought in $474,174 in sponsored research money that same year, roughly 1 percent of the total $46,340,034 in awards recorded for all SU units.

The final decision came in the late fall of 2002 after a series of procedural moves that suggested there was a choice, but there really was not. The University Senate's Academic Affairs Committee voted unanimously to close the College of Nursing; the full senate's vote was very close, 73–68, in favor of closing a program that had been in place since 1943. SU administrators and trustees were deluged with letters of protest from nursing alumni and area health professionals. Part of Freund's closure rationale had a familiar ring. She had adapted Eggers's aspirational catchphrase to higher education's new zeitgeist: closing nursing was necessary "in order to move the University to the next level of academic excellence."[17]

Syracuse University Press

SU Press was another post-9/11 concern. The press's financial state had been a concern since Shaw arrived. It published between 100 and 120 books a year and needed university subsidies of between $300,000 and nearly $450,000 annually to balance its books.[18] That was not unusual for university presses, which tended to publish books that had more scholarly than commercial appeal. Freund was not sure the existence of the press helped recruit faculty or brought the university the prestige it claimed.[19] Yet it had a long history, beginning in 1943 under Chancellor Tolley to foster and disseminate the faculty's scholarly work.

Enter Peter Webber, SU's director of auxiliary services. Webber did a comprehensive business analysis of SU Press and took steps to balance the operation's budget. Among a host of changes, he reduced the number of published titles and reprints by nearly a third, raised prices on some books, and cut positions that were vacant. He suggested more closely analyzing the market potential for new books before signing contracts. A fund-raising campaign was started. By 2003, with Webber guiding it, SU Press was nearly breaking even.[20]

Taking the Show on the Road

New York City fund-raising essentially came to a halt after 9/11, and it was more than a year before it resumed. The Shaws turned their fund-raising attention westward and, in their last four years, took dozens of trips across the country pursuing big "naming" gifts. In California, they visited Dick Clark ('51), "America's Oldest Teenager," and Arthur Rock ('48), the legendary Silicon Valley investor, and developed close relationships with Marilyn ('42) and Bill Tennity and Karen ('68) and Gary Winnick.

At the Winnicks', while Karen and Mary Ann talked about literacy, Gary and Buzz occasionally played one-on-one basketball. After one such visit when Shaw had to borrow sneakers to play, he sent the Winnicks three pairs of SU Nike sneakers, which included a pair for the Winnicks' trainer, with a note, "Perhaps the enclosed will help your game."

The kind of grand Arents events SU had staged in New York were toned down on the road, but the formula of creating spectacle with celebrity guests still held. Marilyn Tennity was awarded an Arents medal in April 2000 in Indian Wells, California, among family and friends. One speaker was Irma Kalish, who had received an Arents medal in 1997 and had been a television scriptwriter for popular shows like *My Three Sons*, *I Dream of Jeannie*, and *Gunsmoke*. As Kalish approached the podium, a pianist played a medley of the shows' theme songs. Marilyn and William Tennity had donated the naming gift for the Tennity Ice Skating Pavilion, which opened on South Campus in 1999, and Marilyn would be a major donor in a future Life Sciences complex.

In Chicago, Renée Schine Crown ('50) was awarded an Arents medal in the Ritz Carlton Hotel on April 3, 2002. Crown and her husband, Lester, had contributed $3 million in the 1980s for the Schine Student Center, in honor of her parents, Hildegarde and J. Meyer Schine. Renée's father was founder and chairman of the 160-movie-theater chain, Schine Enterprises, which was headquartered in Gloversville, New York. Renée and trustee chairman Joe Lampe had grown up together in Gloversville. Crown had recently made another donation to create the Renée Crown University Honors Program, which awards $5,000 annually to seniors to complete their honors capstone project.

At the Ritz Carlton event, Mary Karr, SU's celebrated poet and memoirist, read one of her poems to honor Crown and then introduced "Syracuse University's next poet laureate." Shaw stepped to the podium and read his own Seuss-like verse:

> I am tongue-tied, I am flummoxed,
> I search for words to say,
> to describe just how wonderful is our very own Renée.
> If I pile words upon words, I'll still leave too much out.
> Her many friends will point at me and shout,
> "You fool! You left this out and that and much, much more!"
> In my feeble effort to pay her homage, I'll only make them sore.
> Instead, please join me in gratitude for each and every day,
> that our lives have been touched and blessed by our very own
> Renée.[21]

Away from the pretensions of New York, Shaw could more easily be himself.

*   *   *

The S. I. Newhouse School of Public Communications, led by its dean, David Rubin, was a consistent bright spot through the Shaw era. Rubin came to SU in 1990 from New York University, where he had chaired the journalism department. He earned his bachelor's degree in history from Columbia University and his master's and doctorate in communications from Stanford University. An opinionated and devoted educator—he taught every semester as dean—Rubin took over Newhouse at a time when the nationally renowned journalism school needed strong leadership.[22] Its previous dean, Edward Stephens, had resigned in 1988 after a faculty vote of no-confidence, and the school had been without a permanent dean for two years.

The Newhouse School was an enrollment engine for SU, attracting so many high-quality applicants that the university routinely made "alternate offers" to those not admitted to Newhouse, entering them in another school with the assurance that they could apply to transfer to Newhouse in their sophomore or junior year if their GPA was 3.5 or above.[23] Newhouse would admit about 150 internal transfers a year.[24] In 1990, Newhouse was the source of 810 alternate offers, which shored up enrollment in other schools, like the College for Human Development.[25] The alternate offer was not exclusive to Newhouse applicants, but the school had the lion's share. In 1995, 47 percent of freshmen at human development were there as an alternate because their first choice was not available.

As Rubin renewed and expanded the school's strengths, he furthered good relations with the school's major benefactors, the Newhouse family, which owned the publishing and communications empire Advance Publications, Inc. Major Newhouse family support began in 1962 when Samuel I. Newhouse pledged $15 million for two buildings to house the journalism school. The first building opened in 1964 at a dedication attended by President Lyndon Johnson, who used the occasion to announce an escalation of the Vietnam War after an incident in the Gulf of Tonkin. The second building, Newhouse II, designed to support broadcast television and radio journalism, was dedicated in 1974.

Newhouse's two sons, Samuel Jr. and Donald, attended SU and, after their father's death in 1979, continued supporting the school with annual donations that funded five endowments. Rubin, Jewish like the Newhouses, shared Donald's interest in opera, and they would frequently attend with their wives, Tina Press, who also taught at the journalism school, and Susan Marley Newhouse, who had grown up in Syracuse.[26]

Under Rubin, Newhouse was one of the first schools to assemble a board of advisors, and it was a strong one, composed of top executives who were closely involved with the school professionally and financially. It included Anthony Malara ('58), a former president of CBS television, Robert Miron ('59), then president of Advance/Newhouse Communications in Syracuse, and Steve Rogers ('62), editor and publisher of the *Post-Standard*. Advance was the parent company of the *Post-Standard*. Miron, besides being a top Newhouse executive, was a first cousin to Donald and Samuel Jr.

Donald Newhouse announcing his family's $15 million gift to construct Newhouse III. David Rubin, Newhouse dean, at left, with Shaw. Courtesy of University Archives, Syracuse University Libraries.

In the late 1990s, as the school assessed its space needs—computer labs and an auditorium among them—it determined that a building to contain all this would cost at least $30 million and that "without a Newhouse gift it wasn't going to happen," said Rubin. To demonstrate that the school was not solely reliant on Newhouse largesse, Rubin drew financial assistance from foundations supported by Newhouse media competitors—the Hearst and Knight Foundations—as well as alumni working for Newhouse competitors, which further affirmed the school's reputation within the industry. Yet the Newhouses were hesitant to commit another major gift for a building. Rogers and especially Miron helped make the case with them of the gift's necessity, and when Shaw secured it, the Newhouse brothers made it clear that the gift would honor their father's legacy. Announced in April 2003, the gift, along with previous Newhouse family gifts, was among the largest ever received by the university.

The 74,000-square-foot building, with computer laboratories, a café, and a 350-seat auditorium, would be designed by the

Polshek Partnership architectural firm. James Stewart Polshek, the firm's principal design partner, had worked for I. M. Pei, whose firm collaborated on the first Newhouse building that was completed in 1964. A year after announcing the Newhouse gift, the school reported the start of the Goldring Arts Journalism program, named for Lola ('51) and Allen Goldring, of Long Island, who donated the $1 million to create it. It was the first master's program in arts journalism in the nation.

*   *   *

Martin J. Whitman was one of the university's most generous givers, another of the self-made, Jewish business leaders in New York City. The son of Polish immigrants, Whitman grew up in the Bronx, served in the Navy in the Pacific during World War II, attended SU on the GI Bill, and graduated magna cum laude in 1949 with a bachelor's degree in business administration. He pursued graduate studies at Princeton University and at New York University, earning a master's in economics from the New School for Social Research in 1956. Whitman was the founder and co-chief investment officer of Third Avenue Management. He spoke to SU management classes, gave to the Our Time Has Come campaign, and created a $1 million-plus Martin and Lois Whitman Endowed Scholarship for minority graduate students in the School of Management.

It was his $25 million pledge to rename the management school for which he is most recognized. The donation, announced in 2003, cleared the way for construction of a $40 million, 160,000-square-foot building at Marshall and East Adams Streets, something that had been in the works since completion of the space plan in 1999. The building would be designed by Fox & Fowle Architects, the firm cofounded by Bruce Fowle, a 2001 Arents award winner, for the sum of $4,154,682.[27]

*   *   *

Arielle Tepper was a design/technical theater student when the Shaws arrived. Her mother died in her freshman year and left instructions in her will for Tepper to donate a portion of her estate. While still a student, Tepper made a gift to SU, unusual enough that Geraldine Sheinkopf, an associate director of development, arranged a meeting with Tepper. The two formed a bond, and Sheinkopf introduced Tepper to Mary Ann Shaw, who was a board member of Syracuse Stage.

SU's design/tech program was small, with just a few teachers. Tepper was not happy with it and shared her frustrations with Sheinkopf and Mary Ann, whom she would meet with for lunch each semester. After Tepper graduated in 1994, Sheinkopf told her the university would like her to join the Board of Trustees, and in 1999, at age 23, Tepper became the youngest SU trustee ever.

Tepper had seen much theater in London as a student in SU's DIPA program, and she was determined to produce big theater shows herself. She also understood the difficulty of transitioning from school to professional life in theater and conceived of a program that would provide students with career advice from casting directors, producers, and others in the business. It would be like a study abroad program, only in New York City. Sheinkopf worked on the idea with Tepper, and the program started as a week in New York during spring break and then a few weeks in June. When Sheinkopf died suddenly in 2001, Tom Walsh stepped in, a natural fit with his theater background. A semester program on campus began, with professional directors and writers coming to SU. Tepper provided additional funding to get a longer, more in-depth program started in New York, and the Tepper Semester began there in 2005, largely as Tepper first conceived it, with a mix of SU theater students and students from other schools. "I wanted people to feel that when they came to the school they wouldn't be left in the dark when they graduated," she said.

At Syracuse, as everywhere, life would go on after 9/11. Its ambitions, dreams, and momentum were too powerful to be held back.

CHAPTER 13
Research and More
Reclaiming the Legacy

A DREAM held by economic development officials in the late twentieth century was to replicate the remarkable success of the Stanford Research Park in California and the North Carolina Research Triangle Park. Both had opened in the 1950s with collaborations between universities and technology businesses. Across the United States, close to twenty universities established research parks in the 1970s and another ninety-five in the 1980s.

In New York, area business leaders, among them SU trustee chair H. Douglas Barclay, had been discussing an SU research park before Shaw arrived—it was No. 9 on Eggers's list of priorities for a new chancellor. The state had laid the groundwork with a study in the late 1980s to determine where best to locate several university-based research parks.[1] The city of Syracuse was identified as one place, and the Skytop area of SU's South Campus was selected as the optimal site. The university already had a prime tenant at Skytop—Syracuse Research Corporation (SRC), which had expressed interest in extending its building lease beyond 1999. SRC was created at SU in 1957 as Syracuse University Research Corporation to do high-tech consulting work for the government. It had split off as its own not-for-profit on campus and seemed to embody the perfect research park tenant.

Shaw was cautious about undertaking a research park. "I thought it was a good idea if we could get money for it," he said. Achieving a version of the Stanford park's success, which led to Silicon Valley, would require a host of particular conditions and circumstances, none of which Syracuse had: expensive land, a growing population, an airport with direct flights to many major cities, and a critical mass of university professors who regularly collaborated with businesses.[2] While SU's CASE Center fostered relationships with businesses, restructuring cuts had reduced the number of faculty, especially in technology and science.

Nevertheless, planning began and was led by the Metropolitan Development Agency (MDA), a Syracuse-based business development organization with which Eggers had served and to which Shaw was appointed. The state's Urban Development Corporation (UDC) provided $50,000 for a feasibility study, and the University Hill Corporation, an MDA affiliate, kicked in $10,000. Peter Webber, SU's director of auxiliaries, was put in charge. The park, which was "expected to create up to 2,000 permanent jobs," would encompass ninety acres at Skytop's summit, a location once considered for the Carrier Dome and near to I-481 to the south.[3] The state provided $1.45 million in grants to construct a road with sewer, water, and utilities, and groundbreaking took place on November 21, 1994, an inauspiciously rainy and windy day when SU staff had to scramble to keep the groundbreaking tent from blowing away during the ceremony.[4]

As SRC's lease neared its final days, the company pitched a hard offer: it would construct a building in the research park, but it wanted SU to provide land rent-free.[5] No one could know that in a few years SRC would expand several times over as a major Defense Department contractor with billions of dollars in sales.[6] SU would not concede on the land deal, and SRC moved to a North Syracuse industrial park. Coming on the heels of restructuring cuts, SRC's departure further antagonized professors in engineering and computer science, who saw the company's exit as another indication that SU was letting its research stature slip away.[7] The opportunity to collaborate with SU professors was clearly not enough of an incentive for SRC to stay. In fact, SU's relationship with the company had grown chilly, said Ben Ware, vice president of research. "There was essentially no collaboration."[8]

Other potential research park tenants came along, but none signed up. Sensis Corporation, a Dewitt-based maker of air-traffic, radar, and surveillance equipment, ultimately chose a corporate park in Dewitt. Onondaga County considered the research park for a new crime lab and medical examiner's office. University administrators were concerned about the garish association some would make with the medical examiner's office on campus, and Webber assured them it would be a low-key operation, with only 400 post-mortems a year, delivered in a nondescript van. OnLab made its new home near SUNY Upstate Hospital.

Getting a tenant in the state-funded research park was going to take more state money, and, in 2001, it looked like the university could get some. SU embarked on a planning and lobbying campaign of an intensity not seen since the effort to finance the Dome in the late 1970s.[9] Success came, but dictated by a governor's political priorities, the result looked much different from what anyone at SU had wanted or expected.

The idea for a state-funded building in the research park began as the park itself had, with a business association's white paper. This one was called Vision 2010 and grew out of a planning exercise led by the MDA. It identified environmental systems engineering as a Central New York specialty; there were a number of local businesses in the field, and university research on the topic was already underway. Environmental systems engineering looks at how multiple factors interact on environments and human health, indoor and out.

To support the white paper's findings, the MDA organized a large group of environmental research collaborators that included SU, SUNY ESF, SUNY Upstate Medical University, and dozens of area businesses, named the New York Indoor Environmental Quality Center, Inc. (NYIEQC).[10]

Meanwhile, Edward Bogucz, dean of the College of Engineering and Computer Science, was hiring faculty and seeking grants to support an environmental engineering focus that would align the college with the work of local companies. His goal was to create something similar to SU's CASE Center in computer software engineering, which opened in 1984 with state funding.[11]

In 1999, as Governor George Pataki was gearing up to run for a third term, he announced a competitive funding program for universities to create Strategically Targeted Academic Research (STAR) centers that would focus on high-tech fields and create jobs. SU requested $24.7 million for environmental quality systems research and received $15.9 million, which provided money for capital infrastructure and equipment. The next year, SU learned that Pataki would be proposing another technology initiative, this time to fund new buildings at universities, called Centers of Excellence (CoE). Each CoE would work with businesses focusing on a different technology.

The stars were aligning for SU, and no one was happier than Bogucz. The university had everything the state was looking for: a high-tech focus—environmental engineering—for which it was already receiving state money. It had business partners lined up with MDA support. At last there was an opportunity to get a building that would kick-start its research park. SU, in partnership with the MDA, submitted a proposal for a $35 million CoE grant, but when Pataki identified four CoE sites in his January 2001 State of the State address, Syracuse was not mentioned.

SU's Office of Government and Community Relations, led at the vice president level by Eleanor Ware, and the MDA, led by President Irwin Davis, kicked their CoE strategy into high gear and intensified their Albany effort. Beth Rougeux expertly spearheaded the lobbying, buttonholing every possible political ally. By March, Assemblyman William Magnarelli, D-Syracuse, and Senator Nancy Larraine Hoffmann, R-Fabius, were publicly calling for Pataki to name Syracuse University as a CoE site. In the ensuing months, Rougeux continued to arrange meetings with the governor's senior aides and Senate and Assembly leaders for Davis, Shaw, Ben Ware, Bogucz, and business leaders from NYIEQC.

As the big 2002 election year approached (Pataki and all 211 state lawmakers would be facing a vote), the Republican-controlled Senate launched its own technology funding initiative. It was called Gen*NY*sis (Generating Employment through New York Science) and would fund biotech/health/human performance research. SU unsuccessfully sought $15 million from the Gen*NY*sis program, which it had planned to invest at its Center for Science and Technology building—a disappointing development, but the prize SU most wanted was a building in its research park and that had seemed within sight.

In January 2002, Pataki announced that SU would get a CoE. The announcement was short on specifics but did stipulate one condition—to get $35 million from the state, SU had to raise $105 million from the private sector. SU had been getting financial commitments, but that figure presented a challenge, as headquarters of major manufacturers like Carrier were leaving Syracuse.[12] SU pushed its corporate partners for bigger financial commitments and sought federal funding through Representative James Walsh, who secured $7.6 million for research at the center.[13]

Manufacturers and tech companies were the CoE's natural partners, but it was mall builder Robert Congel and his Pyramid Management Group that pledged enough money to push SU over the $105 million it needed to release state funding. Pyramid was seeking approval for its planned $2 billion megamall, Destiny USA, which it was touting would be the world's "largest green building." Pyramid pledged $45 million and would apply CoE research findings toward its green megadream. Congel wanted the CoE to be the centerpiece of his "Petroleum Addiction Rehabilitation Park" on property in Salina where I-81 and the state Thruway intersect.[14] He had drawings made of a futuristic-looking complex with Syracuse University's S logo on a pedestal at the front of the property. There was no way SU officials could put a CoE there.

In June 2002, Pataki came to SU for a grand, election-year event in Goldstein Auditorium. With 400 dignitaries and public officials in the audience, Pataki pledged $22 million for SU's CoE, which, he said, would be built in SU's research park where other high-tech firms would follow. Both Pataki and Shaw exuberantly proclaimed that Central New York could be the next Silicon Valley.[15] With the STAR money the state had already committed, total state funding for the CoE would be $37 million.

Pataki's electioneering in Syracuse paid off. In October, the area's most prominent higher education leaders, Shaw, Gregory Eastwood, president of SUNY Upstate Medical University, and Neil Murphy, president of the SUNY College of Environmental Science and Forestry, published a column praising Pataki for his high-tech initiatives, and the governor was handily reelected.[16] Shortly after, however, the governor expressed dissatisfaction with the research park site. Pataki's senior policy advisor, Jeffrey Lovell, a Camillus native, was urging his boss to insist that the building be put where it could be seen by as many people as possible.

Shaw's administration considered more visible sites. At Skytop, a building could be put farther south, outside the existing research park but within view of I-481.[17] Or a CoE could be put on parking lot property west of the Dome, where it could be seen from I-81. But when administrators reconsidered all factors, including Pataki's concern for prominence, the best location was next to the Sci-Tech building. It would place the CoE on a public street, College Place, and near the CASE Center where staff could be shared and even more synergetic possibilities existed. SU was applying to the National Science Foundation (NSF) for designation as an Engineering Research Center, which would dovetail with CoE plans and could bring annual NSF funding of $2 million to $4 million. That NSF program only funded projects that were on a campus.

Lovell and Pataki were keen on vacant property within sight of I-690 and Erie Boulevard, at the corner of East Water and Almond Streets. The property had been occupied by Midtown Plaza, which the city had seized for unpaid property taxes and demolished. Before that, it was the site of the L. C. Smith & Corona Typewriter, Inc. factory, and solvents from the factory contaminated the ground.

Nothing about the site near Erie Boulevard appealed to SU administrators, so, in May 2003, Shaw traveled to Albany to tell Lovell why. The site was isolated, a mile northwest of campus, and too small for future expansion. Construction would cost more because of the clean-up needed, and ongoing operations would cost more because the university could not use its existing infrastructure for water, chilled water, steam heat, electric power, and digital networking. If the state wanted the CoE near Erie Boulevard, it would have to provide more money.

By October, no decision had been made and no state money had been released. Bogucz, who had recently been named CoE director, was exasperated. "There just needs to be some place, some physical place, where people can go and say, 'Gee, here are the leading edge technologies that monitor and control environments and leading edge energy systems for buildings and in urban settings,'" he told the

Post-Standard. Even Shaw displayed a rare moment of pique when he told the paper the planned CoE building was never intended to be a showpiece. It would be "a box that you put researchers in, and you have various kinds of rooms that you can control, so that you can do research in. It doesn't add to the landscape anywhere."[18]

The delay was hurting SU. Without a designated site, the university could not design the building or apply for release of funds. Other money that SU was applying for, including grants from the NSF, was being jeopardized because SU could not show firm plans for the CoE. With each passing month, it seemed more likely that some of SU's business partners would pull out. In fact, the university had a scare in 2003 when Carrier closed its manufacturing operation in Syracuse. Fortunately, Carrier's research and design center remained, keeping 300 jobs.

In his January 2004 State of the State address, Pataki confirmed the Syracuse CoE would be built at the off-campus site. He pledged a few weeks later another $4 million to purchase the property from the city, clean up the toxic site, and pay the additional costs Shaw had laid out. Construction would take three years, largely because of the extra time needed to remove toxic materials from the former industrial site.

Nearly five years of planning and intense lobbying had secured SU a new building off-campus in a location it had never considered, while its research park remained empty. Yet the CoE was a major victory for Bogucz, who as dean was struggling to bring the merged College of Engineering and Computer Science into the black. In 2002, the college had a structural operating deficit of nearly $1 million.

Whether the College of Engineering and Computer Science's restructuring could have been better handled is a question that lingers. The drastic cuts—combined faculty in the two colleges were reduced from 108 to 64—were necessary and justified, administrators say, because expenses had continued to increase while research quality had declined.[19] The deep cuts devastated faculty morale, hurt student and faculty recruitment, and cast a pall over the merged colleges that persisted for years. Adding to difficulties was that competition for engineering students had increased—there were at least twenty engineering programs in New York State alone.

In September 2003, when Bogucz was asked to head the CoE, Eric Spina, the chair of the Department of Mechanical, Aerospace, and Manufacturing Engineering, was named the new dean.

*　　*　　*

A few months before leaving his chancellor's position, Shaw committed the university's backing of two research professors who were seeking financial support for projects.[20] He announced the commitment to trustees in May, affirming his and Freund's desire to strengthen SU's research reputation.

The first was a $225,000 loan guaranty, which had been requested by Charles Driscoll, University Professor of civil and environmental engineering. Driscoll's work in the Adirondacks monitoring acid rain's damage to lakes and fish populations and his analyses of mercury levels in Onondaga Lake were widely recognized. Driscoll wanted SU to help purchase land in the White Mountain National Forest in New Hampshire for the Hubbard Brook Research Foundation, another place where he had been doing research. SU would join Cornell University, Dartmouth College, and several not-for-profits, each guaranteeing the same amount. Freund had agreed to cover any call on the university's guaranty with funds from her budget.

The other was for Sheldon Stone, SU's most eminent physicist.[21] Stone was the national spokesman for a $182 million multinational experiment at the Fermi National Accelerator Laboratory (Fermilab) in Illinois that would involve high-energy collisions of atoms to produce subatomic particles, called heavy quarks, using a particle detector array. Heavy quarks and heavy anti-quarks were present when the universe was created but largely disappeared as the universe cooled.[22] Stone was also directing the assembly of the machine that would detect those subatomic particles, using components that themselves took years to construct and needed to be paid for, sometimes before grant money came in.

SU had a recent history of supporting Stone's work. In 1999, SU had lobbied Congressman Walsh to contact NSF director Rita Colwell and to encourage her to fund Stone's research. Funding came and Stone was making progress. Shaw, in 2003, approved a $7.5 million forward-funded account from which Stone could draw. SU was expected to receive about $16 million in research funding through the experiment, known as the BTeV project. In 2005, the project was terminated by the US Department of Energy after being removed from President George W. Bush's budget.[23]

Association of American Universities

SU was ranked 145th nationally in overall research and development spending in 1999, which made vulnerable its continued membership in the Association of American Universities (AAU), the nation's premier organization of research institutions.[24] In the late 1990s, the AAU was looking to expel low-performing research universities, among them SU. The organization used research spending as a primary criterion for membership, and among the AAU's sixty members, only Catholic and Clark Universities had lower research and development (R&D) spending than SU. Another criterion was the number of faculty in one of the National Academies—Science, Engineering, or Medicine—and SU had only one, Josef J. Zwislocki, professor of neuroscience in the College of Engineering and Computer Science (Academy of Science).

Just as Freund was beginning as vice chancellor with a charge to strengthen SU's research profile, the AAU informed SU it was reviewing its membership status. Freund led a committee that prepared a report for the AAU, which expressed SU's belief that it provided the best undergraduate experience of any AAU university. The report emphasized that SU's true quality could not be measured by research dollars alone. Its MFA Creative Writing Program had world-class writers among its faculty, and while Maxwell, Newhouse, and the School of Architecture did not bring in great amounts of research money, they had top-ranked professional programs. SU's new academic plan, as well as its plan to build a new science building, strongly demonstrated SU's commitment to research.

Submission of the report would be followed, administrators presumed, by a visit from an AAU review committee, led by Harold Shapiro, president of Princeton University. But SU's report, authored chiefly by Ben Ware, so impressed the AAU committee that they did not need a site visit, Shapiro told Freund and Shaw on a conference call, and he welcomed SU to continue its AAU membership.[25]

Graduate Programs

The push to rebuild research at the university naturally focused on graduate programs and the need to strengthen their quality. Just as important was the need to clarify graduate program priorities. The student-centered emphasis on undergraduate learning had skewed graduate programs toward teaching, introducing things like the Future Professoriate initiative to help graduate students become better teachers. Meanwhile, the research focus of graduate programs had slipped.

In 2000, David Smith, dean of admissions and financial aid, took over responsibility for graduate admissions and tried to systematically recruit talented research graduate students. Smith found that SU's schools and colleges were even more territorial with their graduate programs than with their undergraduate programs, and he made little headway in turf battles over how recruitment campaigns would be run, as tensions between teaching and research played out anew. "Syracuse never really connected the dots between the talents and capabilities we were seeking to recruit and what they were going to be doing once they got on campus," he said. "Some [graduate students] ended up being really talented teachers but didn't have much to offer in the area of research."

SU never had difficulty meeting overall graduate student enrollment targets because demand exceeded supply, and "you could always fill up with Chinese students if you couldn't find anybody else," Smith said. A coordinated university-wide effort to strengthen graduate student support of research, however, did not gain traction. In 2001, 1,500 graduate students from more than 100 countries were studying at SU.[26]

*   *   *

Hiring and keeping top faculty became a priority in the late 1990s. The 1998 Middle States report had identified a need to improve faculty pay and to reduce workloads and pay disparities, something the University Senate had been calling on for years.[27] Fortunately, SU's endowment investments were growing appreciably, as were most everyone's in the United States in the mid- to late 1990s.

The 1990s economic boom, fueled by deregulation in financial markets, reductions in capital gains taxes, and overheated investments in dot-com and telecommunications firms, created the longest economic expansion in the history of the United States, helped wipe out the national deficit, and multiplied portfolio values.[28]

Two developments signaled the university's improved financial health. One came in 1998 when the university moved $160 million from its restricted, $200 million low-return, rainy-day Plant Fund to its endowment.[29] The 1998–99 year was the last year of the preexisting fiscal restructuring program, under which $3 million was transferred from the reserve to the budget to balance expenses. Thereafter, it was projected that tuition and revenues would amply balance the budget. The other came in 1999, when Standard & Poor's upgraded the university's bond rating (for $231 million in outstanding bonds) from A to A+, citing SU's "successful implementation of fiscal and academic restructuring between 1990 and 1998," leading to "an enhanced financial profile and improved academic standards."[30]

Thus, Shaw loosened the purse strings but, as with most every other financial decision, cautiously and strategically. In early 2000, trustees approved spending $1 million a year for ten years to establish some twenty Trustee Professorships.[31] The professorships granted each recipient an extra $30,000–$50,000 per year until they retired, left the university, or their performance declined. This action would not address the broader issue of pay disparity, but it might help keep the university's best and most vulnerable faculty. With the improved economy, other universities and colleges were actively head-hunting for talented faculty. Rutgers hired three young philosophy professors from SU in one fell swoop, with one telling the *Chronicle of Higher Education* his salary would increase $25,000 per year.[32]

Four faculty who were being wooed by other schools but decided to stay at SU thanks to the incentive funding were Doug Holtz-Eakin, professor and chair of the Department of Economics at the Maxwell School; Mary Karr, poet and professor of English in the Creative Writing Program; Robert Thompson, professor of radio, television, and film at the Newhouse School; and John Yinger, professor of economics and public administration at the Maxwell School.

Trustees also approved the creation of ten Alumni Professor-ships funded by $100,000 a year for up to five years. The money was to be solicited from donors, yet the commitment reflected a new confidence in the university's financial well-being and in its ability to secure funding for the professorships. Another fund, referred to as the Strategic Faculty Development Fund, was designed to reward and retain faculty, usually with onetime payments to cover costs like research and travel expenses, assistance from other scholars, or summer salaries so they could conduct research during those months. It began with $250,000 the first year and was expected to grow as donations came in to $1 million per year in four years. Money would be matched by deans. The first year, ninety-one pro-fessors benefited from the strategic fund.[33]

*   *   *

Under Freund's renewed emphasis on research, other changes were made. Cathryn Newton, who had been chair of the Department of Earth Sciences, was named dean of the College of Arts and Sciences in 2000 and soon began working on a plan to build a new Life Sci-ences complex, which was sorely needed. Existing labs for biology and chemistry were "worse than those found at some high schools," Freund told trustees.

Newton was the daughter of an oceanographer at Duke Uni-versity, had an extensive research background, and had a fighter's instincts, born of her years as the lone woman in the geology pro-gram at SU. She started at the university in 1983 as assistant profes-sor of geology and was named Teacher of the Year in 1991, an award sponsored by the Division of Higher Education and Ministry of the Methodist Church.

She graduated magna cum laude from Duke, earned a master's degree in geology from the University of North Carolina, and a doctorate in earth sciences from the University of California, Santa Cruz, where she developed an interest in invertebrate paleontology and mass extinctions.

As Newton began raising money for the Life Sciences complex, Shaw offered her some advice. "Many of the people whose homes you're going to visit make a lot less money than you do," he told

Cathryn Newton, the first woman dean of the College of Arts and Sciences. Courtesy of University Archives, Syracuse University Libraries.

her. "You have to see things through their eyes, put yourself in the position of the person who has scrimped and saved all their life in order to give money to Syracuse University." Ground would not be broken on the Life Sciences complex until 2006. It would open in 2008 and would be the largest academic building ever constructed at the university: 230,000 square feet, five stories tall, and connected by an atrium to the Center for Science and Technology.

                    *   *   *

As much as SU had reduced enrollment, the university faced a short-age of housing space and a continual need to upgrade its residential housing. Residence hall lounges and study rooms were converted to bedrooms to house an extra 173 students.[34] Upperclass students were moved out of residence halls and into Washington Arms, a brick apartment complex on lower Walnut Avenue. Additional freshmen were put into the former fraternity house of Lambda Chi Alpha, at 809 Walnut Avenue, which the university had purchased in 1997. Tens of millions of dollars were spent installing sprinkler systems, wiring residence halls for Ethernet, renovating rooms, and installing smaller bathrooms.

Marketing

Marketing a stronger, unified Syracuse University to its many, varied and widespread constituencies was a challenge. As SU pushed toward its $300 million Commitment to Learning campaign goal in the spring of 1997, it contracted Ruder Finn, a Washington, DC–based public relations firm, to assess its name recognition and marketing infrastructure. The firm had advised institutions like New York University, Columbia University, and the Massachusetts Institute of Technology. The firm's report was not good.

SU's institutional communications approach was "disassembled and uncoordinated," the firm found, and was having a "deleterious" effect on its image. Part of the difficulty came from competitiveness among SU's schools and colleges, which had increased under restructuring. Schools were promoting themselves independently, and some, like Newhouse and Maxwell, were so strong in their self-promotion that their connection to SU in the public's mind was almost an afterthought, Ruder Finn's report said. SU needed to be proactive, assertive, and coordinated to get its message out.

One consequence of weak public relations was that the local community had a one-dimensional view of SU that was built around sports. While the greater Syracuse community was intensely loyal toward SU athletics, it had little understanding of the progress or depth of SU's changes, the firm found. That observation was reinforced a few years later when Citistates, a civic consulting firm hired by the city of Syracuse, referred to SU as "a fortress on a hill," largely disconnected from the community.[35] SU's community outreach was not self-evident. The thousands of SU students who were mentoring city school students, the professors and students working with businesses through the CASE Center, and the collaborative performances of students and professionals at Syracuse Stage were not the things that came to mind when the public thought about SU.

Image making needed a consistent and concerted effort over time, a fact that Eric Mower, a trustee and ad agency executive, had been unsuccessfully harping on with Shaw for years. "I tried for thirteen years to get him to look at marketing as an opportunity for the university. I got nowhere," Mower said. "He just didn't get it."[36] As with so much else at the university, Shaw saw himself as the change agent. After Ruder Finn's report, SU's new public relations thrust would come from within, and Shaw would lead it. A new Commission on Strategic Communications was formed. The Department of Public Relations was renamed University Communications with five offices: Electronic Media Communications, Internal Communications, National Media Relations, News Services, and Publications. Robert Hill, vice president for public relations, left the university in 1998. Sandi Mulconry, a Newhouse/Arts and Sciences grad, became interim and then associate vice president for university communications. Kevin Morrow was named university spokesman, executive director of news services, and executive editor of the *Syracuse Record*.

A few years later, gearing up for a bigger fund-raising campaign and stung by the Citistates criticisms, Shaw agreed to hire a marketing firm.[37] Lipman Hearne, of Chicago, came on board in December 2003 to conduct marketing research and to analyze SU's institutional health and its branding effectiveness. Not surprisingly, the firm expanded upon critiques that Ruder Finn had laid out six years earlier. Individual schools and colleges remained separate and distinct in their marketing, pursuing their own branding campaigns and soliciting donations for their own endowments. The disparate strategies effectively watered down SU's identity and threatened to burden supporters with multiple requests for donations—from the institution as a whole and from individual schools and colleges. The university's competitive peers were "much more sophisticated," Lipman Hearne wrote.

Furthermore, discontent was stirring again among faculty and deans who felt that athletics was getting attention at the expense of academics and that professional schools were being emphasized to the detriment of others, Lipman Hearne found. The accelerating salary growth of the head basketball and football coaches did not help. Both Boeheim's and Pasqualoni's pay had surpassed Shaw's, and in most years, the differences grew greater. In 2002, Pasqualoni earned $793,538; in 2003, Boeheim earned $838,276, nearly double Shaw's salary.[38]

Faculty expressed other concerns over money—there was not enough to recruit and retain top-notch researchers or to implement the "blending" of academic fields outlined in Freund's academic plan. Efforts to implement Freund's interdisciplinary research and study seemed "scattershot." Faculty questioned whether Shaw's student-centered research university initiative would continue under Chancellor-elect Nancy Cantor.

The marketing firm cited the unsettling statistic that just 39 percent of Syracuse seniors would definitely choose Syracuse if they had to make their college decisions again.[39] More disheartening was that Syracuse still ranked poorly among its twelve peer institutions for scholarship and research.[40] SU's research expenditures lagged all but three of the institutions. It had the highest student acceptance rate (69 percent in 2002). Its retention and graduation rates were below the group average, and its population of nonwhite students was one of the lowest in the group—only Penn State's was smaller. SU was missing out with Asian students, which made up just 5 percent of its student body, while at Boston University, Cornell, New York University, Northwestern, Maryland, Penn, and SUNY Binghamton, they accounted for 12 percent or more of the student body.

As Shaw completed his final months at SU, the advice that trustee emeritus Robert F. Allen had offered in 1991 held as much significance as ever. Allen, the former CEO of Carrier Corporation, had told Shaw that SU needed to hire a top-notch marketing agency to promote itself. Without it, the student-centered research university vision would be lost on the public, and few would appreciate how significantly that vision had changed SU for the better.

I N 1999, Shaw's book *The Successful President* was published by Oryx Press in its American Council on Education (ACE) series (ACE is the nation's largest association of colleges and universities). A short guide for aspiring and current leaders, especially those in higher education, the book presented Shaw's Syracuse University restructuring story as a case study for institutional change. If Shaw's thinking behind actions was not always apparent, the book made it eminently clear that studied management strategies informed most of his actions, and many of them were grounded in firsthand experience. Shaw saw himself as a mentor to his administrators, welcomed questions from them, proffered advice, and assisted people like Freund and Sellars in ways that would help them become college presidents elsewhere.[1]

The Successful President encapsulated much of what those working closely with Shaw had come to understand: He partnered management principles with keen emotional intelligence and clear-eyed observation. He expected his administrators to collect information from all points of view. He assessed and decided, and was consistently transparent about the motives and trade-offs behind decisions. He had a strong ethos of kindness, and he acknowledged work well done. He understood the importance of being seen and being accessible. During nice weather, he frequently took breaks on a bench in the Quad, chatting with whomever came along, and after each commencement, he spent a good hour on the steps of Hendricks Chapel posing for photos with students.

Shaw possessed a rare combination of confidence and lack of pretension that made it easy for him to play the clown publicly, whether donning a bushy orange wig to celebrate SU's 133rd anniversary, reciting goofy poems to the football team after a victory, or screaming himself hoarse at out-of-town pep rallies.

He won people's hearts with unexpected displays of wry humor and simple tastes, as with his lone contribution to an SU cookbook series—a recipe for popcorn: no salt, no butter, no flavorings.[2] "Popcorn is one of those foods which usually isn't cooked badly, but it could be cooked well and the discerning over-indulger will know the difference," he wrote.

Two weeks after the heady victory of the men's basketball championship, Shaw informed trustee Executive Committee members of his plans to retire in a morning telephone meeting on April 23, 2003.[3] He would finish August 1, 2004, in his sixty-fifth year, having served thirteen years as SU's chancellor. The announcement caught nearly everyone by surprise. Just as unexpected was that he planned to stay at SU. He would take a year's leave of absence, he and Mary Ann would live at their recently remodeled house in Skaneateles, and he would write another book, *The Intentional Leader*. After that, he would teach a leadership course at the newly named Whitman School of Management. He would be available to assist the new chancellor, he said.

The implications of Shaw's retirement announcement, coupled with the intoxicating glow of the April 7 NCAA national men's basketball championship, dominated the May trustee meeting, the first since Shaw announced his retirement. He praised his cabinet members via a tip of the hat to Boeheim. They were "working collaboratively as a real team . . . that would make Jim Boeheim proud," he said. Further extolling the coach, he conflated attributes of Boeheim's winning team with values that he himself had modeled through his chancellorship: "Work harder and smarter than the other team, subordinate your ego to the good of the team, and bounce back when you encounter setbacks."

*   *   *

Lampe's seven-year term as chairman of the Board of Trustees would end in May 2004 as Shaw was finishing up. In the meantime, Lampe would chair the search committee for a new chancellor, seeking someone to follow through on Shaw's initiatives. "The person who ends up with this job will not be doing anything drastic to change the university in one way or another. The board is happy with the way that the university is being run and with the path we're on and what Buzz has done there and what he sees in the future," Lampe told the *Post-Standard*, prompting the next day's headlines to read "SU Abuzz about Who Will Be the Next Buzz."[4]

The next Buzz turned out to be a woman, Nancy Cantor, who had been chancellor of the University of Illinois at Urbana–Champaign—a public institution, since 2001. Thirty-two trustees met on a Friday morning in February in the Lubin House gallery and unanimously approved her as the next chancellor. The search committee had interviewed ten candidates in November and December and unanimously chose to ask only Cantor back for a second interview.

On the surface, Cantor could not be more different from Shaw, the small-town Illinois native. Cantor, fifty-one, would be the first woman and first Jewish chancellor in SU's 134 years. A New York City native, she graduated from Sarah Lawrence College and earned a PhD at Stanford. She taught at Princeton before moving to the University of Michigan as dean of the graduate school and then provost and executive vice president. Her specialty was social and personality psychology, and she was a self-professed lover of the arts.

Consistent with Lampe's description of search criteria, Cantor said at her introduction she was not looking to make major changes at the university and had confidence in the senior administrative team.[5] She praised the work of SU's Center for Public and Community Service, saying that the hands-on experience students received through the program critically shaped their education. "They can't be trained in ivory towers," she said.[6]

Trustees also appointed Cantor Distinguished Professor of Psychology and Women's Studies in the College of Arts and Sciences. Her husband, Steven Brechin, was appointed professor of sociology in the Maxwell School and the College of Arts and Sciences.

In preparation for her stay at the chancellor's residence, $400,000 of improvements were undertaken to replace the boiler, upgrade electrical and plumbing systems, paint, replaster, and repair the

Nancy Cantor, SU's first woman chancellor, being introduced by Shaw in 2004. Courtesy of University Archives, Syracuse University Libraries.

house's four fireplaces.[7] John Couri ('63), the cofounder, former president, and CEO of Duty Free International, Inc., was named the new chairman of the Board of Trustees.

Shaw's public retirement event in April 2004 was lighthearted and relaxed, true to his style all along.[8] A three-foot-tall ice sculpture of Buzz Lightyear, a character from the children's movie *Toy Story*, was a centerpiece on the main table, and blue Buzz Lightyear tablecloths covered the others. Since the movie's release in 1995, Shaw had quoted the lead character's signature line in several speeches—"To infinity and beyond." Several hundred people attended the free event at the Schine Student Center's Goldstein Auditorium.[9] At the

Buzz and Mary Ann Shaw after they received Syracuse University honorary degrees in May 2004. The Post-Standard/Dennis Nett.

reception, Lampe gave Shaw the keys to a 2004, black, four-door Lexus RX330 sport utility vehicle. Send-off gifts from trustees were traditional. Eggers had received a house. Weeks later at commencement, Shaw swapped out his floppy orange mortarboard hat for a driver's cap.

Shaw was named a University Professor, an honored status granted by trustees. As University Professor, he would receive nine-elevenths of his chancellor's salary.[10] At the same time, trustees also bestowed University Professor status on John Palmer, former dean of the Maxwell School, and Charles Driscoll, professor of environmental systems engineering. Mary Ann would work part-time as a community relations associate in SU's Office of Government and Community Relations.

Recognitions, honors, and tribute articles rolled in. Both Shaws were awarded Arents medals—the highest honor bestowed on SU alumni—even though they were not alumni. They received honorary degrees, Mary Ann being the first wife of a chancellor to receive one. Joining the Shaws with honorary degrees were Lampe, chairman of the Board of Trustees since 1997, and Josef J. Zwislocki, SU professor of neuroscience who retired in 1992.

Mary Ann received a Post-Standard Achievement Award in 2004 for her work developing SU's Literacy Corps, through which 170 students volunteered in Syracuse public schools; for organizing Success by Six, the United Way's outreach to children of poor families; and for her work on the proposed Syracuse children's hospital. She had made public service an integral part of SU students' experience through the creation of the Center for Public and Community Service (renamed the Mary Ann Shaw Center for Public and Community Service when she left). Some 5,000 students annually were performing public service, half of them through SU courses that had a public service component. Mary Ann pushed to establish the Arts Adventure Program (later called PULSE), which provided undergraduates with low-cost tickets to performing arts events at Syracuse Stage and the Famous Artist Broadway Theater series.

*   *   *

To end this portion of the university's history when Shaw stepped down as chancellor would leave it incomplete. After the Shaws moved out of the chancellor's residence at 300 Comstock Avenue, they stayed active in Central New York affairs for another six years, and each of them continued their community work in ways that would affect Syracuse far into the future.

Despite the widely held perception of Syracuse University as the fortress on a hill, separate and apart from the city of Syracuse, under Shaw the university and the city had become more engaged than they had ever been. The university had forged new agreements with the city to improve South Crouse Avenue and Marshall Street, SU had initiated a mortgage program for employees to purchase houses in the city, and the university had worked out agreements with the city to allow SU to have peace officers.

The real pioneering work with the community that set the stage for the incoming chancellor was the new relationships developed because of Mary Ann. While her husband served on boards like the Syracuse area Chamber of Commerce and the MDA, just as chancellors before him, Mary Ann pushed to connect SU with the Syracuse City School District and area preschool programs. She had strong relationships with people in the United Way, the Salvation Army, and area hospitals.

In May 2003, Shaw was named chairman of the MDA, an economic planning and development organization that for decades had had an outsized influence on the shape of Syracuse and Onondaga County. Asked in an interview as outgoing chancellor what the city and county could do to help SU, Shaw said, "Give me 1,000 apartments downtown and employers [who] start encouraging young people to live there, and you'll see a different kind of environment."[11] With the MDA's help, that statement proved self-fulfilling, and downtown Syracuse became a more welcoming place for SU students to live and recreate.

In 2009, while still MDA chairman, Shaw led meetings that would join the MDA and the Chamber of Commerce, two business organizations with distinctly different memberships, cultures, and focus. The two organizations had a history of not working together, but as the business landscape changed, it was clear they needed to collaborate. The MDA had roughly 150 invitation-only members who were mostly corporate CEOs and saw themselves as the community's business elite, the ones who made the big projects happen, like the Carrier Dome and the Center of Excellence. They crafted regional strategic plans that drew in state and federal money and pushed for tax breaks and other incentives to try to keep big businesses from leaving town. However, big businesses, like Carrier and New Venture Gear, were leaving town, and the MDA's clout was eroding.

The Chamber of Commerce was more of a networking association for its 2,000 members, providing them with group health insurance and other benefits. It recruited conventions to Syracuse, lobbied for pro-business policies, endorsed political candidates, and ran an incubator for new technology companies.

An opportunity to join forces came as each organization welcomed new presidents. Shaw led negotiations for five months and, in early 2010, a new agency was introduced: CenterState CEO. It was the area's first unified voice for economic development.[12] The MDA and the chamber agreed to comingle and reduce staff and merge expenses and operating costs. Each would keep its separate legal status and liabilities.

Rob Simpson, CenterState CEO's new president, remembers Shaw leading those meetings: "He could sit there and command the presence of the room for an hour without saying a word. And at the end he would reflect in a very succinct way, not only what he heard but the action items that people had agreed to. He kept us to deadlines. He offered great strategic observations. He made a welcoming environment for us to have really difficult conversations."[13]

Mary Ann's work on behalf of young children had begun early in her career. While still in Madison, Wisconsin, she had worked on a campaign to improve facilities at the University of Wisconsin Children's Hospital. Children needed much different things in a hospital than adult patients, she said. "They have to have very specialized treatment and facilities, and their families have to be totally involved."[14]

After arriving in Syracuse, she soon learned about the overcrowding and run-down condition of the pediatric ward at Upstate Hospital and heard from doctors about their decades-long desire for a specialized children's hospital. The idea had been a nonstarter, for no one could agree where a children's hospital should be or even if it was necessary.

By 2003, Dr. Gregory Eastwood, president of Upstate, and Dr. Thomas Welch, the new chair in the Department of Pediatrics, decided they would build a children's hospital within a new addition at Upstate, and they asked Mary Ann to chair the children's hospital fund-raising committee. She brought calm, focus, and determination to the task, said Eileen Pezzi, Upstate's vice president of development since 1996. "She knew how to lead and you wanted to follow her. She leaned on us, worked with us, let us fly on our own. All ideas were good ideas, but at the end of the day, she brought it all together."[15]

Pezzi had reached out to Tom Golisano, the chairman and founder of Paychex, Inc., a payroll-processing company in Rochester, and a perennial New York gubernatorial candidate. Golisano came for a tour of Upstate's pediatric unit, where he met Eastwood, Welch, Pezzi, and Mary Ann Shaw. They showed Golisano the same over-crowded and makeshift accommodations they had been showing Syracuse business leaders—too many cribs in a room, mothers sleeping on floors, beds in hallways. Weeks later, Golisano agreed to let Pezzi follow up with him in a visit to Rochester. Pezzi could bring anyone, and she chose Mary Ann, who had much more experience asking for big gifts from wealthy donors. The two strategized, traveled to his office, made their pitches, and returned in October 2005 with a com-mitment from Golisano for a $6 million naming gift for the children's hospital at SUNY Upstate Medical University. The gift was the largest the hospital had ever received from an individual donor, and it put the fund-raising campaign well over its $15 million goal.

It was yet one more success for Mary Ann Shaw, who had come to Syracuse University as the chancellor's wife and had proven her-self to be so much more. Her time in Syracuse marked her as one of the most influential people in the history of the city and the univer-sity to have never held public office or interviewed for her job.

Conclusion

The single greatest challenge facing SU, Shaw told trustees in 1999, was "the gap between our aspirations and our resources. We are all too aware of the disparity between our resources and our commit-ment to our shared vision as the nation's leading student-centered research university." All through his tenure he had cited that chal-lenge, calling for more financial support from trustees.

Whatever SU's vision of itself—and it is modified with each new chancellor—the university's perpetual need has been for more money, a bigger endowment. It is a problem shared by many higher education institutions, public and private. While Shaw did not find a donor on the legendary scale of Phil Knight, the Nike founder who bequeathed hundreds of millions of dollars to his alma maters, the Shaws secured tens of millions of dollars in gifts that propelled pro-grams and new construction.[16]

With help from his cabinet and deans, in his final months Shaw prepared a statement of needs and challenges his successor would face.[17] Some would be unavoidable, regardless of how the new chancellor chose to guide SU. Others presumed the incoming chancellor would continue the path Shaw had charted. As he had done throughout his tenure, Shaw candidly acknowledged the university's shortcomings.

The budget would need to be closely monitored. It was projected to break even for the next five years with little in anticipated gains. That meant that unforeseen circumstances could send SU's fortunes plummeting again. "Changes in the external environment could easily cause our fiscal situation to deteriorate," Shaw wrote.

Of particular note was the budget challenge of intercollegiate athletics, which accounted for 5 percent of the university's spending. Athletics had been paying its own way, even contributing bowl revenues to the general fund. With the recent defection of teams from the Big East hurting television contract revenues and ticket sales flat or declining in football, Shaw projected athletic budget deficits of $2.7 million in 2004–5 and as much as $3.5 million in later years. As Shaw saw it, money for athletics would need to come from a reallocation of funds, which would mean lowering salary increases or cutting staff, raising tuition, increasing the size of the freshmen class, or some combination of all. Increasing freshmen enrollment by fifteen students would generate roughly $1 million to $1.5 million annually. In fact, Shaw had already adjusted the 2004–5 tuition increase from 6 percent to 6.4 percent to generate an extra $450,000 for athletics.[18]

There would be other financial challenges as well: Faculty and staff salaries were still not competitive and needed to be raised. Money that had been supporting strategic increases above the standard 3 percent, which was coming from a special faculty development fund, would run out in 2005, according to Shaw's budget plan. There was still no comparable supplemental funding to bring staff salaries to a competitive level. "In the matter of closing that discrepancy we have made little progress."

Shaw had laid the groundwork for a new fund-raising campaign that was slated to raise at least $550 million by 2012, and he had allotted an extra $554,000 to get it started, with a silent phase beginning in 2005.[19] "Reaching and exceeding the next campaign's goal are critical to the University's future," he wrote.

Multiple building projects were underway or in the design phase, with timelines for all of them: Hinds Hall was being renovated for the iSchool (School for Information Studies); Slocum Hall was scheduled to be renovated for the School of Architecture; planning for the Life Sciences addition to the Center for Science and Technology was slated for completion by 2005; and construction of Newhouse III was to begin that same year. Projects identified in the space plan would cost more than $200 million and add $6 million to the operating budget. In addition to the space plan's building projects that were moving ahead, the university had published in 2003 a master plan created under supervision of Virginia Denton, SU's director of design and construction. The plan was drawn up by Bohlin Cywinski Jackson Architecture, the same firm that had designed Apple's flagship retail stores for Steve Jobs, including the glass cube in Manhattan.[20]

The richly illustrated, 275-page master plan concisely distilled SU's building history, identifying design principles that carried through for more than a century, as well as design mistakes and shortcomings. New building opportunities were suggested within SU's campus framework with an emphasis on design, campus unity, and aesthetics over cost, and perhaps for that reason, or perhaps not to call attention to the firm's nearly $2 million in fees, the master plan is not mentioned in any trustee meeting notes.[21] One of its elegant proposals that addressed the perennial issue of campus parking was a two-block-long underground garage for 900 vehicles beneath Walnut Park.[22]

One mention of the Campus Plan is in a 2004 written memo to Lou Marcoccia from Eric Beattie, who had replaced Denton after her October 2003 retirement. Marcoccia had asked Beattie to identify the issues involved if SU were to demolish the Tolley Building instead of rehabilitating it. The Tolley Building was one of the oldest buildings on campus, designed by Archimedes Russell, constructed in 1888, and listed on the National Register of Historic Places. Through Shaw's tenure, it had housed the top administrative offices, yet it was structurally in need of $5–$10 million of work, so much so that administrators were concerned about the upper stories collapsing in high winds.

Beattie presented a host of reasons for preserving Tolley, including anticipation of a protracted battle with preservationists and negative publicity if the university moved to tear it down. In addition, he cited the 2003 Campus Plan's call to foster "the physical preservation of historic and residential buildings."

The Academic Plan, in its third year in 2004 and calling for strategic partnerships between areas of academic strength, needed more work and funding. Shaw also highlighted problems with student retention, student alcohol abuse, the need to upgrade and modernize the university's oversized dorms, and the need to get all faculty using the new computer technologies that had been introduced.

That Shaw explicitly conveyed SU's needs as he departed underscored how well he had managed and monitored so many aspects of SU life. It was not for lack of attention that needs persisted. Running an institution with thirteen schools and colleges, 18,500 students, 4,766 full- and part-time faculty and staff, and a $746 million budget that included a $22 million athletics program is an extraordinary balancing act. When that university has a modest financial cushion and is primarily funded by tuition and auxiliary revenue, the challenge becomes even more trying.

In times of financial stress, if more students are admitted without adding proper support, the quality of students and instruction can slip, and rebuilding both can take decades. The temptation to enroll more students, especially during the post-9/11 recession, was constant, and to Shaw's credit, he resisted it. Through the transparency of his restructuring process from the very first days, faculty and trustees had seen the quality improvements that came when enrollment matched the university's resources. While some called for enrollment increases to provide a quick infusion of money to increase faculty pay or to reduce workload or to hire star faculty, plenty of trustees and faculty argued to keep enrollment steady and manageable, with no more than 3,000 freshmen entering in any given year.

With his vision to become the nation's leading student-centered research university, Shaw had directed the most extensive restructuring process in the institution's history through one of the most perilous times in its history. Steering SU through an increasingly competitive field with fewer resources than many competitors, he had shown himself to be smart, resolute, and, at times, flinty. After budget cuts of more than $60 million and the loss of some 600 jobs, the university had become smaller and stronger. Shaw had launched SU on a path of strategic strengthening and long-range planning that resulted in significant improvement in national reputation and rankings, increased quality of students, and a renewed sense of purpose and commitment on campus.[23] Faculty diversity improved and the campus was revitalized with physical improvements and more major construction about to begin.[24]

The university boasted that between 1991 and 2001 (when inflation rose 30 percent), the market value of its endowment increased by 350 percent. Annual fund-raising increased from $29.7 million in 1991 to $61 million in 2001. Eggers Hall had opened (1994), and Goldstein Alumni and Faculty Center (1997), MacNaughton Hall for the College of Law (1998), and the Tennity Ice Skating Pavilion (2000) were built. Ground was broken for the Whitman School of Management (2003), and plans were being developed and money was pledged for Newhouse III.

The bigger story was the rising prominence of Syracuse University in Central New York, something that was happening almost by default. In just three years, between 2000 and 2003, Central New York had lost 7,200 manufacturing jobs, nearly 20 percent of its manufacturing total. The Syracuse metropolitan population declined by 10,000 between 1990 and 2000 and was still losing people, according to census figures.[25] With the closing of factories and the departure of corporate headquarters from the area, SU had become Onondaga County's second biggest employer, and its influence as a power broker was growing.[26]

So too were SU's concerns over the condition of the city of Syracuse—the two were more interdependent than ever. The city's reputation and quality of life affected SU's ability to recruit students and faculty. Unlike the corporations that had once dominated Syracuse but then left town, SU was not going to relocate.

The currency that Shaw and Mary Ann brought to their subsequent work with the MDA and children's hospital campaign came from their identity with and their success at SU. The "fortress on the hill" was becoming the benevolent powerhouse reaching down the hill. Looking back to 1991, the search committee members and trustees who selected Shaw deserve credit for their good instincts and sound choice, for selecting a leader who fit perfectly the needs of the time.

When Shaw left, the budget was in the black, new creative programs were being launched, major construction was underway, and a healthy culture of frankness and caring was in place. Parts of the university still needed work, and the institution needed much more money to continue improving and needed to hone its institutional message and get it out to the world. How and whether his successor would carry all that forward would be the story in the years ahead.

APPENDIXES

NOTES

WORKS CONSULTED

INDEX

APPENDIX A
Ad Hoc Advisory Committee's Assessment Methodology

To assess schools, the Ad Hoc Advisory Committee started with 1982–83 data and compared enrollment, tuition revenue, tuition discounts (financial aid, which varied school to school), average SAT scores of admitted freshmen, number of applications to schools, and an estimate of money each school "earned" above its budget or was paid to subsidize its budget. It looked at projected high school graduation numbers for the Northeast, SU's principle source of students at the time.

The committee weighed *demand* according to the number of prospective student applications and credit hours taught at each college and school. They determined the *centrality* of each by gauging how much other schools and colleges at SU depended upon it for instruction. The College of Arts and Sciences, for example, offered instruction to virtually all students and had a high centrality. The College of Law offered instruction only to law students and had a low centrality. *Quality* assessments were not easily comparable on a spreadsheet, with different factors determining quality, college to college. Nevertheless, the committee did make quality conclusions about each college and school.

Internal Ranking of Schools and Colleges with Budget Cuts and Add-ons, 1991–92

1990–91	FB/OH Percentage	Category	Vincow's Cuts (Add-on)	Shaw's Cuts (Add-on)
SU Average	103			
Architecture	121	1	($90,000)	($90,000)
Arts and Sciences	166	2	$2,750,000	$2,750,000
Computer Information Science	–53	3	$1,045,000	$950,000
Education	2	3	$1,280,913	$1,280,913
Engineering	–39	3	$2,860,000	$2,860,000
Human Development	180	2	$165,000	$150,000
Information Studies	–26	3	$165,000	$150,000
Law	77	1	$0	$0
School of Management	87	2	$440,000	$440,000
Maxwell	152	2	($1,080,000)	($1,080,000)
Nursing	–21	3	$220,000	$200,000
Public Communication	134	1	($360,000)	($360,000)
Social Work	–21	3	$165,000	$150,000
Visual and Performing Arts	181	1	($225,000)	($225,000)

This table lists the FB/OH numbers arrived at by the Ad Hoc Advisory Committee and the restructuring category in which the committee placed each school. The budget cuts and add-ons were proposed in Vincow's December 1991 report, and most of the cuts and add-ons in Shaw's final plan, released in February 1992, were identical. Shaw, in his report, did not refer to the categories of schools, which was deemed bad for morale. Revenue was estimated by multiplying the number of credit hours taught in a college or school by the tuition per credit hour.

The FB/OH number was an index that represented a college's/school's revenue in relation to the money the university budgeted for it. If an entity's "revenue" equaled the budgeted amount, its FB/OH would be 100 percent. If its FB/OH exceeded 100 percent, the program was "earning" more than it was budgeted and was viewed as "profitable." "Profit" helped the schools and colleges that were not covering their costs. Conversely, if a program's FB/OH was less than 100 percent, the university was "subsidizing" it. Colleges and schools with an FB/OH substantially below 100 would be candidates for major cuts or mergers.

The name FB/OH looked like a ratio but was not. It was an attempt to remind those considering FB/OH numbers that the university was paying for fringe benefits (FB) (health insurance, retirement) and overhead (OH) (heating, maintenance, lights, some portion of the library's cost, and other administrative services) as well as salaries and expenses.

Sources: Ad Hoc Advisory Committee Report on the Schools and Colleges, *Syracuse Record*, Sept. 16, 1991; Gershon Vincow, Restructuring Plan for Academic Affairs, *Syracuse Record*, Dec. 16, 1991; Kenneth Shaw, Chancellor's Report on Restructuring, *Syracuse Record*, Feb. 17, 1992.

Administrative Consultants Hired by SU

The consultants who reviewed SU's administrative and academic support divisions, with their area of review, were:

Suzanne H. Woolsey, executive director, Commission on Behavior and Social Sciences in Education at the National Academy of Sciences (overview coordinator)

David Lieberman, senior vice president, University of Miami (business and finance)

John Hayes, director of development, Dartmouth University (development)

John F. Bumess, senior vice president of public affairs, Duke University (public affairs)

William A. Diagneau, director of university facilities, University of Rochester (facilities administration)

Richard J. Towle, vice president for administrative services, Boston University (human resources and security)

Bobbie Knable, dean of students, Tufts University (student affairs)

APPENDIX D

The 33 Initiatives

Quality

Total quality management program
Campus space allocation
Energy conservation
Printing and graphics services study
Computing services strategic plan
Improved classroom opportunities through smaller classes
Active learning opportunities
Basic math skills
Integrate research into teaching
Assess academic programs
Improve the faculty reward system
Program overlap review
University governance
Refine academic fiscal plans
Enhance cooperation between academic affairs and administrative services
Enhance cooperation between academic affairs and student affairs
Enhance undergraduate recruiting, scholarship, and loan initiatives

Caring

Fund drive to support scholarship endowment
Enhanced orientation
Improved academic advising
Improved student retention
Strengthened services for graduate students

Human resources plan
Retired faculty association

Diversity

Chancellor's commission on pluralism
Initiative to hire African American and Latino faculty

Innovation

Chancellor's fund for innovation
New teaching awards
Common educational experience for undergraduates
Blending liberal and professional studies
Full-cost accounting system

Service

University neighborhood community forum
Open office hours for chancellor's cabinet officers

APPENDIX E
The Grateful Dead

The Grateful Dead played in Syracuse on Saturday, October 20, 1984. It was the final concert of their eleven-concert eastern US tour, and after Syracuse they headed home to Berkeley, California. The SU event was everything for which Dead concerts were infamous: van loads of Dead Heads—fans that followed the band to as many shows as they could— descended upon the campus and lingered for days after, with scores of drug arrests as well as drug and alcohol overdoses that kept police and emergency medical crews busy.

The Dead concert made money, though, so the university drew up a condition under which the band could return: it could play at SU only if the concert was in the middle of a three-day, back-to-back concert cluster in three different markets. The Dead would have to play a concert in another market the day before the Dome appearance and play another concert the day immediately after the Dome show in a different market, according to terms discussed in a November 18, 1988, letter from David Marsden, of Monarch Entertainment, to Pat Campbell. The idea was to get the Dead Heads in and out and eliminate camping on the Quad. The condition effectively guaranteed the end of the Dead at the Dome, since the band most always had two days of rest and travel between shows in different markets. SU did try to schedule a Grateful Dead concert in April 1989, to which the Dead said their spring tour was "already set."

Students' Changing Attitudes about SU

The research firm Clark, Martire & Bartolomeo, Inc. regularly conducted surveys of prospective and enrolled students regarding their perceptions about Syracuse University.

Prospective Students

The following data reflect changing perceptions of prospective students between 1990 and 1996. The percentages are respondents who held excellent/very good perceptions about:

- Course offerings and programs: 75% vs. 94%
- Academic advising: 68% vs. 85%
- Good job after graduation: 74% vs. 88%
- Ability to gain entry into a good graduate/professional school: 76% vs. 88%
- Campus life: 70% vs. 79%
- Availability of student housing: 68% vs. 89%
- Attractive campus: 68% vs. 81%
- Fun 75% vs. 89%

Enrolled Students

The following data reflect changing attitudes of enrolled students who held excellent/very good perceptions about the identified topics, the first figure from student responses in 1994, the second from 1996.

- Academic quality: 68% vs. 80%
- Faculty commitment to teaching: 21% vs. 24%
- Faculty accessibility outside the classroom: 29% vs. 37%
- Willingness to tell others proudly about attending SU: 52% vs. 65%

Source: Clark, Martire & Bartolomeo, Inc., "A Strategic Study: Current and Potential Undergraduate Students," Feb. 1997, SU Archives, Shaw Collection.

SU's Peer Colleges, 2001

In 2001, SU ranked tenth for retention rates among thirteen peer colleges:

Boston University
Case Western Reserve University
Duke University
Emory University
Georgetown University
New York University
Northwestern University
Tulane University
University of Rochester
University of Southern California
Vanderbilt University
Washington University

9/11 Response Committees

Emergency Response Committee, chair, David Smith. Established guidelines to ensure a smooth transition for faculty, staff, and students who would be called to military service. At the time, SU had ten active reservists, fifteen inactive, and two who had been called to duty.

Logistics Committee, chair, Lou Marcoccia. Developed protocols to handle sudden, unexpected events requiring special attention to transportation or inventory needs, access to buildings, energy management, power loss, or biological contamination.

In- and Out-of-Class Special Activities, chair, William Pollard.

DIPA Program, chair, Ron Cavanagh. Contracted special personnel to be stationed at main entrances of DIPA centers and created evacuation plans.

Crisis Communication, chair, John Sellars.

Campus Safety, chair, Thomas Wolfe. Reviewed response protocols to be used if campus became unsafe because of internal strife or external events.

International Education, chair, Pat Burak.

Hate Crime Prevention, chair, James Duah-Agyeman.

Source: Chancellor's Report to the Board of Trustees, Nov. 2, 2001, SU Archives, Trustee Collection.

Notes

All collections and papers referenced in these notes are found in Syracuse University Archives, Special Collections Research Center, Syracuse University Libraries, unless otherwise noted.

Introduction

1. William Ihlanfeldt, "A Report on the Recruitment, Financial Aid, and Retention Strategies of Syracuse University," Dec. 1991, Shaw Collection.

2. John Palmer, interview with author, Dec. 1, 2015.

1. Team Shaw: Getting Started

1. Before joining Crouse-Hinds in 1965, Witting had been a leading figure in television, credited with bringing the likes of Sid Caesar, Jackie Gleason, and Bishop Sheen to network TV.

2. Michael Sawyer and Bruce Hamm, Report on Chancellor's Search, June 1991, Eggers Collection.

3. Until Shalala forwarded Shaw's name to the search committee, he had not been on the committee's radar.

4. Donna Shalala quotes in this chapter are from an interview with the author, May 4, 2016.

5. Robert Smith and Fred Pierce, "'Buzz' Earns Praise from Colleagues," *Post-Standard*, Apr. 26, 1991.

6. Unless otherwise noted, all Kenneth Shaw quotes in this chapter are from interviews with the author on Mar. 14 and June 27, 2016.

7. Eric Mower, interview with author, Aug. 11, 2016.

8. Mary Ann Shaw, interview with author, Mar. 14, 2016.

9. Jake Crouthamel, Dome Report to New Chancellor, 1991, Shaw Collection.

10. Donald J. Haviland, "Becoming a Student-Centered Research University: A Case Study of Organizational Change" (PhD diss., Syracuse University, 1999), 44.

11. The meeting occurred July 20, 1991.

12. Shaw's criteria for his own writing and speeches were that they be under-standable to someone with an eighth-grade education, like his mother. "She didn't have the benefit of a big vocabulary. But she understood anything that came be-fore her. The truth is, there are a lot of people with big vocabularies, but they still benefit from having things said directly, honestly, and quickly." Kathryn Lee, his speechwriter, masterfully put Shaw's ideas into a form that was clearly recognized as Shaw's voice.

13. In 1990–91, the national average (mean) for all students was 999. A perfect score is 1600.

14. US Bureau of the Census, "Projections of the Population of the United States, College-Age Men and Women." No. 381, 1967; No. 470, 1971; No. 704, 1977.

15. Kenneth Shaw, chancellor's report to trustees, Nov. 8, 1991, Trustee Collection.

16. Robert F. Allen, budget report to trustees, May 4, 1991, Trustee Collection.

17. Samuel Weiss, "The Hard Times Roll on Syracuse Campus," *New York Times*, Oct. 29, 1991.

18. Melvin Eggers, staff assessment note, [1991], Eggers Collection.

19. A major criticism of the committee's report was that it favored the colleges from which committee members came.

20. Chancellor's Ad Hoc Advisory Group, "Report on the Schools and Colleges of Syracuse University," Sept. 1991, 1, Shaw Collection.

21. In 1991, SU had six colleges and eight schools. When referred to collectively, to avoid burdensome distinctions, "school" and "college" are used interchangeably.

22. Haviland, "Becoming a Student-Centered Research University," 66.

23. William Ihlanfeldt, *Achieving Optimal Enrollments and Tuition Revenues* (San Francisco: Jossey-Bass, 1980).

24. Ihlanfeldt, "A Report on the Recruitment, Financial Aid, and Retention Strategies of Syracuse University," Dec. 1991, Shaw Collection.

2. Restructuring: Building on Strengths

1. John Palmer to Eleanor Gallagher, memorandum regarding SU values, June 18, 1991, Shaw Collection.

2. Robert Smith, "SU Unveils $28 Million in Cutbacks," *Post-Standard*, Sept. 12, 1991.

3. At that same meeting, Shaw urged cabinet members, who would confront rage and ire over faculty and staff cuts, not to "take the anger personally."

4. John Palmer, interview with author, Dec. 1, 2015.

5. Syracuse University tax return Form 990, 1992.

6. Haviland, "Becoming a Student-Centered Research University," 190.

7. The survey was sent to 315 faculty; 139 responded.

8. John Hogan to Chancellor Shaw, memorandum, "SWAT Review of Reports to the Chancellor," Jan. 17, 1992, Shaw Collection.

9. The administrative side included student affairs, business and finance, facilities administration, university relations, human resources, and the chancellor's office.

10. Shaw, chancellor's report, Feb. 17, 1992, 13, Shaw Collection.

11. In a 1997 report to the Middle States Commission on Higher Education, SU claimed to have completed twenty initiatives. Several, like the program overlap review and the retired faculty association, never got off the ground.

12. Wiggins was chair of the Department of Religion.

13. Ronald Cavanagh, interview with author, Apr. 5, 2016.

14. Trustees' Executive Committee meeting minutes, Feb. 4, 1994, Trustee Collection.

15. Stephen Burd, "NEH Ends Program to Reward Teaching," *Chronicle of Higher Education*, Sept. 9, 1992.

16. Ruth Stein, who worked as a teaching consultant at the Center for Supported Learning, coauthored several books on teaching strategies with Sandra Hurd, a professor of law and public policy in the School of Management. *Building and Sustaining Learning Communities* and *Using Student Teams in the Classroom* both came out of their work at the Center for Supported Learning.

17. Michael Flusche to Vincow, memorandum concerning John Alan Robinson/ supported resignation program, Dec. 6, 1993, Vincow Collection.

18. Flusche's method presumed that salary increases were an indicator of a professor's quality. For tenured faculty members eligible for the supported resignation program, their previous five years of salary increases were added and compared to the five-year sum of their department's average salary increases.

19. "Syracuse University Staff Workforce Reduction Program," Oct. 28, 1991, Shaw Collection.

20. Shaw cabinet meeting notes, Dec. 2, 1991, Shaw Collection.

21. Doug Mell, "Shaw Says Faculty Will Need 'Catch-Up,'" *Wisconsin State Journal*, Sept. 21, 1989, 1A.

22. Baker made the request in Aug. 1992.

23. Michael Burke, "Doubletalk," *Daily Orange*, Apr. 11, 2016.

24. Jon Palfreman, "Prisoners of Silence," PBS *Frontline*, aired Oct. 19, 1993.

25. Storch v. Syracuse Univ., 233 N.Y.S.2d 823 (App. Div. 1995).

26. Biklen was named dean in 2006. Fifty-two professors, members of the Commission for Scientific Medicine and Mental Health, signed a letter that called Biklen's appointment a "major step backward in the vitally important effort to promote science and combat pseudoscience in mental-health care." *The Scientific Review of Mental Health Practice* 4, no. 1 (Spring–Summer 2005), https://www.srmhp.org/0401 /media-watch.html.

27. Strait was dean from 1981 to 1984, ran the Case Center for five years, and returned as dean from 1989 to 1992.

28. Strait, interview with author, Dec. 12, 2015.

29. Watson and Tolley forged the IBM/SU relationship in the 1940s, and Watson donated the naming gift for Watson Hall (1954) on SU's campus. John Robert Greene,

with Karrie A. Baron, *Syracuse University*, vol. 4, *The Tolley Years, 1942–1969* (Syracuse: Syracuse Univ. Press), 56.

30. Haviland, "Becoming a Student-Centered Research University," 127.

31. Ibid.

32. Ben Ware, interview with author, Dec. 14, 2015.

33. Shiu-Kai Chin, interview with author, Dec. 3, 2015.

34. Strait, interview with author, Dec. 15, 2015.

35. Piper Fogg, "Syracuse U Professor Resigns," *Chronicle of Higher Education*, Apr. 21, 2006.

36. Greene, *The Tolley Years*, 15.

37. John Hogan to Shaw, memorandum concerning Carrier Dome Plant Fund, Oct. 16, 1991, Shaw Collection.

38. David Smith, interview with author, Jan. 7, 2016.

3. Image Making: Shaping and Promoting the New SU

1. Ronald Cavanagh, interview with author, Apr. 5, 2016.

2. TIAA-CREF, "Theodore M. Hesburgh Award for Faculty Development to Enhance Undergraduate Teaching," 1996, Shaw Collection.

3. Robert Diamond, Theodore M. Hesburgh Award application, Jan. 3, 1996, Vincow Collection.

4. Shaw address to trustees, Nov. 7, 1997, Trustee Collection.

5. William Safire, "B.C./A.D. or B.C.E./C.E.?" *New York Times Magazine*, Aug. 17, 1997, http://www.nytimes.com/1997/08/17/magazine/bc-ad-or-bce-ce.html.

6. Shaw to Donna Arzt, Mar. 19, 1998, Trustee Collection.

7. *Chicago Manual of Style* (Chicago: Univ. of Chicago Press, 1993).

8. Enrollment had averaged at 2,500 full- and part-time students the prior five years.

9. Shaw, interview with author, Naples, Florida, Mar. 14, 2016.

10. Michael Simpson, "The Evolution of Utica College from Branch Campus to Independent College of Syracuse University," Apr. 1993, Shaw Collection.

11. Simpson to Utica College associates, letter, Oct. 1992, Shaw Collection.

12. Simpson to Shaw, letter, Apr. 30, 1993, Shaw Collection.

13. "SU's Mascot," Syracuse University, http://cuse.com/sports/2001/8/8/mascot.aspx.

14. Peter Webber to Lou Marcoccia, "Executive Summary Logo and Mascot Selection Status Report," Aug. 22, 1995, Shaw Collection.

15. Ibid.

16. The verse quoted in the report is from Rudyard Kipling's *The Law for the Wolves*: "Now this is the Law of the Jungle, as old and as true as the sky; and the Wolf that shall keep it may prosper, but the wolf that shall break it must die. As the creeper that girdles the tree trunk, the law runneth forward and back. For the strength of the pack is the wolf, and the strength of the wolf is the pack."

17. Shaw, email to author, Jan. 21, 2018.

4. Making Connections: Public Service and the Digital Age

1. Dave Tobin, "Questioning SU—Students Who Conducted Hard-Hitting Survey Get an Education," *Post-Standard*, Oct. 17, 2013, A14.

2. William Coplin, interview with author, Feb. 1, 2016.

3. Pamela Heintz, interview with author, Jan. 26, 2016.

4. Ben Ware, "'93 Forward!," Vincow Collection.

5. Ibid.

6. Ware to Joan Carpenter, memorandum, Feb. 27, 1992, Vincow Collection.

7. Shaw, interview with author, Mar. 14, 2016.

8. David Smith to Shaw, memorandum, Aug. 13, 1992, Shaw Collection.

9. People stockpiled food and water, refused to fly, and waited with bated breath for midnight, January 1, 2000. The federal government set up a Y2K command center, a consumer hotline, and a website (www.y2k.gov). Little disruption occurred.

10. Ware, interview with author, Skaneateles, New York, Nov. 20, 2015.

11. PeopleSoft software was not the only software the university acquired, but it was the largest single system. Ware, interview, *Syracuse Record*, Mar. 29, 1999.

12. Ware to Vincow, email regarding purchase of PeopleSoft student system, Sept. 19, 1996, Vincow Collection.

13. Shaw to Executive Committee of the Board of Trustees, Dec. 3, 1999, trustee minutes, Trustee Collection.

14. Caliber Learning Network news release, Aug. 1, 2000, Freund Collection.

15. The restriction forced those wanting internet access to subscribe with a national internet service provider, like Earthlink or Mindspring.

5. Campus Life: Managing the Village

1. Vincow address to trustees' Executive Committee, Mar. 5, 1993, Trustee Collection.

2. Syracuse University played a leading role in establishing the principle of in loco parentis in a precedent-setting 1928 New York State Appellate Division case, *Anthony v. Syracuse University*. The court upheld the university's right to dismiss a student for violating the student contract to abide by SU's behavior code. In the case of Beatrice Anthony, she was dismissed for not being "a typical Syracuse girl."

3. John Robert Greene, with Karrie A. Baron, Debora D. Hall, and Matthew Sharp, *Syracuse University*, vol. 5, *The Eggers Years* (Syracuse: Syracuse Univ. Press), 263.

4. Robert Shields, "Music Students Stage Sit-in," *Daily Orange*, Dec. 5, 1991.

5. Shaw cabinet meeting notes, Dec. 9, 1991, Shaw Collection.

6. Shaw cabinet minutes, Jan. 27, 1992, Shaw Collection.

7. Robert L. Smith, "Report: Students Should Hear SU Rape Cases," *Post-Standard*, Mar. 17, 1993.

8. Callahan, interview with author, Dec. 28, 2017.

9. Lauren Wiley, "Man Rapes Student near Quad," *Daily Orange*, Dec. 5, 1994.

10. Kristen Nye, "Hazing Sparks Six Suspensions," *Daily Orange*, Aug. 31, 1995, A1.

11. Shaw to Mr. and Mrs. Gerald C. Hilton, letter, Mar. 2, 1995, Shaw Collection.

12. Shaw, interview with author, Naples, Florida, Mar. 14, 2016.

13. Eleanor Ware, interview with author, Nov. 10, 2015.

14. Shaw cabinet meeting notes, Sept. 11, 1991, Shaw Collection.

15. In New York State, peace officers have most but not all police powers, receive less training than police officers, and need special training to carry firearms.

16. "Peace Officer History of Enhancement to Campus Security," Human Services and Government Relations Collection.

17. After 9/11, SUNY ESF president Cornelius B. Murphy Jr. changed campus policy to allow peace officers to carry firearms under particular circumstances. Murphy memo to Shaw, Feb. 26, 2004, Human Services and Government Relations Collection.

18. Harvey Kaiser, SWOT report, Office of Facilities Administration, June 1991, Shaw Collection.

19. Shaw, interview with author, Mar. 14, 2016.

20. Beth Rougeux, interview with author, Apr. 5, 2016.

21. A 281-hour training program was approved in June 1996.

22. "Peace Officer History of Enhancement to Campus Security," Human Services and Government Relations Collection.

23. House parties were also underway on neighboring Clarendon Street and Euclid Avenue.

24. Eleanor Gallagher married Ben Ware on Mar. 7, 1998, and changed her surname to Ware shortly after.

25. Woodstock '99, https://en.wikipedia.org/wiki/Woodstock_%2799.

26. Gloria Wright, "Student Judicial Cases Soar at SU," *Post-Standard*, Sept. 20, 1999.

27. Editorial, "Binge Drinking Colleges and Universities Wage an Important Battle with Alcohol Abuse," *Post-Standard*, Sept. 1, 1999.

28. Dan Gonzalez, "SU, City Back Police Patrols," *Post-Standard*, Sept. 24, 1999.

29. "Syracuse University East Neighborhood Initiative," SU Real Estate Office report, Nov. 17, 1993, Human Services and Government Relations Collection.

30. Anastasia Urtz to Shaw, memorandum concerning Neighborhood Patrol Initiative, Nov. 30, 1999, Human Services and Government Relations Collection.

31. Chancellor's report to trustees, May 12, 2001, Trustee Collection.

32. The Remembrance Scholarship program was proposed by David Smith, dean of admissions and financial aid. The annual competition for thirty-five, $5,000 awards requires applicants to research the tragedy and its victims. The awards and the annual convocation were created to preserve the memory of Pan Am Flight 103.

33. Each figure, built on a welded steel armature coated with fiberglass and synthetic stone, weighed an average of 225 pounds and required a four-person crew with machinery to move.

6. Diversity: Upholding a Value

1. "They love the education they got that set them on their paths to the middle class. A lot of them were poor coming in. But they didn't like the on-campus experience, the social experience, what they regarded of racism in the classroom." Robert Hill, interview with author, Oct. 26, 2016.

2. George William "Billy" Hunter, an attorney, played football for SU, the Washington Redskins, and the Miami Dolphins. He was one of the youngest US attorneys ever and is a former executive director of the National Basketball Players Association. Suzanne De Passe is a former Motown executive and a film producer.

3. Larry Martin to faculty and staff, memorandum concerning Coming Back Together V, Sept. 1, 1995, Student Affairs Collection.

4. Nicole Taylor, "Martha's Vineyard Has a Nourishing Magic for Black Americans," *New York Times*, Aug. 22, 2017.

5. Sean Kirst, "Finally, SU Says Thanks," *Post-Standard*, Nov. 17, 1995.

6. Michael Flusche to Vincow, diversity study for Middle States report, June 1, 1993, Vincow Collection.

7. Shaw and Paul Wisdom, "The Black Challenge to Higher Education," *Educational Record* 50 (1969): 351–59; also in *The Campus and the Racial Crisis* (Washington, DC: American Council on Education, 1970). Another of his contributions: "A Case Study: The President's Role in Creating a Healthy Racial/Ethnic Climate," in *The Lurking Evil: Racial and Ethnic Conflict on the College Campus*, edited by Robert Hively (Washington, DC: American Association of State Colleges and Universities, 1990).

8. $140,000 was to add three faculty positions to African American Studies, and $200,000 was to add five minority faculty positions across campus.

9. Tom Boyd, SU director, employment practices and equal employment opportunities, to Professor Paul Salomone, memorandum regarding approval of search plan proposal, Dec. 15, 1994, Shaw Collection.

10. Shaw to cabinet members, memorandum regarding follow-up on diversity in employment practices, 1994–95, June 14, 1995, Shaw Collection.

11. Women's Studies at SU received approval as a concentration in 1982, a minor in 1989, and a major in 1991. It began offering a graduate certificate in 1987. Diane Lyden Murphy, *History of Women at Syracuse University*, exhibit in Eggers Hall.

12. Vincow to Shaw, Women's Studies Program, Sept. 25, 1992, Shaw Collection.

13. Ad Hoc Faculty Committee on Women's Concerns, Nov. 9, 1992, Shaw Collection.

14. Diane Murphy and Marie Provine, "Responding to Sexual Harassment at Syracuse University," Apr. 26, 1993, Shaw Collection.

15. "Military's Ban on Gays Protested Nationwide," staff report, *Chronicle of Higher Education*, Apr. 17, 1991.

16. Michelle N-K Collison, "Many ROTC Units under Fire," *Chronicle of Higher Education*, Nov. 8, 1989.

17. Maria Olson, "Shaw Rejects Appeal on ROTC Disclaimer," *Wisconsin State Journal*, May 8, 1990.

18. Phil McDade, "Pressure on ROTC Continues," *Wisconsin State Journal*, Nov. 26, 1990.

19. Shaw to Dick Cheney, letter, Sept. 30, 1991, Shaw Collection.

20. Shaw to Lesbian and Gay Collective of Syracuse University, letter, Dec. 9, 1991, Shaw Collection.

21. National Defense Authorization Act for Fiscal Year 1996, Pub. L. 104–106, S. 1124, 110 Stat. 315, enacted Feb. 10, 1996.

22. Anthony DePalma, "2 Universities Give Gay Partners Same Sex Benefits as Married Couples," *New York Times*, Dec. 24, 1992.

23. Shaw, interview with author, Nov. 3, 2015.

24. Frank Brieaddy and Paul Reide, "SU: Scouts' Gay Policy Ends Dome Fundraiser," *Post-Standard*, Apr. 28, 2001.

25. Despite long-standing criticisms that the university gouged the Boy Scouts for the event, it was not a huge moneymaker for SU. The university charged the Scout Council about $100,000 to cater and host the event and netted between $10,000 and $20,000, according to a May 14, 1996, memo to Shaw from Marcoccia regarding Dome receipts, in the Shaw Collection.

26. Bruce Carter, interview with author, Dec. 14, 2016.

27. Gil Troy, *The Age of Clinton: America in the 1990s* (New York: St. Martin's Press, 2015), 275.

28. Trustees' Student Affairs Committee minutes, May 11, 2001, Trustee Collection.

29. Trustees' Executive Committee minutes, Feb. 4, 2000, Trustee Collection.

30. Trustees at a Nov. 2002 Academic Affairs Committee meeting noted the "alarming lack of males enrolled at universities across the nation."

31. Tom Mortenson, "What's Wrong with the Guys?" fact sheet, Pell Institute for the Study of Opportunity in Higher Education, Washington, DC, 2003.

32. Stephanie Strom, "A Sweetheart Becomes Suspect," *New York Times*, June 27, 1996.

33. Greene, *The Eggers Years*, 228.

34. Nicholas Steffans, "Naked Bike Riders Protest Sweatshops," *Daily Orange*, Mar. 27, 2000.

35. Fred O. Williams and Jay Tokasz, "New Era, Union Reach Deal," *Buffalo News*, June 5, 2002.

36. Webber, interview with author, Jan. 29, 2016.

37. Shaw, interview with author, June 27, 2016.

38. Middle States analysis of SU's periodic review report, Aug. 2003, Shaw Collection.

39. Neil Strodel, interview with author, Sept. 26, 2016.

40. Eleanor Ware to Shaw, diversity training proposal, Feb. 14, 2001, Human Services and Government Relations Collection.

41. The incident occurred at Darwin's Bar, at 701 S. Crouse Avenue, May 7, 2002.

42. The university ultimately placed Sigma Alpha Epsilon fraternity on interim suspension and took unspecified action against Levine. Nancy Buczek, "SU Apologizes, Suspends Fraternity," *Post-Standard*, May 10, 2002.

43. Kevin Flynn, "Shooting in the Bronx: The Overview," *New York Times*, Feb. 14, 1999.

7. Intercollegiate Athletics: A New Era

1. Although Slive soon left to become commissioner of the Great Midwest Conference, Glazier became a partner with BS&K in June 1991. Cynthia Jones, Glazier's colleague, joined him, and they established a lucrative niche for BS&K representing schools facing possible NCAA charges.

2. Alexander Wolff and Armand Keteyian, *Raw Recruits* (New York: Pocket Books, 1990).

3. Frank Brieaddy, "A Calm Boeheim Says There's Nothing to This," *Post-Standard*, Mar. 7, 1990, C1.

4. Under NCAA rules, an institution is obligated to declare an athlete ineligible once school officials become aware of an infraction. Staff Reports, "SU Chaos: 7 Out Then In," *Post-Standard*, Feb. 9, 1991.

5. FOC members were David Bennett; Howard Johnson, associate vice chancellor for academic affairs and professor of mathematics; Travis Lewin, professor of law; Nancy Sharp, associate professor of newspaper; A. Dale Tussing, professor of economics; and James Wiggins, professor and chairman of the religion department.

6. Trustees' Executive Committee meeting minutes, Jan. 3, 1992, Trustee Collection.

7. Jim Boeheim, with Jack McCallum, *Bleeding Orange* (New York: Harper Collins, 2014), 153. © 2014 by Jim Boeheim and Jack McCallum. Courtesy of Harper Collins Publishers.

8. Mike Fish, "SU Hires Compliance Expert," *Post-Standard*, Mar. 6, 1992.

9. Sean Kirst, "Now, a Test for SU's Administration," *Post-Standard*, May 12, 1993.

10. Lindsay Kramer, "Chancellor: Boosters Meant Well," *Post-Standard*, Feb. 13, 1992, A9.

11. Associated Press, "Top Syracuse Booster Is Asked to Leave Post," Feb. 12, 1991.

12. Tom Foster, "Investigation Cost SU $875,000 in Legal Fees," *Post-Standard*, Oct. 3, 1992.

13. NCAA, "Syracuse University Infractions Report," Oct. 1, 1992, Shaw Collection.

14. Shaw remarks on NCAA report of sanctions, press conference, Oct. 1, 1992, Shaw Collection.

15. Charlie King, "Mario Cuomo, Hard-Nosed on the Hard Court," *Daily News*, Jan. 6, 2015, http://www.nydailynews.com/opinion/charlie-king-mario-cuomo-hard-nosed-hard-court-article-1.2067381.

16. Shaw to Mario Cuomo, letter, Oct. 7, 1992, Shaw Collection.

17. Mike McAndrew and Mike Waters, "SU Player Suspended Following Bar Brawl," *Post-Standard*, Jan. 9, 1993, A1.

18. Ibid.

19. Shaw to Jake Crouthamel, letter, Jan. 12, 1993, Shaw Collection.

20. Mike Waters, "SU Writes Rule Book on Players' Behavior," *Post-Standard*, July 30, 1993.

21. Moten holds the title of all-time leading scorer for the Big East.

22. Boeheim, *Bleeding Orange*, 173.

23. Ibid., 175.

24. Ibid., 201.

25. Ibid., 208.

26. The freeze option is a complex, running-based strategy in which plays change in the moment according to the positioning or movements of the defense.

27. Donnie Webb, "MVP Graves Wins Raves," *Post-Standard*, Jan. 2, 1992.

28. Sarah Layden, "Coach P Leads SU's Employee Salary List," *Post-Standard*, Nov. 16, 2000.

29. Bill Kellar, director of Nike Football Sports Marketing, to Pasqualoni, Feb. 10, 1994, Shaw Collection.

30. Donnie Webb, "Shaw to Angry Fans: 'Get a Life,'" *Post-Standard*, Nov. 17, 1999.

31. Donnie Webb, "SU Tickets Thrown for a Loss," *Post-Standard*, Sept. 7, 2001.

32. Shaw, interview with author, Nov. 3, 2015.

33. Jake Crouthamel, "SU Football Fans Have High Energy—and Expectations," *Post-Standard*, Dec. 21, 2003, C3.

34. Greene, *The Eggers Years*, 125.

35. "Title IX," Wikipedia, https://en.wikipedia.org/wiki/Title_IX.

36. Athletics reported to Marcoccia's office.

37. Lou Marcoccia to Shaw, memorandum, Apr. 20, 1992, Shaw Collection.

38. "Q&A: Jake Crouthamel," *Orange Exclusive*, Apr. 2003.

39. Sean Kirst, "The First Dallas Cowboy," *Post-Standard*, Jan. 20, 1993.

40. In 2001, the athletic department launched a direct-mail appeal for nonrevenue sports, with an initial focus on women's sports.

41. Associated Press, "Women Sue Syracuse University to Start Lacrosse Team," May 10, 1995.

42. Tom Leo, "Crouthamel Says Football Rates Break," *Herald American*, July 23, 1995.

43. The US Court of Appeals for the Second Circuit found that plaintiffs lacked standing to sue and that some of their claims were moot because of actions the university had taken since the women had filed suit.

44. Jim Naughton, "More Colleges Cut Men's Teams," *Chronicle of Higher Education*, Feb. 21, 1997.

45. Trustees' Executive Committee meeting minutes, Mar. 7, 1997, Trustee Collection.

46. Paul Riede, "Tennis Lawsuit Settled," *Post-Standard*, Mar. 27, 1999.

47. Associated Press, "Syracuse Coach Resigns," May 8, 1999.

48. "Q&A: Jake Crouthamel," *Orange Exclusive*, Apr. 2003.

49. Big East teams had played in NCAA championship games nine times.

50. Boeheim, *Bleeding Orange*, 95.

51. Shalala, interview with author, May 4, 2016.

52. The eight senators were Jon S. Corzine (D-New Jersey), Christopher J. Dodd (D-Connecticut), and Robert C. Byrd (D-West Virginia), John W. Warner (R-Virginia), Arlen Specter (R-Pennsylvania), Joseph Lieberman (D-Connecticut), John D. Rockefeller IV (D-West Virginia), and George Allen (R-Virginia and the son of NFL head coach George Allen).

53. Mike Waters, "Crouthamel Says, 'I Was Speechless,'" *Post-Standard*, July 1, 2003.

8. New Entrepreneurism: Commerce on Campus

1. Shaw to cabinet officers, memorandum regarding cost containment targets, Aug. 28, 1991, Shaw Collection.

2. Shaw address to trustees, Nov. 1, 2002, Trustee Collection.

3. Webber, interview with author, Jan. 29, 2016.

4. Thomas Evans (Bond, Schoeneck and King) to C. Frank Harrigan, City of Syracuse Corporation Counsel, letter, Sept. 25, 1992, Shaw Collection.

5. Flusche, interview with author, Apr. 19, 2016.

6. Business improvement and lighting districts are taxing entities that businesses pay into to get extra street maintenance and more attractive street lights.

7. Greene, *The Eggers Years*, 251.

8. The fallout shelter tax break, which reduced the hotel's property tax bill some 20 percent, was a vestige of Cold War civil defense planning, adopted by the city of Syracuse in the 1960s to encourage parking garage development. The Berlin Wall came down in 1989, and the Soviet Union disbanded in 1991.

9. Fiscal 2002–3 operating budget variances, trustees' Executive Committee meeting minutes, Aug. 1, 2003, Trustee Collection.

10. Marcoccia to Shaw, memorandum concerning Carrier Dome event receipts, May 14, 1996, Shaw Collection.

11. Carrier Dome SWOT report to Shaw, 1991, Shaw Collection.

12. Responding to Crouthamel's suggestions about nonathletic events at the Dome in a Nov. 6, 1990, memo, Eggers wrote, "No wrestling and definitely no boxing in my time." Eggers Collection.

13. Frank Brieaddy, "Wrestling and Roller Derby Are Interested, Jake," *Post-Standard*, Dec. 18, 1986.

14. Marcoccia to Shaw, memorandum regarding Dome events, Oct. 31, 1991, Shaw Collection.

15. Shaw to Marcoccia, handwritten note, Aug. 24, 1994, Shaw Collection.

16. Mary Ann suggested the songs to her husband in a fax, Jan. 3, 1994, and Shaw passed along the suggestions to Crouthamel.

17. South Korea has a large Methodist population, and SU's Methodist affiliation (it was founded as a Methodist College) helped attract Methodist students. Shaw, interview with author, Nov. 2–3, 2015.

18. This was a good decade before Skype, FaceTime, or other video-conferencing capabilities.

19. Thomas Cummings to Shaw and Vincow, "Asia and Pacific Rim, New Enrollment and Revenue Targets," Sept. 3, 1998, Vincow Collection.

20. Investopedia, "Asian Financial Crisis," http://www.investopedia.com/terms /a/asian-financial-crisis.asp.

21. Beth McMurtrie, "Foreign Enrollments Grow in U.S. but So Does Competition from Other Nations," *Chronicle of Higher Education*, Nov. 16, 2001.

22. Mike McAndrew, "Manny's Fortune Smiles on SU," *Post-Standard*, Nov. 10, 1999, A1.

23. SU Budget Office report, enrollment assumptions, Aug. 21, 1991, Shaw Collection.

24. Lampe, interview with author, May 2, 2016.

25. Cummings, interview with author, Mar. 12, 2016.

26. The Euro currency did not circulate until 2002. https://en.wikipedia.org /wiki/History_of_the_euro.

27. Trustees' Executive Committee meeting minutes, Mar. 10, 2000, Trustee Collection.

28. DIPA enrollment report, 2001–10, Freund Collection.

29. DIPA cost comparisons, 2010, Freund Collection.

30. Trustees' Executive Committee minutes, Jan. 3, 1995, STrustee Collection.

31. Resolution to sell real estate, Oct. 6, 1997, Trustee Collection.

32. Previously, degrees were only awarded by the college in which a matriculating part-time UC student was enrolled.

9. Work Environment: Building Community

1. Bruce Carter, interview with author, Dec. 14, 2016. During Shaw's time, Carter was an associate professor of psychology and, later, director of the Honors Program.

2. David May to Eleanor Gallagher, memorandum concerning SUIQ issues, Jan. 11, 1991, Human Services and Government Relations Collection.

3. David Smith, interview with author, Jan. 7, 2016.

4. Michael Flusche, interview with author, Apr. 19, 2016.

5. Joan Carpenter to Shaw, memorandum concerning employee recognition program, Jan. 5, 1994, Shaw Collection.

6. Neil Strodel, interview with author, Sept. 26, 2016.

7. SEIU representatives, interview with author, Apr. 7, 2017.

8. On Sept. 5, SU football played its home-opener against Tennessee. SU lost to tenth-ranked Tennessee 33–34 in front of 49,550 fans.

9. Neil Strodel, interview with author, Sept. 26, 2016.

10. Peter Webber, interview with author, Jan. 29, 2016.

11. Strodel, interview with author, Sept. 26, 2016.

12. Shaw report to trustees' Executive Committee, July 2001, Trustee Collection.

13. Trustees' Budget Committee minutes, Nov. 5, 1998, Trustee Collection.

14. Human Services and Government Relations goals report, 2002–3, Human Services and Government Relations Collection.

15. In 1993, SU counted 7,185 beds in its residence halls, 5,000 in the neighborhood east of the university, and 1,605 south of the campus.

16. There were nearly 600 fewer students living in the east neighborhood in 1993 than in the spring of 1991 (1,884 down from 2,465). SU East Neighborhood Initiative, Nov. 1993, Shaw Collection.

17. City of Syracuse Zoning Administration Study of East Neighborhood, 1990, Shaw Collection.

18. The Syracuse Neighborhood Initiative, designed to revive the city's housing stock, was launched in 1999 with a $5 million grant from the federal Department of Housing and Urban Development.

19. During moderate to light snowfalls, a melt system kept the roof clear. The Dome's temperature would have to be raised to at least 75 degrees Fahrenheit, making game crowds uncomfortable.

20. Mike Waters, "Manager of Syracuse's Carrier Dome Worries about Its Roof with Every Snowstorm That's Predicted," *Post-Standard*, Dec. 14, 2010.

21. Shaw to Marcoccia, note regarding Patrick Campbell's description of snow maintenance on the Dome roof, Nov. 15, 1995, Shaw Collection.

22. Greene, *The Eggers Years*, 165.

23. Office of Government Relations briefing, "Planned Replacement of the Carrier Dome Roof," 1997, Human Services and Government Relations Collection.

24. Gloria Wright and Erin Duggan, "Dome Worker Falls 60 Feet to His Death," *Post-Standard*, June 9, 1999.

25. John O'Brien, "OSHA Inspectors Missed Hatch," *Post-Standard*, July 17, 1999.

10. Reassessment: Adjusting Course

1. Gwenn Judge, interview with author, Oct. 4, 2016.

2. Haviland, "Becoming a Student-Centered Research University."

3. Shaw, chancellor's report, trustee meeting, Nov. 8, 1991, Trustee Collection.

4. For the comparison, Haviland used SAT percentile rankings rather than raw scores because the College Board had adjusted the SAT scoring for the class entering in 1995, which essentially raised raw scores above what they had been previously.

5. Haviland, "Becoming a Student-Centered Research University," 190; adjusted for inflation.

6. David Smith, interview with author, Oct. 3, 2016.

7. Office of Enrollment Management, planned changes for fall 2002, Freund Collection.

8. David Smith, email response to author inquiry regarding waitlist and alternative offer strategies, Aug. 13, 2017. SU had not had a waitlist since at least 1973, perhaps ever.

9. Office of Enrollment Management, enrollment report, Apr. 1, 2004, Shaw Collection.

10. Haviland, "Becoming a Student-Centered Research University," 215.

11. Ibid., 224.

12. Pamela McLaughlin, interview with author, Aug. 29, 2017.

13. Haviland, "Becoming a Student-Centered Research University," 247.

14. McLaughlin, interview with author, Aug. 29, 2017.

15. Greene, *The Tolley Years*, 76.

16. Research spending declined from its high of $33,124,499 in 1987–88 to $24,942,118 in 1996–97, dollars adjusted for inflation. Haviland, "Becoming a Student-Centered Research University," 234.

17. Between 1988–89 and 1996–97, engineering's research spending declined from $11,945,047 to $4,182,113, Maxwell's increased from $1,263,042 to $2,872,373, and information studies went from $580,608 to $1,421,588. In arts and sciences, which experienced big cuts and departures of top research faculty, spending declined from $7,729,655 to $5,878,005.

18. Karen W. Arenson, "Undergraduate Education Is Lacking, Report Finds," *New York Times*, Apr. 20, 1998.

19. "Administrative Performance Review of Kenneth A. Shaw," Dec. 9, 1996, Shaw Collection.

20. Shaw, interview with author, Mar. 14, 2016.

21. Vincent Tinto, *Leaving College: Rethinking the Causes and Cures of Student Attrition* (Chicago: Univ. of Chicago Press, 1993).

22. A-SPIRE Plan, May 2001, Freund Collection.

23. In May 1992, rioting broke out in Los Angeles County after four police officers were acquitted of using excessive force in the videotaped arrest and beating of Rodney King. Over six days of rioting, 63 people were killed, 2,383 people were injured, and more than 12,000 were arrested. "1992 Los Angeles Riots," Wikipedia, https://en.wikipedia.org/wiki/1992_Los_Angeles_riots.

In 1994–95, over eleven months, former NFL football star O. J. Simpson was tried and acquitted of two counts of murder. The trial was deemed the most publicized trial of the century, and national surveys showed dramatic differences in the assessment of Simpson's guilt or innocence between black and white Americans. "Race Factor Tilts the Scales of Public Opinion," *USA Today*, Feb. 5, 1997.

24. Division of Student Affairs, "Co-curricular Fee Proposal," Dec. 2001, Academic Affairs Collection.

25. Comprehensive reviews are conducted every ten years.

26. "Administrative Performance Review of Kenneth A. Shaw," Dec. 9, 1996, Shaw Collection.

27. "Our horizon for improving student quality was 20 years." David Smith, interview with author, Oct. 3, 2016.

28. Shaw address to trustees, Nov. 6, 1998, Trustee Collection.

29. J. L. Nicklin, "A University Takes Financial Steps to Offer the Personal Touch," *Chronicle of Higher Education*, Dec. 18, 1998.

30. At the same time, Freund's husband, Thomas Kniesner, was appointed as a professor in the Departments of Public Administration and Economics at the Maxwell School.

31. Freund, interview with author, Feb. 2, 2016.

32. Trustee minutes, Dec. 3, 1999, Trustee Collection.

33. Trustees' Academic Affairs Committee meeting minutes, Nov. 1–2, 2001, Trustee Collection.

34. Trustees' Executive Committee meeting minutes, Sept. 8, 2000, Trustee Collection.

35. An example of a major structural obstacle: Faculty members' career advancement came from recognition by peers within their discipline, salary increases were determined by their dean or faculty chair, and they had spent years teaching and researching, usually by themselves. A-SPIRE offered few or no incentives for faculty to contribute to a different field through collaboration.

36. Trustees' Student Affairs Committee meeting minutes, Oct. 31, 2002, Trustee Collection.

37. Freund, "Academic Affairs Report to Trustees," Nov. 2003, Freund Collection.

11. Development: Raising Money

1. Greene, *The Tolley Years*, 181.

2. Between 1945–46 and 1948–49, enrollment rose from 5,716 to 19,698.

3. Greene, *The Tolley Years*, 167.

4. Greene, *The Eggers Years*, 61.

5. Ibid., 107.

6. The Book, chancellor search, 1990, Shaw's margin notes, 2, Shaw Collection.

7. Shaw also had a tradition of visiting the football team in the locker room when they won and of reciting a poem he had scribbled out at the game. "Look out, Mabel, Syracuse is going to run the table," was a typical line.

8. H. Douglas Barclay, interview with author, Oct. 19, 2015.

9. Josh Barbanel, "High School in Rare Link with College," *New York Times*, Jan. 25, 1993.

10. The consumer price index had risen 2.9 percent in 1992, and similar protests were happening at colleges across the country. William Celis III, "Colleges Increase Fees Again," *New York Times*, Apr. 7, 1993.

11. At Lubin House, Eggers and Safire once lunched with Edward Albee, who had just completed a series of creative writing program lectures on the SU campus.

12. The Safire Room would be the most lavish room in the library, with wood paneling, a coffered ceiling, custom-cut moldings, matching furnishings, and large wooden window shutters. Refurbishing the former classroom cost nearly $200,000.

13. The most valuable books, such as first editions of William Cobbett, would be kept in the library's secure archive.

14. Handwritten note on letter from Mark Weimer, SU Library curator of special collections, to Shaw, May 31, 1994, Shaw Collection.

15. The Herald Companies operated the *Post-Standard*, the *Herald Journal*, and the *Herald American*, and were part of the Newhouse family holdings.

16. At Newhouse, Safire, Janklow, Mel Elfin ('51, editor of special projects for *U.S. News & World Report*), and David Rubin, Newhouse dean, presented a seminar on "The Media Force." At Schine, Robert Menschel and five others talked about "The Arts under Siege." At the Hall of Languages, Safire, Janklow, and writer Mary Karr talked about "The Profession of the Writer." Bleier also talked to Newhouse students about media, and Menschel talked to School of Management students about investing.

17. Greene, *The Tolley Years*, 159.

18. "Bronx High School of Science," Wikipedia, https://en.wikipedia.org/wiki/The_Bronx_High_School_of_Science#Notable_alumni.

19. "Jewish Quota," Wikipedia, https://en.wikipedia.org/wiki/Jewish_quota.

20. Robert Menschel, interview with author, Aug. 16, 2016.

21. The university provided space, a salary, and fringe benefits.

22. Thomas Walsh, interview with author, Apr. 13, 2016.

23. Lubin House also became the site of more frequent trustee Executive Committee meetings.

24. Ken Johnson, "Milton Avery Revisited," *New York Times*, Nov. 5, 1999.

25. In 1959, the team went 11–0 and won the national championship.

26. Michigan Tech, in Houghton, Michigan (population 7,000), had an enrollment of 6,336 in 2000.

27. The division was formerly known as the Division of University Relations.

28. Fisher, telephone interview with author, Aug. 8, 2016.

29. "A good chancellor has a sense of who is going to be most effective in establishing the kind of relationship where money can come." Shaw, interview with author, June 27, 2016.

30. Shaw, interview with author, June 27, 2016.

31. "We want to move from being a competitive national research university to a very competitive one, and . . . that will require doubling our endowment and reserves,

so that we can draw approximately $80 million annually for a host of improvements." Shaw to trustees, May 15, 1999, Trustee Collection.

12. 9/11: Retrenchment

1. For the student who lost a parent in the 9/11 attack, SU provided full tuition for the remainder of the student's time at SU. For students with a supporting parent, guardian, or spouse who lost employment or income because of 9/11, SU provided special grants for the remainder of the academic year.

2. Shaw, interview with author, Nov. 2, 2015.

3. Editorial, "Back to Normal, Football Game Signals Central New York Is Picking Up and Moving Ahead," *Post-Standard*, Sept. 25, 2001.

4. "'Islam Is Peace' Says President," White House, https://georgewbush-white house.archives.gov/news/releases/2001/09/20010917-11.html.

5. The interdisciplinary BA in religion and society was introduced in 2002 in the College of Arts and Sciences.

6. The lecture series was the idea of Robert Menschel, who made it possible with a generous gift. Most speakers cost between $10,000 and $20,000. Menschel had been impressed by a similar lecture series at Bowdoin College, in Brunswick, Maine, where his daughter was a student. Between 2001 and 2004, the series brought in thirty-five high-culture icons and media moguls, among them Barry Diller, David McCullough, Salman Rushdie, Mort Zuckerman, Richard Leaky, Garrison Keillor, Joshua Bell, and Neil deGrasse Tyson. Michael Flusche, associate vice chancellor of academic affairs, oversaw the series. In Oct. 2002, William Safire spoke. Year after year, Safire would complain to Menschel that Flusche's speakers were too liberal.

7. Chancellor's address to the community, Oct. 2, 2001, Trustee Collection.

8. Trustees' Budget Committee meeting minutes, Oct. 31, 2002, Trustee Collection.

9. Chancellor's report to the trustees, Nov. 2, 2001, Trustee Collection.

10. Chancellor's Ad Hoc Advisory Group, "Report on the Schools and Colleges of Syracuse University," Sept. 1991, 15, Shaw Collection.

11. Chickadonz, interview with author, Apr. 13, 2017.

12. Kenneth Ma, "Syracuse U to Pay $1.1 million in Dispute over Uncertified Nursing Program," *Chronicle of Higher Education*, Apr. 6, 1999.

13. Ailenn E. Gallagher, "Nursing Report Admits SU Faults," *Daily Orange*, Oct. 20, 1998.

14. Ibid.

15. (1) 119 Euclid Avenue, Dean's Office and Admissions; (2) 426 Ostrom Avenue, Public Health and Child and Family Studies; (3) Drumlins Complex, two buildings, Sport Management and Advancement; (4) Peck Hall, 601 E. Genesee Street, Marriage and Family Therapy; (5) Bernice M. Wright Lab School South Campus; (6) Lyman Hall, Food Studies; (7) Sims Hall, Nutrition, Social Work, Research Center, IT.

16. Trustees' Executive Committee meeting minutes, Aug. 2, 2002, Trustee Collection.

17. Eggers in 1985 had called for Syracuse University to advance to the "next tier of excellence." The Book, chancellor search, 1990, 6, Shaw Collection.

18. SU Press Board of Directors meeting minutes, July 17, 2001, Freund Collection.

19. Trustees' Academic Affairs Committee meeting minutes, Nov. 1–2, 2001, Trustee Collection.

20. Trustees' Academic Affairs Committee meeting minutes, May 10, 2003, Trustee Collection.

21. Program for Renée Crown event, Shaw Collection.

22. In 2002, Rubin began hosting a weekly public affairs program, *Ivory Tower*, on the local PBS affiliate WCNY. He continued hosting it for fourteen years.

23. "Growth and the University," enrollment report, 1996, Vincow Collection.

24. Rubin, interview with author, Feb. 26, 2016.

25. Ad Hoc Advisory Group, "Report on Schools and Colleges," Sept. 1991, Shaw Collection.

26. Rubin suspected his Jewish heritage was among the reasons he was hired as dean of the Newhouse School, because it would resonate with the Newhouse family. Rubin, interview with author, Feb. 26, 2016.

27. SU 990 tax returns, 2001, 2002, 2003.

13. Research and More: Reclaiming the Legacy

1. The study, commissioned by New York's Urban Development Corporation (UDC) was conducted by the management consulting firm Arthur D. Little.

2. High population densities around the nation's big urban centers create heavy residential demand that drives up the cost of all vacant land. Industrial land typically sells for roughly one-third of the cost of residential land, but the only way to maintain large tracts of affordable land near major urban centers is to create industrial, or research, parks. "Los Angeles' Industrial Land: Sustaining a Dynamic City Economy," Department of City Planning and the Community Redevelopment Agency, Dec. 2007.

3. Rick Moriarty, "Industrial Park Wins Grant," *Post-Standard*, May 21, 1991.

4. Robert L. Smith, "Earth Turned at SU to Start Building Research Park," *Post-Standard*, Nov. 22, 1994.

5. Webber, interview with author, Jan. 29, 2016.

6. David Tobin, "SRC in Cicero Meets Army Challenge to Save Lives," *Post-Standard*, May 2, 2010.

7. Edward Bogucz, dean of the College of Engineering and Computer Science, was distraught over SRC's move. "We have this captive company, on our campus, and you're going to let them move? No! Figure out some kind of deal that makes it attractive to them. There was nothing in the decision that related to the value to the university of having that company in our midst." Bogucz, interview with author, May 5, 2016.

8. Ben Ware, interview with author, Dec. 14, 2015.

9. Greene, *The Eggers Years*, 151.

10. Among the businesses that agreed to invest in Centers of Excellence research were Niagara Mohawk, McQuay International, Syracuse Research Corporation, Carrier Corporation, Welch Allyn, EMC2 Corporation, NYIEQ Center, Inc., and Healthway Products Company.

11. A 1999 report on the CASE Center noted $98 million in state, federal, and corporate funding between 1984 and 2000. Freund Collection.

12. Michelle Breidenbach, "Research Facility Support Lagging," *Post-Standard*, Mar. 12, 2002.

13. Chancellor's report to trustees, Nov. 1, 2002, Trustee Collection.

14. Rick Moriarty, "Congel Puts Full-Court Press on University," *Post-Standard*, Sept. 22, 2002.

15. Nancy Buczek, "Excellence Center for CNY," *Post-Standard*, June 6, 2002.

16. Pataki garnered 49.4 percent of the vote, Carl McCall 33.5 percent, and Tom Golisano 14.3 percent.

17. Moving the CoE south of the existing park would require extending utilities, estimated to cost $1.5 million. The university asked Congressman Jim Walsh for assistance getting an off-ramp from I-481 that would lead to the research park.

18. Michelle Breidenbach and Nancy Buczek, "CNY Waits for Millions Pataki Pledged for Center," *Post-Standard*, Oct. 8, 2003.

19. Haviland, "Becoming a Student-Centered Research University," 127.

20. Shaw to trustees' Executive Committee, memorandum regarding financial matters, May 28, 2004, Trustee Collection.

21. Briefing supporting Sheldon Stone loan request, n.d., Freund Collection.

22. Sarah Layden, "SU Has Big Plans for Tiny Particles," *Post-Standard*, Oct. 19, 2000.

23. "BTeV Experiment," Wikipedia, https://en.wikipedia.org/wiki/BTeV _experiment.

24. Charles Phelps to Debbie Freund, email concerning SU's AAU status, Sept. 18, 1999, Freund Collection.

25. Freund, interview with author, Feb. 2, 2016.

26. A-SPIRE Plan, May 2001, Freund Collection.

27. Senate Budget Committee, report on faculty and staff salaries and compensation, Oct. 18, 1999, Trustee Collection.

28. "1990s United States Boom," Wikipedia, https://en.wikipedia.org/wiki /1990s_United_States_boom.

29. Julie L. Nicklin, "A University Takes Financial Steps to Offer the Personal Touch," *Chronicle of Higher Education*, Dec. 18, 1998.

30. Bond Rating Update, *Chronicle of Higher Education*, Nov. 12, 1999.

31. Trustees' Executive Committee resolution, Feb. 4, 2000, Trustee Collection.

32. Robin Wilson, Jeff Sharlet, and Julianne Basinger, "Rutgers U Scores a Triple against Syracuse," *Chronicle of Higher Education*, Sept. 21, 2001.

33. Chancellor's report to trustees, Nov. 3, 2000, Trustee Collection.

34. David Kohr to Marcoccia, email regarding temporary housing, July 18, 2002, Shaw Collection.

35. Neal Peirce and Curtis Johnson, Citistates Group, "Closer Ties to Universities and Colleges Would Benefit Region," *Post-Standard*, July 1, 2002.

36. Eric Mower, interview with author, Aug. 11, 2016.

37. Shaw responded to the Citistates report with an inventory of SU/community partnerships in a letter to the editor, "SU Is Not a 'Fortress on the Hill,'" *Post-Standard*, July 21, 2002.

38. SU 990 tax return, 2004.

39. Lipman Hearne, "Syracuse University Self-Assessment Research Interim Report," Feb. 2004, Freund Collection.

40. Peer institutions identified by Syracuse University for Lipman Hearne's comparison: American University, Northwestern University, Boston College, Penn State University (University Park), Boston University, SUNY Binghamton, Cornell University, University of Maryland (College Park), George Washington University, University of Pennsylvania, New York University, and the University of Rochester.

14. Transition: Out of the Spotlight

1. Freund, interview with author, Feb. 2, 2016; Sellars, interview with author, June 23, 2016.

2. Proceeds from the cookbook series went to the United Way.

3. Trustees' Executive Committee meeting minutes, Apr. 23, 2003, Trustee Collection.

4. Nancy Buczek, "Wanted at SU: A People Person with Big East Savvy," *Post-Standard*, Feb. 5, 2004.

5. Nancy Buczek, "Shaw: You're Going to Love New Chancellor," *Post-Standard*, Feb. 7, 2004.

6. Ibid.

7. Chancellor's residence improvements, Mar. 3, 2004, Shaw Collection.

8. For Eggers's farewell celebration, which was a $75-per-person, black-tie event, Eggers and wife Mildred rode into the Carrier Dome in a horse-drawn carriage.

9. Nancy Buczek, "Shaws Driving Away from SU in SUV," *Post-Standard*, Apr. 16, 2004.

10. 9/11 is a common salary formula for administrators moving to teaching. It presumes administrators work eleven months (with a month's vacation), and professors work nine months. University Professors also receive a bourse, or stipend, for secretarial help, travel, and expenses. Budget-wise, a University Professor is not associated with any unit so does not add to the budget of any unit.

11. Nancy Buczek, "Kenneth 'Buzz' Shaw Reflects on University, Community," *Post-Standard*, July 31, 2004.

12. Rick Moriarty, "Two Agencies Share a Mission to Foster Economic Growth," *Post-Standard*, Jan. 8, 2010.

13. Rob Simpson, interview with author, Feb. 12, 2016.

14. Mary Ann Shaw, interview with author, Nov. 2, 2015.

15. Eileen Pezzi, interview with author, Jan. 26, 2016.

16. Between 1991 and 2001, market value of the endowment increased by 350 percent. Annual fund-raising increased from $29.7 million in 1991 to $61 million in 2001.

17. Shaw, "SU's Long-Range Challenges," Oct. 8. 2003, Shaw Collection.

18. Nancy Buczek, "Plan: Use SU Tuition Money for Athletics," *Post-Standard*, Jan. 15, 2004.

19. Chancellor's report to trustees, May 10, 2003, Trustee Collection.

20. "Projects," Bohlin Cywinski Jackson, https://bcj.com/projects/apple-store -fifth-avenue-new-york.

21. Bohlin Cywinski Jackson was paid $1,868,686 in 2001 and 2002. SU 990 tax return, 2001, 2002.

22. Syracuse University Office of Design and Construction, Bohlin Cywinski Jackson, and Urban Workshop, *Syracuse University Campus Plan, 2003*, Syracuse University Design and Construction Collection.

23. In 1990, 23 percent of entering freshmen were in the top 10 percent of their high school class; in 2003, 41 percent.

24. Minority faculty made up 10 percent of the total in 1991, 16 percent in 2003.

25. Editorial, "Why Forbes Ranked Syracuse so Far Down," *Post-Standard*, June 18, 2001.

26. SU employment statistics summary, 2002–3, Human Services and Government Relations Collection.

Works Consulted

Boeheim, Jim, with Jack McCallum. *Bleeding Orange.* New York: Harper Collins Publishers, 2014.

Galpin, W. Freeman. *Syracuse University.* Vol. 1, *The Pioneer Days.* Syracuse: Syracuse Univ. Press, 1952.

Gorney, Jeffrey. *Syracuse University: An Architectural Guide.* Syracuse: Syracuse Univ. Press, 2006.

Greene, John Robert, with Karrie A. Baron. *Syracuse University.* Vol. 4, *The Tolley Years.* Syracuse: Syracuse Univ. Press, 1996.

Greene, John Robert, with Karrie A. Baron, Debora D. Hall, and Matthew Sharp. *Syracuse University.* Vol. 5, *The Eggers Years.* Syracuse: Syracuse Univ. Press, 1998.

Haviland, Donald J. "Becoming a Student-Centered Research University: A Case Study of Organizational Change." PhD diss., Syracuse University, 1999.

Hurd, Sandra N., and Ruth Federman Stein. *Building and Sustaining Learning Communities: The Syracuse University Experience.* Bolton, MA: Anker Publishing, 2004.

Ihlanfeldt, William. *Achieving Optimal Enrollments and Tuition Revenues.* San Francisco: Jossey-Bass, 1980.

Issacson, Walter. *The Innovators: How a Group of Hackers, Geniuses, and Geeks Created the Digital Revolution.* New York: Simon & Schuster, 2014.

Marchand, Donald A., and Forest W. Horton Jr. *Infotrends: Profiting from Your Information Resources.* New York: John Wiley, 1986.

Packer, George. *The Unwinding: An Inner History of the New America.* New York: Farrar, Straus and Giroux, 2013.

Shaw, Kenneth, A. *The Intentional Leader.* Syracuse: Syracuse Univ. Press, 2005.

———. *The Successful President: BuzzWords on Leadership.* ACE series. Phoenix, AZ: Oryx Press, 1999.

Stam, David H. *What Happened to Me: My Life with Books, Research Libraries, and Performing Arts.* Bloomington, IN: AuthorHouse, 2014.

Stiglitz, Joseph E. *The Roaring Nineties.* New York: W. W. Norton, 2003.

Syracuse University Office of Design and Construction, Bohlin Cywinski Jackson, and Urban Workshop. *Syracuse University Campus Plan, 2003.* Syracuse: Syracuse University, 2003.

Tinto, Vincent. *Leaving College: Rethinking the Causes and Cures of Student Attrition.* Chicago: Univ. of Chicago Press, 1993.

Troy, Gil. *The Age of Clinton: America in the 1990s.* New York: St. Martin's Press, 2015.

Wolff, Alexander, and Armand Keteyian. *Raw Recruits.* New York: Pocket Books, 1990.

Index

Italic page numbers denote illustrations.

289

Engineering, College of: dean of,
267n27; merger of, 29, 34, 47–48;
restructuring and, 46–49, 169,
173; women in, 103–4
Engineering and Computer Science,
College of: dean of, 49, 218, 223;
enrollment in, 168; faculty of,
164, 217, 224; interdisciplinary
collaboration and, 180; research
programs and, 173, 218, 278n17;
restructuring of, 222; SRC and,
217, 282n7
Engineering Research Center, 221
enrollment. *See* student enrollment
entrepreneurial initiatives, 137–50;
Auxiliary Services and, 137–39;
for Carrier Dome, 144–45,
276n12; Crouse–Marshall
Street improvement project, 139,
140–41, *141*; DIPA and, 138,
147–49, 276n26; international
students and, 138, 145–47,
276n17; Sheraton University Inn
and, 141–44, *142*, 275n8, 276n12;
Tolley increase in, 184; University
College and, 138, 149–50, 276n32
Ephron, Nora, 197
ERIC (Educational Resources Infor-
mation Center), 171
Ericson, Kirsten, 133–34
ESPN, 135, 204
Evensky, Jerry, *39*
Executive Committee, 186–87

facilitated communication (FC),
44–46
Facilitated Communication Institute,
45
Facilities Management, Office of,
12–13
faculty: African American and
Latino, 97–98, 106–7, 169, 271n8;
Chancellor's Citation for, 154;

hiring and retention of, 225–27;
impact of restructuring on, 169,
172–74; layoffs of, 28, 40–42;
minority, 97–98, 106–7, 169, 244,
271n8, 285n24; morale of, 17,
32–33, 34, 38–39, 207, 222; part-
time, 169, 243; recruitment of,
96, 222, 225; research programs
and, 30, 225–27; retreats for, 174;
salary increases for, 267n18; in
science and engineering, 103–4;
Ken Shaw's interactions with,
173–74; SUIQ and, 153; supported
resignation of, 41–42, 48, 166,
267n18; tenured, 41–42, 98, 107,
267n18; women, 97, 98, 107
Faculty Oversight Committee (FOC),
112, 273n5
Faculty-to-Faculty Teaching Consultancy, 40
Fair Labor Association (FLA), 105
fair-wage initiative, 157
Falge, John, 86
fallout shelter tax break, 143, 275n8
Family Nurse Practitioner program,
207, 208
Famous Artist Broadway Theater
series, 237
FAN (Freshmen Advocacy Network),
37
FB/OH (Implicit Fringe Benefit/Over-
head), 21, 22, 49, 51, 251–52
FC (facilitated communication),
44–46
Federal District Court, 131
Federal Emergency Management
Agency (FEMA), 159
Federal Reserve, 76
Fendler, Janos, 30
Fermi National Accelerator Labora-
tory, 223
Fiesta Bowl, 52, 70, 75, 122–23, 125
Final Four, 118, 121

Shaw, Mary Ann (*cont.*)
   committee and, 3; on songs for
   Carrier Dome, 276n16; storm
   damage and, 159; Marilyn Tennity
   and, 91; Tepper and, 215; on Tow-
   son State University position, 7
Shaw, Sara Ann, 9, 12
Shaw, Susan Lynn, 9
Shaw, William, 4
Sheinkopf, Geraldine, 215
Sheldon, Thomas, 188
Sheraton Hotel & Conference Center,
   LLC, 143–44, 174
Sheraton University Inn and Confer-
   ence Center, 141–44, 142, 275n8
Shields, Joseph, 81
Sigma Alpha Epsilon, 108–9,
   273nn41–42
Silicon Valley, 216, 220
Silver, Sheldon "Shelly," 163, 164
Simmons, Nancy, 128
Simmons, Roy, Jr., 128, 147
Simpson, Michael K., 62
Simpson, O. J., 175
Simpson, Rob, 239
Sims, Lazarus, 118
S. I. Newhouse School of Public
   Communications. *See* Newhouse
   School
60 Minutes, 45
skating rinks, 90–91, 210, 244
Skytop Apartments, *158*, 161
Skytop area, 216, 217, 221
Slive, Michael, 111, 273n1
Slocum Hall, 242
Slocum Heights apartments, 158–59
Slutzker, Emanuel "Manny," 147
Slutzker, Lillian, 147
Smith, David: on admissions policies,
   53–54; Emergency Response Com-
   mittee and, 263; on financial aid,
   168; graduate research programs
   and, 225; portrait of, *53*; on

student quality, 279n27; on SUIQ,
   153; on voice response technol-
   ogy, 75
Smith, George D., 91
Smith, Horace, 175
smoking, 91–92, 117
Smullen, Bill, 150
snow storms, 161–63, *162*, 277n19
soccer (women's), 131, 133
Social Work, School of, 70, 143,
   178–79, 180, 208, 281n15
softball (women's), 132, 133
Soladay, Doris, 112, 130
Soling, Chester P., 185
Sorkin, Aaron, 197
South Africa, 104
South Campus, 86, 158–59, 216
Southern Illinois University, 7–8, 27
South Korea, 146, 276n17
space plan, 180–81, 205, 206, 214,
   242
Space Planning Advisory Committee,
   180–81
SPD (Syracuse Police Department),
   84–85, 86, 90, 270n21
Spina, Eric, 223
SRC (Syracuse Research Corpora-
   tion), 216, 217
staff: in College of Engineering, 48;
   layoffs and voluntary departures
   of, 42, 166; morale of, 17, 28,
   144; restructuring and, 169; sala-
   ries of, 43, 156, 157; strikes by,
   155–57, 164–65, 277n18
staff recognition program, 153–54
Stam, David, 78, 171
Stam, Deirdre, 78
Standard & Poor's, 177
Stanford Research Park, 216–17
Stanford University, 101
STAR (Strategically Targeted Academic Research) centers, 218–19,
   220

As a journalist for twenty-five years in upstate New York, **David T. Tobin** won numerous state and local awards for feature writing, his news blog, and beat reporting, as well as for his coverage of business and finance and sports issues. He lives in Marcellus, NY.